MW00424225

299

The Path
of the
Universal Christ

CLIMB THE HIGHEST MOUNTAIN SERIES

The Path
of the
Universal Christ

Mark L. Prophet · Elizabeth Clare Prophet

The Everlasting Gospel

SUMMIT UNIVERSITY ❧ PRESS
Corwin Springs, Montana

THE PATH OF THE UNIVERSAL CHRIST
by Mark L. Prophet and Elizabeth Clare Prophet
Copyright © 2003 by Summit University Press
All rights reserved

No part of this book may be reproduced; translated; electronically stored, posted or transmitted; or used in any format or medium whatsoever without written permission, except by a reviewer who may quote brief passages in a review. For information, please contact Summit University Press, PO Box 5000, Corwin Springs, MT 59030-5000.
Tel: 1-800-245-5445 or 406-848-9500.
Web site: www.summituniversitypress.com
E-mail: info@summituniversitypress.com

Library of Congress Control Number: 2003100579
ISBN: 0-922729-81-6

SUMMIT UNIVERSITY ❧ PRESS
Climb the Highest Mountain, Summit University Press,
Keepers of the Flame, *Pearls of Wisdom,* Teachings of the Ascended Masters,
Science of the Spoken Word and ❧ are registered trademarks.
All rights to their use are reserved.

Layout and design: Lynn Wilbert

Printed in the United States of America

Cover: "From Beyond," a painting by Nicholas Roerich.
Nicholas Roerich Museum, New York, N.Y. Used by permission.

Note: Because gender-neutral language can be cumbersome and at times confusing, we have often used *he* and *him* to refer to God or the individual. These terms are for readability only and are not intended to exclude women or the feminine aspect of the Godhead. Likewise, our use of *God* or *Spirit* does not exclude other expressions for the Divine.

07   06   05   04   03   6   5   4   3   2   1

To all who look for salvation in this age,
to all who know that the hour is come
when the true worshipers shall worship
the Father-Mother God in Spirit and in Truth,
to all who would climb the highest mountain,
we dedicate this volume as the next step.

Note to the Reader

The *Climb the Highest Mountain* series has been outlined in thirty-three chapters by the Ascended Master El Morya. This book contains chapter 15, "The Christ."

Contents

Section 4 · You Can Become the Christ   34

Section 5 · The Path of Personal Christhood   52

Introduction

To the student of life's mysteries:

This is the book that was written in the hearts of men long before it was written with pen and sword.

The myth of simplicity regarding religion must be exposed for what it is—just that. Religion, the science that teaches man how to bind himself to God, is not simple. The concept that makes people think that if a religious doctrine is true, they should be able to understand it with study and self-immolation is altogether misleading. The fact that learned men expect to study a lifetime to master only one discipline and yet feel that anything along religious lines that cannot be understood in an evening's discussion must either be untrue or too complicated to bother about, is a tragic misconception that deprives many of life's sweetest and most sacred mysteries.

Religious doctrine on this planet remains in the dark ages in its awesome tomb of untouchability. Those too advanced in their thinking to accept beliefs that have decayed with the centuries have thrown out religion altogether. Let them also not neglect to slay the myth of simplicity and to consider the fact that there is a science and a religion that explain the destiny of man, his origins and his raison d'être. Let them not fail to reconsider the simple truths of life ingrained in every heart and mind as keys to a vast compendium of knowledge that the LORD has hidden from the worldly-wise and made known to the pure in heart.

In this volume we set forth this knowledge as it has been given to us directly by the Ascended Masters, who from inner levels of consciousness guide all mankind who are willing to give ear to the voice of the Ancient of Days, who has promised to write his laws in their inward parts so that all might know him from the least unto the greatest.

Those who close their ears to progressive revelation have muzzled the ox whose golden tongue would give forth the secrets of the ages. To stop the voice of the Almighty in this time of world need and world travail is to seal the doom of the planet, for without knowledge and assistance from on high, mankind cannot hope to survive this age of crisis. Without vision the people perish.[1] This is a book of vision.

The truth we present in this work is by no means final; it is a foundation that can lead all to higher truth and ultimately to the summit of their own being. It contains the keys to the Golden Age if mankind will accept and act on it. It contains the facts long hidden by the dark ones who have deliberately (consciously) removed from the archives of the world every shred of knowledge that would give humanity liberation from every form of bondage—physical, mental or emotional.

The true teachings of the Christ have likewise either been removed from the scriptures, or they were omitted from the start. The works of others whom the LORD sent to illumine the Path such as Origen of Alexandria have been anathematized or burned. The few keys that remain available to the masses are taught as mysteries and given without explanation for their blind acceptance, or as has been the case, their blind rejection. Both are part of an ancient plot to defraud the sons and daughters of God of their ancient spiritual heritage, which comes down from the retreats of Lemuria and Atlantis, lost continents of the Pacific and the Atlantic. These civilizations sank beneath the sea because the people ceased to be governed by cosmic law, and the science of that law became distorted and abused or withheld altogether.

The truth we set forth herein is the truth of the ages, the laws whereby the universes were framed. This is the truth that is locked in the memory of the atoms and cells composing the earth's crust and the being of man. This is the truth that every soul knows, but through lack of proper training and education has remained a lost art lying dormant just beneath the surface of the mind until it is brought to the fore by contact with the Light and renewed with the Teachers who stand waiting in the wings ready to disclose the missing links to the puzzle of life.

All that man requires to complete his evolution and fulfill his divine plan will be revealed to him through the indwelling Christ and the memory of the soul awakened, quickened and mobilized into action by the Heavenly Hosts. Nothing will be withheld from those who pursue the knowledge of the Law of Life as the hounds of heaven, for all is in readiness, all is waiting for the moment of their desiring to have, to hold and to be more of God, more of consciousness, more of life.

If the concepts in this book disagree with your own, do not feel the need to make an immediate assessment before you have all the facts. Put new ideas on the shelf until you have further proof and explanation. Put your own ideas on the shelf and maintain, above all, an open mind. One of the devil's great weapons is to make people feel they must immediately accept or reject—classify and package every new idea presented to them, for he knows that with this attitude, no progress can be made.

And thus, as you read this series, seek to assimilate the whole panorama of Truth in each multiform part. The glossing over of these parts may well abort your assimilation of the delicate filigree patterns that unfold the magnificence of your own soul's comprehension of the laws of cosmos—mysteries from far-off worlds, from the Pleiades as well as from the sun of our own solar system—mysteries from the sands of the Sahara and the tall pines of Darjeeling. You will find herein the wisdom of the ages, the thoughts of a Christ, a Buddha and the savants and servants of the LORD. You will find knowledge of a different kind—knowledge that has been withheld from the masses, knowledge that has been guarded in the retreats of the Masters.

As Diogenes with his lantern roamed the streets in search of an honest man, so you, the reader, must raise the torch of honor and without bias seek Truth within these pages. From here, you will learn the true teachings of Christ, of your own identity, of nature and of life itself. And in the process, you will find that power by which each man can become the god of his own universe, the king in his own kingdom, the priest of his own temple, thereby responding to the fiat of the Logos: "Take dominion over the earth!"[2]

Your new-found freedom will come not alone from the formed but from the unformed as well, not just from what is said but from what remains unsaid; for words are but cups into which the mind must pour the substance of experience and devotion, the distillations of soul knowing, the formulations that are idling just beneath the surface of awareness waiting to be energized by the Christ mind.

Not what is written alone with pen and ink will be the new-found freedom released through understanding in your life, but what you think and do, showing yourself approved unto God by the living measure of your active understanding—

this will practically enhance the world in which we live and serve as an avant-garde message to all the ages to come.

Christ is not the Christ alone of the Andes, of America, of India, of any one nation. Christ is the Light emanation, the Solar Logos, the living Word, by whom all things were created, as referenced in the Gospel by the Beloved John. Man, in reality, is destined to be a triumph of attainment.

The key you have in your hand may be wisely used or critically examined. Man can do both. The choice is his. He can, if he wish, wisely use the teachings presented herein and also still critically examine them. And if he be willing to forsake dogma for Christ, love for hatred and wisdom for confusion, he will find the answers he has long sought. These words are hieroglyphs charged with that meaning that can change your life and your world into the beauty God intended man to manifest.

To you is given the key in hand. If you must judge it adversely, we ask humbly that you will first lay aside all your prejudices and opinions until you have read the last word of the last chapter of this series and sought to understand it. For here is the key that will unlock the door of your freedom as nothing has ever unlocked it before. Here is the key that comes from higher realm, a message for all ages of true Christ dimension.

Man, know thyself. Man, accept the instrument of your liberation. Mankind, be firm and awake, for the day is at hand. The Golden Age must first be posited within ere it manifest without. As the spinning wheel of life conspires so marvelously to produce the flax so gossamer and filmlike that will one day become a garment of solar radiance, a garment of attainment, a wedding garment you will then wear as living devotion and love's perfect shields against all delusion, all confusion and all misunderstanding.

Open the door of your heart without bias, bigotry or delay to a renewal of your life in the alchemical furnace of He who loves you most. May the angels from the realms of glory sit on your shoulder as you pursue these words and ever guide you into the Truth you seek.

Sincerely, in service to humanity,

Mark L. Prophet

Elizabeth Clare Prophet

MARK AND ELIZABETH PROPHET
Messengers of the Masters

The Christis

If thou shalt confess with thy mouth the
Lord Jesus, and shalt believe in thine heart that
God hath raised him from the dead, thou shalt
be saved.

For with the heart man believeth unto
righteousness; and with the mouth confession
is made unto salvation.

For the scripture saith, Whosoever
believeth on him shall not be ashamed.

For there is no difference between the Jew
and the Greek: for the same Lord over all is
rich unto all that call upon him.

For whosoever shall call upon the name
of the Lord shall be saved.

PAUL TO THE ROMANS

Wherefore God also hath highly exalted him, and given him a name which is above every name:

That at the name of Jesus every knee should bow, of things in heaven, and things in earth, and things under the earth;

And that every tongue should confess that Jesus Christ is Lord, to the glory of God the Father.

PAUL TO THE PHILIPPIANS

Section 1

The Mystery
of the Christ

*"No man can say that Jesus is the Lord,
but by the Holy Ghost."*[1]

T HE ACKNOWLEDGMENT OF JESUS AS
the Son of God, as the Christ, is a
prerequisite to the understanding of the Christ. For if man cannot see and acknowledge the Christ in the one whom God sent
to be the perfect example to the age of the only begotten of the
Father,[2] then he is not capable of acknowledging the Christ as
his own identity and his own potential. And if he cannot
acknowledge the Christ as his own potential, then he can never
be saved. Thus we begin to study the mystery of the Christos,
of the ineffable Light which lighteth every man that cometh
into the world.[3]

The apostle Paul says that "there is no difference between
the Jew and the Greek: for the same Lord over all is rich unto
all that call upon him. For whosoever shall call upon the name
of the Lord shall be saved."[4] This Lord before whose Presence
we bend the knee was personified in the man Jesus, who held
the office in Hierarchy of the Christ for the two-thousand-year
cycle that began with his ministry in Galilee.

By calling upon the name of Jesus as the incarnation of the Christ, man is saved through the power of the Christ that God has already placed within man. By calling upon the name of the Lord, he releases the full potential of the Christ within his own being, which enables him and allows him to rise to the victory of the Christ that Jesus demonstrated in his three-year ministry.

The modern world is inundated with more religious organizations than there have ever been in any previous century. Some have endured for thousands of years. Men think that the mysteries of the Christ are simple to determine. Many do not even recognize that there is any mystery in the concept of the Christ. And yet the concept of the Christ remains to the present day the greatest mystery that has ever challenged the mind of man.

In recent years, science (the behavioral sciences in particular) has placed emphasis upon the subconscious mind and its behavior patterns, probing the id, the ego and the superego, apart from any concept of the Christ. It is becoming increasingly obvious that religion does not thoroughly understand all of the mysteries of the mind of man and of nature. Science has many answers and chooses, in many cases, to ignore the old religious landmarks. Religion, too, has many answers, and in some cases chooses to ignore the markings of science. A synthesis of religion and science produces profound revelations in thought. Nowhere is this more self-evident when correctly understood than in the mystery of Christ.

It is the Christ in every race, in every nation and people that establishes a congruency with the Almighty and a unity whereby there are no differences. All differences are dissolved in the Christ. For that same Lord is within all and over all—"rich," that is, flowing with abundant blessings to all who call upon him.

Those who fail to acknowledge the Christ in Jesus—

through pride, intellectual sophistication, arrogance or rebellion against God—cannot rise to their own Christ identity, to the potential of Christhood in themselves. And thus, they effectively delay their progress on the Path and their salvation (their self-realization through self-elevation). And so, the act of acknowledging the Son of God, Jesus, is the first step in understanding the true nature of the Christ.

The Historical Jesus: Christ the Man

Two thousand years ago there lived upon this planet the historical person of Jesus. Born in Bethlehem of Judea and raised in the community of Nazareth, the man Jesus was well known to his contemporaries. His ministry was filled with dynamism, with service and with an impact that has endured to the present day. Although many other figures have also made their mark upon the screen of world history, none have inspired us as much as the beautiful figure of the Master-Teacher, Jesus.

All historical figures receive a subjective treatment from historians, writers and evaluators of the past. Jesus was no exception, and it goes without saying that the early apostles and teachers in the Church expressed their own concepts of the Master in the form of the spoken and written word. Saint Paul, the great theologian and apostle, revealed the mysterious figure of Christ Jesus to mankind in the early Church in a somewhat different manner than others had previously recognized him. The mental and emotional patterns of early Church leaders caused them to hold differing opinions of the Master's mission and purposes.

Nowhere do we find any recording of Jesus' actual words transcribed and written down by himself, but everywhere we find interpretations of the Christ and of his purposes. Because this is so, it is essential that we examine his life with a view to a determination of his purposes and his intent—of the meaning of his life for ourselves and for all mankind.

Mary, the mother of Jesus, comes to give her perspective on his life and mission: "The conflicting views held by men concerning the life and ministry of my son are legion. Therefore, as a cosmic mother, I extend to you today the lamp of knowledge containing the precious oil of the mystery of Christhood in order that the role that he outpictured may be better understood by those who yearn to identify more closely with the Christ here and now....

"God did not design one house to be builded upon the shifting sands of human misdirection and another to be builded upon the rock of Christ Truth. From the beginning God intended that all should express the great purity, truth and victory of the Christ, which my son Jesus showed forth in his Galilean embodiment.

"I know full well that orthodox interpretations, although stemming from well-intended effort on the part of many who have nobly served our cause, do not convey the correct understanding of my Son's mission and teaching. This problem has arisen as the result of inherent weaknesses, deletions and inaccuracies in the worded structure of certain biblical passages and through traditional concepts woven like a cocoon of ignorance around embodied truth. To dispel illusion, then, I come with lamp in hand to rephrase the old story of 'peace on earth, good will toward men.'

"The angels sang, not alone to the infant babe whom I held so tenderly in my arms as I revered him in my heart, but also to each mother's son who had ever been born, who ever was and who should ever be blessed and begotten of the Father. For God, the celestial Spirit, the Progenitor of every heart of radiant identity, in his own great heart of love, of mercy and of justice, could not possibly deny to any of his sons the treasures that are embodied in the concept of the Christ. The birth in the stable revealed, to the amazement of mortals, that the vastness of the Cosmic Christ, the immortal design of the Son of God, could descend in lowly mien even in the midst of elemental animal life while attended by angelic and cosmic hosts.

"The wonder of Jesus was not in his humanity, but in the divinity of the Christ, which manifested through his humanity. Not only have men made of him a personality, a person likened unto their own image, but also they have been obsessed with the idea that this blessed Son carried out a mission that was unique to himself and to the ages. I do not deny the uniqueness of his message and service; but I affirm that it is a unique manifestation that all have the opportunity to outpicture, but which only the few realize.

"I do not imply here that each individual has the same life plan or pattern, but I do wish to convey to all that the high hope held by the Father for each of his beloved sons and daughters is one of coequality, and that this destiny contains within it the essential pattern and holy strands of the Christ, the only begotten of the Father, full of grace and truth. The Christ is the chief cornerstone upon which the entire temple is builded. The Christ of every man is the unique mediator between the personality that must evolve in the world of form, referred to as the lower self, and the individualized focus of the Father, the I AM Presence that issued forth from the center of the great flame of God-Being.

"Men have uttered the name of God and cloaked it with human vanity. They have used the name I AM to lay claim to every paltry thing in life; and yet Being, God-Being, eternal life, has escaped them. Thus, the sacred Word, I AM, has been denied the full expression of its inherent power and reality in their world and consciousness.

"I seek, then, to convey to every son of heaven the mighty reality of life that is his. I am a cosmic mother, and as much your mother as I am the mother of beloved Jesus. Some who are adherents of the Christian faith call me the Mother of God. To those of the protesting branch of orthodox Christianity, this seems a sacrilege; for men may well ask, 'Who is worthy to be the Mother of God?' But this concept, when understood to mean the mother of the embodiment of the Divine Spirit, reveals the glorious truth that every mother who understands that which was spoken—'and the Word was made flesh and dwelt among us'—may be 'the Mother of God.' "[5]

Jesus, the Messiah

The concept of a Messiah was not new to the Israelites, nor to the Hebrew people. They had for years prior to the birth of Jesus awaited an event of such importance, fulfilling ancient prophecies and bringing new hope to their nation as well as to the Gentiles.

Jesus was the incarnate Messiah, the one prophesied by the prophets of Israel. He came to restore the true teaching of the prophets to the people of Israel. We find that the chief priests and scribes, the Pharisees and the Sadducees, were greatly concerned because Jesus was restoring these teachings to the people. In the beginning of his mission he stood in the synagogue quoting the prophecies of his own coming, and he said: "This day is this scripture fulfilled."[6]

He came to give to the people of Israel the key to the incarnation of God. When they accused him of saying that he was the Son of God, he quoted their own scripture, Psalm 82:* "Behold I have said, ye are gods."

However, Jesus' mission was not for the Jews alone. Saint

---

*It was Jesus, in his earlier embodiment as David, who wrote the Psalms.

Paul considered himself to be the apostle to the Gentiles (the non-Jews), for he was so appointed, and he exerted every effort to declare this phenomenon of God to the Gentiles everywhere upon earth. The success of Paul's service to life is attested to in the expansion of Christianity. He, together with Saint Peter, was one of those who succeeded in telling the good news of the coming of the Master to the earth and in laying the foundation for early Christianity.

Somewhere, however, in all of the writings and concepts about Jesus is a missing link, or perhaps it would be better to say, an incorrect concept concerning the Master Jesus. Perhaps one of the reasons this incorrect concept has not been refuted in our time is that most individuals have feared to tread upon a concept so universally acknowledged by Christians. Few dare even to speculate upon it publicly for fear of religious taboo or ostracism.

The Divinity of the Christ:
The Only Begotten Son

M ANY CHRISTIAN MEN AND WOMEN feel that their entire hope for survival in the world to come, or perhaps even in the present, lies in what they have termed the divinity of Jesus the Christ. Without Christ, their life lacks meaning. With Christ, their life becomes full of meaning. They look for, hope for and wait for a World Saviour—one who has the power to reach into their own lives and change those lives for the better, and permanently so. They see in the presentation of Jesus the Christ such a man of God, such a Son of God—in fact, one whom John declared to be none other than the only begotten of the Father: "For God so loved the world that he gave his only begotten Son, that whosoever believeth in him should not perish, but have everlasting life."[1]

But who is the only begotten Son of God? The only Son of God is the Universal Christ, the Cosmic Christ (the terms are synonymous). *Christos* is a Greek word meaning "one anointed of the Light." The Son of God who is the only begotten is the Light-emanation of the Father-Mother God individualized.

The Son of God is one Son, one descent of one Universal Light; but of this universal Light-body Jesus said at the Last Supper, as he held the single loaf of bread, "This is my universal body of Light which is broken for you." He revealed the mystery again of the Law of the One, one Universal Light who is one Son of God. But he breaks the bread and gives us each a piece of it. In that very act he is saying, "I am restoring to you that same Universal Christ that you have forgotten and lost in your descent into this world."

When he said, "I am the bread of life which came down from heaven,"[2] he affirmed that he was that bread that is the Cosmic Christ. He was speaking out of the personhood of that only begotten Son, the Christ, because that Christ was fully integrated in the human being Jesus. They were one and the same. They were merged together. There was no difference between Jesus the human being and Jesus the Christ. That is why he is our Saviour. That is the example he set.

When Jesus served Holy Communion to the apostles, he said, "Take, eat: this is my body, which is broken for you." If that body is broken into a million pieces, just as every drop of the ocean contains the whole ocean, that piece of that bread is still the fullness of that Universal Christ. And that Universal Christ you call to as your beloved Christ Self. You may also call that Christ Self your Higher Self or your Higher Consciousness.

The wine that Jesus gives is the essence of the Spirit of the I AM Presence. He says, "This do ye, as oft as ye drink it, in remembrance of me"[3]—in remembrance that I came and was with you and I was the embodiment of that Universal Christ. We partake of the Body of Light each time we celebrate Holy Communion.

The Divinity of Every Son and Daughter

The holding of the concept of the divinity of Christ does not detract from any man's sonship under the divine aegis, but rather contributes to the whole. But somehow the idea that the sin that so easily besets us is ever at hand has imbued mankind with a spirit of self-condemnation. Man deems himself unworthy of receiving the cherished gift of divine Sonship except through the person of the man Jesus.

We believe that the Master Jesus was divine. We believe that he was the only begotten Son of the Father, but we believe also that you and I are divine—that we, too, in a very real sense, are the only begotten of the Father.

Just how this is possible will be explained clearly, for it is a postulation and affirmation of the inner revelations that God has made to us. We hope that it will not be desecrated by condemnation, criticism or judgment until such a time as the reader has examined the fabric of the whole thought rather than a part. We do not say this out of fear for ourselves, but for the joy that this true revelation brings to those who are able to receive it, and in their ability to receive it, to expand their own consciousness of the Presence of God and to achieve greater realization of the great hope there is for every man, woman and child upon this planet.

When you completely understand this revelation, you will realize full well that the greatest fear, if any fear can be said to have possessed the mind of Jesus, was the fear that men would worship him, that they would make out of him and of his person an object of their affection without following the message of regeneration that he left.

"In the Beginning Was the Word…"

The role, the title, the vestment of Messiah or Saviour or Son of God, is not so much personal as it is universal. When God created man in his own image, he could fashion him in none higher, for there is no higher image than the Image of God. Saint John declares: "In the beginning was the Word, and the Word was with God, and the Word was God." He also declares that "without him [the Word] was not any thing made that was made."[4]

It has been commonly accepted by men that through Christ the worlds were framed by the Word of God—that the Christ was, in effect, the Word incarnate—the Word that became flesh. This antedates, then, the existence of the man Jesus, who said, referencing this Christ of his being, "Before Abraham was, I AM."[5]

In truth, then, not only Jesus, but all men created in the Image of God were vested in the beginning with the original pattern or gift of the divine sonship. The gift to man, then, of the only begotten Son of God is a spiritual gift given to all, that all must receive, that all must believe in order to possess and be possessed by it. The only saviour that man in truth has, is God through Christ. Thus, the only begotten Son of God is seen as a high image to which all may be exalted and with which all may be totally identified.

At first this may seem almost a desecration, until one pauses to think that in the beginning God created man in his own image. As there is none higher than God, certainly to be in the image of the Christ or the image of the only begotten is wholly in keeping with the Father's intent to give of himself to man.

The Universal Logos

One of the great fallacies in human thought and reason is that because there is but one God, there can be but one Son of God. This was never the divine intent. The Christ is not Jesus per se, although he, himself, certainly became the Christ. The Christ is the Word, or the Logos. The Logos was the Word that went forth, by which all things were made. And when the Logos spoke "through" Jesus, the Logos said, "Before Abraham was, I AM." You can say the same thing. And it will be true of you too, because the I AM, the Divine Being, existed long before our flesh form in any of our embodiments, and the I AM will continue to exist.

The Universal Christ Spirit, the Logos, this second person of the Trinity existed, then, in the consciousness of God from the Beginning. For God is a Spirit, and the Spirit of God sent forth by the power of his own cognition and majesty the Son, or the radiance of himself, the Solar Logos, the Universal Logos, the Word that went forth and by its vibratory action shook all things into manifestation. And therefore, all things are a manifestation of the mind-stuff of God.

This universal consciousness, this Light, this *emanation—* energy *man*ifest*ation* of God—is the only Reality in the universe, the only begotten of the Father. This great Reality exists in every human heart and is the Holy Christ Self, the Mediator between the earth man and the heavenly man that is above each individual. For God has said, "I will draw nigh unto you if you will draw nigh unto me."[6] If we understand this, then, we must be receptive to the great creative intelligence that gave us birth.

Waves Upon the Sea

We must recognize that there has been a lie fostered by malintent upon man to create the illusion that there is and can be only one son of the Father.

There is only one begotten Son and that is the Universal Christ. Jesus was a manifestation of that and demonstrated for all time that resurrection that he so ably represented in his Palestinian mission. However, we today have the same opportunity that he did, and in his own words, we may draw the recognition of this truth; for he has spoken, saying, "He that believeth on me, the works that I do shall he do also; and greater works than these shall he do; because I go unto my Father."[7]

We must recognize, then, that each time a universal soul who has attained to his Christ stature goes back to the heart of God, he carries with him the richening of his own earth experiences. And thus the Godhead gains in transcendence and transcendent power. And the power of infinity is itself multiplied because man has served the divine cause.

The sons of God are like the waves upon the sea, like the sand by the seashore, like the stars of the heaven innumerable. We all exist in the consciousness of God in the Divine Image. If man is made in the Image of God and his likeness, there is no higher. How, then, could there be one son above the other? How could one individual, per se, stand above the other except through the use of opportunity. For God is a God of justice, and when men serve him and devote themselves to him, he honors their efforts. For it is written that every jot and tittle of the Law shall remain in effect. It is also written that for whatsoever a man doeth, he shall receive the just reward.[8]

Section 3

The Universal Christ:
The Chart of Your Divine Self

THE SPECIFIC FUNCTIONS OF THE individualized Universal Christ are (1) to mediate between the absolute perfection of God, the I AM Presence, and the lesser states of manifestation that are yet becoming that perfection, and (2) to transform that which has not fully arrived at this blessed state of perfection.

Mediation and transformation are achieved in many ways. The Universal Christ insulates the paradise of absolute God-purity from the negative traits of the human consciousness, which have no permanent Reality. It also connects man with his divinity and transmits to him the high vibratory action of that Holy Presence, rendering it intelligible to the lesser manifestation.

The Christ acts as the Mediator between God and man, and therefore the Universal Christ becomes identified at the midpoint between God and man. This is necessary because God's eyes are too pure to behold iniquity,[1] and therefore, the I AM Presence is absolutely unaware of any evil anywhere.

The Christ possesses the simultaneous power of knowing the perfection of God and also of knowing the needs of man.

There is one God who is individualized again and again, one times one times one, in the God Presence above us. There is one Universal Christ, one only begotten Son of God, one individualization of that Christ in Jesus multiplied many times over in the Holy Christ Self of each of us, the middle figure in the Chart. (See Chart of Your Divine Self, facing page 22.) Jeremiah foresaw and foretold this Mediator, naming that Christ Self as The Lord Our Righteousness.[2]

The Individualized Trinity

We have a great ministry before us in presenting to the world the true understanding of who is Father, who is Son and who is Holy Spirit. We see these three aspects of the Trinity represented in the Chart of Your Divine Self. The three figures are the signs of the levels of our inner divinity that we are intended to realize in the New Age.

Various religions have grown up about each of these individual components. And so, there has grown up an argument as to what God is. People say God is Krishna or God is Father or God is Son or God is Holy Spirit, and there have also been cults of the Mother. There is an argument because we do not realize that God is a great sphere of consciousness. This diagram of Being is a likeness, a representation on canvas of the flaming sphere of consciousness that actually is the permanent Self, the permanent life.

This Chart is actual. It is in three and four dimensions of Being. And it shows that there is a pulsating sphere of God consciousness that is quivering just above you in this moment and a crystal clear stream of consciousness that is flowing through you.

You see three Persons. You see the Father, the Son and the Holy Spirit. Three is the real mystical power of God. We find through the teachings of the Ascended Masters that the real revelation of life is that all manifestation of the sons and daughters of God is this Trinity.

We all believe in a Universal God and perhaps a Universal Christ and perhaps a universal soul. But the understanding of identity as God's individualization of himself as the Trinity where we are gives us a very personal contact. It gives us personal power, personal wisdom and personal love. The Chart is a Trinity of you in manifestation, and you see it as a threefold action in your life. (See p. 22.) This Trinity is only separated in time and space. In fact, God the Father, the Son and the Holy Spirit* within us is intended to be realized as one essential Light through the mastery of time and space.

The upper figure in the Chart of Your Divine Self is the I AM THAT I AM, the center figure is the individualized Christ Self, and the lower figure is the soul in the state of evolving Godward. This Trinity of Being is more than a religious repetition of words. It is one of the greatest keys to understanding. It is the simple statement: *God is within you.*

But how is he within you? Why is he within you? And how do we discover this magnificent focal point of energy as the means to release that energy of the Word?

The I AM THAT I AM

Wherever God is, he is always Principle and Person, impersonal energy and a personal personhood. The I AM THAT I AM is a living fire, and this living fire descends into the clay vessel. It is written that "the light shineth in darkness; and the darkness comprehended it not." But "the Word was made

*We find the same Trinity in the East as Brahma, Vishnu and Shiva.

flesh, and dwelt among us (and we beheld his glory, the glory as of the only begotten of the Father) full of grace and truth."[3]

Thus, when the Light became a person, we understood the Light. It was a living person who walked among us, who needed to eat, who needed to sleep, who needed to rest, who needed to get away from the burdens of the world and go into the ship or go into the mountain and pray, who felt pain, who had agony, who died on the cross and who proved the flame of the resurrection spirit. We find that God descending into form takes on characteristics that we can understand because we experience them, too. And by the very reality of that person, the realness, the humanness, we discover how that Light works in us.

We must know that God loved us, that he so loved us that he gave to us the individualization of himself. And if we do not understand this Trinity, this life, this energy, this polarization of God as the core of our being, then we are actually denying the existence of that God, and we are depriving ourselves of the power, the wisdom, the love, the life, the determination, the Word itself to challenge darkness in this age.

The first recorded revelation of the I AM THAT I AM was to Moses. God told him, "This is my name for ever, and this is my memorial unto all generations."[4] That name was given not to Moses alone, not as a private experience, not because we should worship him, but because we should become that I AM THAT I AM. That revelation becomes an archetype. It becomes a pattern of the unfoldment and the evolution of God where you are and where I am.

That name is not simply a repetition of someone's surname. I AM THAT I AM is the statement of eternal Being. Whose being? First of all, the being of Moses; it was the moving stream of Moses' own God consciousness. Secondly, it was your being, my being. It was the Universal Light. It was that I AM Presence that is the individual God-awareness of you and me and every son and daughter of God.

The great legacy of Aries, East and West, is that we have the name I AM—and that name is power. (In the East the name of God is the OM.) When you say the word *I AM* and you mean "God," everything that follows is fulfilled by the power of your I AM Presence. It's not just the power of positive thinking or affirmation. The name itself of God, *is* his Presence. When you pronounce it, the Light of God is where you are, because the sounding of the name is equivalent to the Being.

The Universal Christ

The second figure in this Chart, the middle figure, is the Universal Christ. John wrote: "God sent his only begotten Son into the world, that we might live through him."[5] The eternal life the Son brings is the reigniting of the divine spark that has gone out, or almost gone out, so that we are no longer sensitive to it in our hearts.

Who is this Christ? It is Christ Jesus, and it is the Universal Christ. John spoke of this Light, and he said, "That was the true Light, which lighteth every man that cometh into the world."[6] We are all ignited by Christ, by the Christ Light. This personal figure of Christ is the manifestation of Christ with us as the Mediator between ourselves and the Father, the I AM Presence.

A Christ, *Christos,* an "anointed one," is one who is anointed with the Light of his I AM Presence and that Universal Son of God. Jesus told us that this anointing is accessible to all: "If a man love me, he will keep my words: and my Father will love him, and we will come unto him, and make our abode with him."[7]

This Christ has manifested to us in many ways. We have seen glimpses of that Christ in Melchizedek, King of Salem and priest of the Most High God. We have seen glimpses of that Christ in the virtue and love of our friends and loved ones. We find the Light of Christ, as through a prism, reflected and refracted through all of us in some portion. We are all the manifestation of that One, and therefore, we have a right to put on the whole mantle of that Sonship. For this was the purpose of his coming.

The Mediator

The Christ Self is a very personal Presence. When you hear God talking inside of you as conscience, warning you of danger or telling you something you must do, that is your own personal Christ Self. Sometimes you don't do what it says, and you find out afterward you made a big mistake.

The individual Christ Self, the middle figure in the Chart, is the Mediator between Spirit and Matter, between heaven and earth. The Christ Self is your teacher, your minister, rabbi, priest, psychiatrist, friend, brother on the Path.

You can visualize a figure-eight pattern from the upper to the lower figure in the Chart. At the nexus of that figure eight is the Word, the personification of the Christ, the eternal Saviour. Mediating between the outer self and the permanent atom of being is that Inner Guru, that Inner Light, that Second Person of the Trinity, the advocate before the Father, before this fountain of life and consciousness and energy.

God gave us this Light, this Mediator, this Son because we could no longer approach the Godhead, the mighty I AM Presence. We are in a state of karma and imperfection. God is the Absolute, all perfect. If we were to merge with that God in our state of imperfection, we would be annihilated. Therefore, we must become one with our Christhood, truly fulfilled in the Light, yet aware of the human condition as Jesus was. We must become mediators.

As we put on our Christhood, the Light continues to increase and increase and increase until 51 percent of our being is Light. That it is enough Light for the soul to ascend to God. Clothed upon with that mantle of Christhood, that soul, then, is wearing the deathless solar body, the wedding garment, and will not be annihilated upon entering into the kingdom of God. The kingdom of God is the I AM THAT I AM.

God gave this Cosmic Christ that whosoever believeth in him should not perish but have everlasting life.[8] That Cosmic Christ is manifest in Jesus. God has promised us that we can be heirs with Jesus of that Christ that he bore. But we ourselves must do it. We must do his works and follow in his footsteps.

Your personal Christ Self is your Real Self, the energy, or nucleus, that you must become. When you put on the vibration and the consciousness of the living Christ, then that living Christ descends as a mantle, as it has done over all the saints and mystics East and West. Then, whatever your name is, you become the one who is known as the Christ.

In connection with the mystery, we know that in the origin of names, a man who was a blacksmith might bear the name of John for his first name. If his work and service to life was that of a smith in old England, he would become known by the name "John, the Smith," or depending on his calling, "John, the Baker," or "Peter, the Shoemaker," and so on. Later on in the use of language, the "the" was dropped as superfluous, and he became known simply as "John Smith," "John Baker," or "Peter Shoemaker." In the same way, Jesus, who became the Christ, came to be known as Jesus Christ.

The Personhood of the Christ

Jesus, by his surrender—"not my will, but thine, be done"[9] —allowed his temple to be totally occupied by the Second Person

The Chart of Your Divine Self

of the Trinity. And therefore, he walked the earth in the fullness of the Personhood of the Christ. This is the real individualization of the God flame, the Person behind the person, even as the I AM is the Principle behind the principle in us all. When you become that Self, your soul will merge ultimately with the permanent atom of being, the I AM Presence, on the path of the ascension. Thus, Jesus, the man portrayed in the lower figure in the Chart, put on the garments and the fullness of the Inner Christ as the center figure in the Chart and ascended into the Presence of the white Light and the I AM THAT I AM.

A Codification of Doctrine

Jesus unveiled and gave to us the great teaching of the Universal Christ, but Church councils, not having the real Holy Spirit and fervor of this revelation, have sought to codify into doctrine and dogma things that Jesus never taught.

Early Church Fathers decided to allow only a narrow perspective of what he taught that eliminates the understanding that *you* are the son of man, that each one of us is the son of man—which simply means the "*son* of *man*ifestation."[10] *You* are the Light of manifestation of your I AM Presence this very moment. That son of manifestation is a soul who has descended into these dense bodies and this concrete, physical world. The soul has free will, but the soul is not permanent. The soul becomes permanent when she becomes the bride of the Universal Christ. That fusion of the soul with that Universal Light is called the alchemical marriage.

Jesus, the Son of man, was the full incarnation of the Son of God. This we know. This we believe. The Council of Nicea and other church councils, confusing the Universal Son of God and the Son of man—the question of Jesus' divinity and his divine Sonship—decided that the human, flesh-and-blood Jesus was the only begotten Son of God. They decided the rest of us were sinners, that God only created one Son, and the only way we could be saved was simply to believe in him. Jesus did not teach this, but they made it church doctrine.

They codified a doctrine of original sin, a stain that could never be removed, whereby all the rest of these billions of souls that God sent forth could never rise again because of one act of one person described in the allegory of Adam and Eve.

Nowhere will you find written that Jesus said that he was the only Son of God, that he was the exclusive Son of God. The apostle said, "Let this mind be in you, which was also in Christ Jesus."[11] It is lawful for us to seek to embody that Universal Mind, who is the Son of God.

The Lord Our Righteousness

Jeremiah called the Universal Son The Lord Our Righteousness, and he prophesied his coming.[12] The Lord Our Righteousness, the middle figure in the Chart, is the Son of God with us. It is the coming of the Inner Teacher, or the Inner Guru.

Jeremiah's prophecy is not the coming of the Saviour. The Lord Our Righteousness is coming two thousand years after the birth of Jesus Christ, in the age of Aquarius today. It is the prophecy of the coming into awareness of each individual's own Christ Self, his own Real Self, and that is the Second Coming of Jesus Christ. The First Coming is the coming of the avatar of the age. The Second Coming is the quickening within your heart.

We salute this Universal Christ in every age by many names. That Inner Light and that Inner Being, the Christos, the Anointed One within us, is also known in the East as Krishna. By any other name, by any other mask, it is still the same eternal Light.

We find that when we are willing to stand in the presence of that One, in the presence of the real Light, the true Light and not its shadow, that The Lord Our Righteousness, our own righteousness within, begins to teach us, begins to realign our being with the inner blueprint, begins to show us the way. And The Lord Our Righteousness gives us an understanding of the office of the Christ.

The office of the Christ is to continually be the voice of conscience that tells us the Real from the unreal, what is True, what is untrue, what is lawful, what is not lawful, what is the right use of God's Light, his Law, his love, his wisdom, his power. The Holy Christ Self is our great teacher and our saviour.

The Lower Figure in the Chart

The lower figure in the Chart is a vessel for the Holy Spirit. You are depicted here standing in the violet flame of the Holy Spirit, invoking that flame. This is the age when we understand our God as a consuming fire.[13] Moses said it. Paul said it. And Jesus taught it.

This Holy Spirit energy is a pulsating violet flame, the highest spectrum in the color range. It is the sacred fire and the Third Person of the Trinity that is the fullness of love made manifest, and it is for the cleansing of the temple.

Jesus, the man, is the lower figure in the Chart. Jesus is the human being like you and me. He had a body like ours. He came into incarnation the same way we did, through his mother, Mary. He was at the time of his incarnation the full incarnation of the Christ. He was the Word incarnate. He was the full manifestation of what we should become. He was the great example for us for this two-thousand-year period to walk in his footsteps.

The Son of Man

At various points in his mission, Jesus asked those close to him who they thought he was. He desired to differentiate between his humanity and his divinity. When referring to himself as the man Jesus, he called himself the Son of man. Thus, he said to his disciples, "Whom do men [men who look at my outer self] say that I the Son of man, am?"

Their reply was, "Some say that thou art John the Baptist: some, Elias; and others, Jeremias, or one of the prophets." Thus having heard the testimony of those who observed only his human personality, Jesus tested Peter's spiritual discernment: "He saith unto them, But whom say ye that I am?" Peter recognized the Reality of the Son of God made manifest in the Son of man; and therefore, he declared with the authority of the Only Begotten who also dwelt in him, "Thou art the Christ, the Son of the living God."[14]

Jesus then blessed Peter, for he knew that in order to discern the Christ in Jesus (the Son of man) Peter had to be attuned to the Christ within: "For flesh and blood hath not revealed it unto thee, but my Father [the I AM Presence through the divine Mediator] which is in heaven. And I say also unto thee, That thou art Peter, and upon this rock I will build my church."[15] Upon this scientific principle, this understanding of the Christ who lives in every man and woman whom God hath made, Jesus laid the foundation of his Church.

It is recorded that Jesus charged his disciples "that they should tell no man that he was Jesus *the* Christ." This title he bore because his Christ Self-awareness completely enveloped his human consciousness until the Son of God and the Son of man were no longer separate as they appear in the Chart as the middle and lower figures. No longer two but one, the human was transformed and transfigured until it became the full realization of the Christ-potential in living, breathing awareness. Jesus the man became Jesus the Christ, and his mission was to show all men how they, too, might become the Christ. Because he knew of his trial to come and the persecution by the carnal mind of all who reunite with the Christ, Jesus charged them to remain silent on the subject of his attainment. The hour would come when all would know that he was the Son of God, and when his time was come, all would be fulfilled.

Upon the occasion of Lazarus' death, Jesus questioned Martha concerning her belief in him and his power to raise her brother from the dead. Answering in the faith she had been taught by her Lord, Martha said, "I believe that thou art the Christ, the Son of God, which should come into the world."[16] Thus, Martha also recognized the divinity of the Christ as the real identity of the man Jesus. Her belief in the Christ was a necessary prerequisite to the raising of Lazarus. Through her consciousness of the Christ, Jesus anchored the resurrection flame that restored the body of him who was dead.

Let us further clarify the terms *Son of God* and *Son of man*. The Son of God is the Holy Christ Self, the Cosmic Christ. The Son of man is the soul who has become one with that Christ by passing his initiations. It is the Son of man who therefore bears the iniquities and the burdens and the karma and by whose stripes we are healed. The Son of man is the one who is essentially Christ incarnate, perhaps not wholly perfected, not wholly having balanced one hundred percent of the karma, but nevertheless, the Christ is ensconced firmly in that temple.

When individual man, yet in the state of becoming whole, allows the Christ to enter his being and minister to the needs of all, the mercy of God dispensed by the hand of the Mediator is made tangible to the souls of all upon earth. At that moment, the lower self becomes the mediator between the Christ Self and every other part of life evolving Godward. Through the one who consecrates the tabernacle of his four lower bodies as the dwelling place of God and the focus for the Christ, untold millions are touched by the light: and "I [Jesus], if I [the Christ] be lifted up from the earth, will draw all men unto me [unto Jesus the Christ—for through self-mastery the son of man and the Son of God are become one]."[17]

The Master's greatest desire was that they should not mistake the Son of man (Jesus) for the Son of God (the Christ). Should confusion arise regarding the source of his humanity (in Christ) and the source of his divinity (in God), the Saviour knew that generations to come would not worship the Christ, but the man Jesus—in whom they had beheld the "glory *as of* the only begotten" of the Father-Mother God, whom he so perfectly personified in grace and in truth.

For this reason, "Jesus cried and said, He that believeth on me, believeth not on me, but on him that sent me. And he that seeth me seeth him that sent me."[18] We cannot fail to note this final, almost desperate, plea made to all who would hear him: "You who believe in me, the one whom you have known as Jesus, although you may not realize it, believe in the Christ, the Divine Mediator. You who have seen me, have seen the Christ Light of the only begotten Son, which I have borne in the Father's name."

The Ascended Master Jesus sums up this entire question when he says, "I AM your Jesus, Son of God, Son of man. I AM your twin on the road of life, and we shall walk and talk together until your victory is won."[19]

The Crystal Cord

The crystal cord is the line that connects the upper figure in the Chart, the I AM Presence, with the Holy Christ Self and the lower figure. It is called the "thread of contact." The crystal cord has been reduced in many to a mere thread. Yet, over that crystal cord, as tiny as it is today, flows the power of your I AM Presence.

That power comes all the way from the Great Central Sun, the spiritual Sun behind the sun, through the individualized Presence of God, through the Christ Self, and finally, that cord goes through the crown chakra and fastens in the heart. The Light that passes over the crystal cord keeps the threefold flame, the divine spark in the heart burning. We can qualify God's Light that comes to us over this thread of contact with our decrees and our prayers and all that we send out into the world.

We are intended to expand the threefold flame and also to expand the dimension of the crystal cord. Think of it now as a thread of contact. By contrast, the diameter of the crystal cord of those in ancient Golden-Age civilizations was one foot. Imagine how much more Light poured from the God Source, how great the infiring of the mind, how great the Light in the chakras. This explains how people could precipitate their own food and levitate objects. What man has done, man can do. This is the law of the Brotherhood. What we have done once, we can do again. And this is the great hope of our path today.

The Keystone in the Arch

Our knowledge of the Hierarchy is that many other sons of God have gone before Jesus in all ages and planetary systems since the worlds were born. We know that there are great Cosmic Beings and those who are called Gods and Goddesses who have been in heaven for aeons. Why is Jesus still the principal one and the one whom we claim as our Lord and Saviour? Why is Jesus the keystone in the arch of being?

All who are on planet Earth today, having not fulfilled the fullness of our Christhood, must now enter in. And God has opened the door for our entering in to the path of the return of our Sonship through one individual, and that individual is Jesus Christ.

And so he says, "I AM the door. I AM the shepherd of the sheepfold."[20] He tells us that "no man cometh unto the Father, but by me."[21] The "me" he is referring to is the Christ that he embodies. It is the Universal Christ. Each one of us comes to the heart of our I AM Presence through our own Holy Christ Self—but not until we will bend the knee and confess that Jesus Christ is the full incarnation of the Word, is the full incarnation of Christ.

Jesus Christ is unique because he came, chosen by God the Father of all other sons of heaven, and he volunteered in answer to that call to incarnate to be the avatar. That means the God-manifestation, the God incarnate, or the Word incarnate. Jesus volunteered to be the Word incarnate and to set the example for what all people of earth should accomplish in the Piscean age, which is the internalization of the threefold flame, the Christ flame, the internalization of the Holy Christ Self walking the earth, truly embodying the Christ.

Many people in the world today are unable to acknowledge Jesus Christ except as a good rabbi and a good teacher and a prophet. They are unwilling to see or to bend the knee or to bow before the Christ of him in order that they might receive the Christ in themselves. But this is what our Father says to us. "If you will not acknowledge the Christ in my Son whom I have sent, who has lived for you, who has given his life for you, who has carried the balance of the 25,800-year karma coming due at the end of Pisces, has borne it for you as the bearer of your karma for two thousand years, if you cannot see the Christ in him, then you will not see the Christ in yourself." For he was the great examplar of the incarnation of the Word. The testimony is there. The life is there. He was the perfect example (or, let us say almost perfect—since the human condition is not perfect).

The evolution of this planet is so far behind the manifestation of Jesus Christ that God has said, "You have turned your back on the Christed ones, on your own Christ Self and your own Christ path for so long, that this is the initiation you must pass. You must be willing to bend the knee before a flesh-and-blood Son who may not have appeared perfect to the people of his time but who was the perfection of the incarnation of the Christ."

There are individuals and peoples on the planetary body who have not heard of Jesus Christ, who have their own religions and their own faith and cannot see why he is any better than anyone else. We do not deny that there are souls in heaven, saints in heaven and Ascended Masters who have attained to that level who may never have known Jesus Christ on the outer. But everyone who has ascended must come to that perfect love of the Son of God, of the Universal Christ. At a certain moment on the Path when you come that close to God, you do see the Ascended Master Jesus Christ, you do see him as the Lord and Saviour. And you do recognize that he is the keystone in the arch of the Piscean age, and none of us could get through this age without his intercession.

The Holy Christ Self of every son and daughter of God upon this planet is one with Jesus Christ. In order to ascend, every Hindu, every Buddhist and everyone else of every other religion must make peace with his own Holy Christ Self. In that process, he will know the love of this Son of God.

Christ in You, the Hope of Glory

Universal love, through the person of the Universal Christ, which manifested in Jesus so effectively, made him indeed appear to be the only begotten Son of the Father. For in the age in which he lived and in that which was to follow, there were few, if any, who could measure up to the high standards of sonship that he manifested, albeit he so kindly and prophetically declared, "Greater things shall ye do because I go unto my Father."[22]

It has been his will, even as it is the will of God the Creator, to assist all men in manifesting the intent and purpose that he, the Christ, the Divine Logos himself, envisioned for man at the moment of creation. For "by him [the Universal Christ] were all things made," and with the advent of creation, the Father's hope did not come forth to bring only one son out of captivity. The beautiful imaging of his own heart and love in perfect manifestation was not limited alone to the Logos but was intended to bring all people into perfect manifestation. Therefore, would it not be a great failure on the part of God himself if only one son could be the only begotten of the Father, if only one manifestation could truly express him?

The entire hope of God, then, is for the perfect expression of the perfect divine man to come forth in every son of his heart and manifest in every child of his intent. "Be ye therefore perfect, even as your Father which is in heaven is perfect."[23] God has never raised a hurdle so high that man cannot leap over it.

This, then, is the true forgiveness of sins: the acknowledgment and recognition that it is Christ in you that is the hope of glory—that it is Christ in every man that is the hope of glory; that Christhood is, in truth, possible of attainment. This is possible not so much through the acceptance of the person of a world saviour in the figure of the historical Jesus or even of Jesus as the great Master-Teacher, but rather through the acceptance of the figure of Christ, the example, for oneself as affirmation of the great manifestation of the Universal Christ who lived in Jesus.

The mystery of the Christ is the mystery of reality—the reality of every man. There is no greater reality than this reality of the Christ. Through this reality, all life comes into its own dimension—all life is translated and transfigured in meaning into regeneration and into the fullness of universal purpose.

This concept brings joy, not only to God but also to the man Christ Jesus, for how could a great, wise Master-Teacher, one who was called the only begotten Son of God, fail to rejoice, even as the angels in heaven rejoice, at everyone who turns from darkness and embraces the fullness of that Light that God really is?

If you were the only sinner on this planet, the only individual who had karma, God would have sent his only begotten Son, the Cosmic Christ, the Universal Christ, to embody through the Son Jesus that your soul might be saved for the path of victorious overcoming. And you are saved, not in the sense of the absolution of your karma, or sin, but in the sense that you have been taken on by Jesus, you have been supported by Jesus. He goes through the atonement for your karma even as you must work out that karma, every jot and tittle of the Law. Jesus would have incarnated for you and you alone, because God has anointed him to this office.

We contemplate, then, the love of the Father, the Father Principle and Person, the love of the Universal Son, the Principle and the Person, in the person of Jesus Christ.

Section 4

You Can Become the Christ

WHAT DOES IT MEAN TO BE A Christ? Any man or any woman can be a Christ, and all are destined to become Christs. Jesus became the Christ in the same manner that you and I can become the Christ, in the same manner that all the Ascended Masters have become the Christ, for God expects all of us to become Christs.

The Path That Jesus Walked

The Ascended Master El Morya explains some of the path that Jesus walked in preparation for his mission to show the example of the Christ to the world: "Many of you understand the journey of Jesus our Lord to the Far East, and you understand the purpose of his journey taken when a teenager, as many of you who are here today are. It was in pursuit of the teachers of the Far East and a teaching itself. It was preparatory to his final years in Palestine.*

"And so he did meet the great lights of India, and he did take the teachings of Hinduism and Buddhism and make them come alive. And he did challenge, therefore, the priesthood, the classes who denied to the poor, the full flowering of that Spirit. And he preached to the poor and he gave them back the dignity of life. And for this, they who held the reins of power in religion sought to take his life as they did later in Palestine.

"Beloved ones, I point out to you one of the most pernicious errors of orthodoxy this day, and it is the lie that Jesus is the only Son of God, and furthermore that Jesus came into embodiment in the full mastery of Christhood and did not himself have to follow the Path and realize his own inner God-potential before beginning his mission.

"These things are plain in scripture, but the scriptures have been read and reread so many times that the true intent is no longer heard by the soul. The layers of misinterpretation and then the removal of the very keys themselves have given to Christianity today a watered-down religion that does not have the fervor or the fire to meet the challengers of civilization—whether it be in World Communism or in pornography or all manner of perversion or immorality that does steal the Light of the soul.

"Beloved ones, I tell you, nothing can move forward in life unless the individual has a true understanding of God and his relationship to that eternal Spirit. Therefore, realize that Jesus did not come from God a new soul, born for the first time in his incarnation in Nazareth. Nay, I tell you! He was embodied as Joshua, the military hero of the Hebrew people.[1] He was

---

*The story of Jesus' journey to the East, during the years from 12 to 30 on which the Bible is silent, is told in ancient Buddhist manuscripts found in Leh, Ladakh. For additional information about Jesus' life during these years, see *The Lost Years of Jesus,* by Elizabeth Clare Prophet.

embodied as Joseph and wore his coat of many colors as the favorite son and did go through all manner of trial and persecution by his own brothers who were jealous of him; and yet he found favor in the sight of Pharaoh.[2]

"Beloved hearts of Light, you know the soul of Jesus in Elisha, the disciple of the prophet Elijah.[3] And you know that Elijah came again in the person of John the Baptist as was prophesied and as it is written.[4] Jesus gave to his own disciples the confirmation that this John the Baptist was Elias come again,[5] thereby ratifying the teaching of reincarnation. Yet it is still denied by those Bible-quoting Christians who have determined to say it is not so. And I will tell you *why* they say it is not so: it is because they do not want to accept their accountability for their own past karma!

"You cannot believe in reincarnation unless you will also stand, face and conquer the deeds of the past. Thus, the non-accountability, due to the upbringing of children in the West today, does not prepare warriors of the Spirit to meet the inroads that are being made by all forces of lust and greed after this nation's light and after this citadel of freedom.

"Understand, then, that your understanding of the one God and the one Christ enables you to see that that one God and one Christ has vouchsafed to you the I AM Presence and Christ Self as the manifestation of pure divinity—not many gods, but one God. And the pure Son of God is the Universal Christ whose body and bread are broken for you. And therefore, as partakers of the Light, as one with the Holy Christ Self, you also may pass through the initiations of discipleship as Jesus did. And you ought to look forward to and expect the fullness of that Christ dwelling in you bodily.

What One Can Do, All Can Do

"Wherefore evolution of a spiritual nature? Why have the prophets come? Why have the avatars appeared? Because they are favorite sons and all the rest are sinners? I tell you, *no!* And it is the most pernicious lie, as I have said, for it stops *all* short of the mark of that high calling in Christ Jesus of which the apostle spoke.[6] And none dare become heroes or leaders or examples. And those who do are set on a pedestal of idolatry rather than seen as the example!

"What one can do, all can do. And this is the philosophy of the Darjeeling Council that we would impart. We would quicken and enliven you, as God has empowered the saints to do, to unlock that potential of your heart, that divine spark, and to show you that lifetime after lifetime you have been moving toward that point of the courage to *be* who you really are and not to accept the philosophy that you are evolved from animals and that you cannot exceed the matrix of the animal creation.

"Beloved ones, what shall be left of a planet?—a scientific humanism? What shall be left?—world socialism and all shall become drones in a planetary movement controlled by moguls of power East and West?

"Beloved hearts, this is the goal of sinister forces. And let none deny that there is an Antichrist.[7] For the Antichrist is every force within and without the psyche of man that would put down that true and living God within you. Realize that this is not of necessity a person who will appear at a certain time, but it is the decision on the part of many to embody the destructive forces of the universe to put out the Light of freedom, nation by nation.

"Without the understanding of the equation of Armageddon, without the understanding of free will, it is impossible to realize that some have chosen the left-handed path of destruction, of the Lie and of the Murderer. And without accepting this, it is impossible to understand so-called human behavior, which is not human at all, but it is *devil* behavior and the behavior of devils incarnate.

"Do I sound like a fundamentalist Christian? *Well, I am!* [applause] Remember well: I came first to adore.[8] I was transformed. I was transfigured. I was, if it need be said, the first 'born-again Christian.'

"Beloved hearts, I say it only that you realize that saints East and West, whether or not they have contacted Jesus the man in his life or since, have had the conversion to Christ. And they have perceived that Christ in Buddha. They have perceived that Christ in Krishna. And let none deny it, for when you deny the Son of God in one who has outpictured that virtue and love, you effectively close the door to that Light coming into your own temple.

"Thus, you see, a religious teaching that denies the calling of the individual to embody the living Christ is, in fact, calculated by dark forces to deny the open door to divinity to every son of God. John said, 'Beloved, now are we the sons of God...,'[9] and this he learned with his head upon the breast of Jesus.[10]

"Therefore, understand the meaning of the trek to the Himalayas by the teenager Jesus. Those lost years—eighteen in number—show the great preparation of this soul of Light, this Son of man, this one who truly embodied the full effulgence of our God. It shows that by his example he left for you a record of the path of discipleship—that it is true, that it is legitimate.

"And in the ancient texts of the Vedas and the teachers of India, stored in the Himalayas and held in the heart of unascended masters, there is that living record—the law written in the very body temples of those who have kept the vigil of that which was held in the ancient temples of Lemuria. For those teachings of the Law of God that were there were transported to the caves and retreats of the Himalayas before the sinking of that continent. Thus, going back, far back beyond all recorded history, you find the lineal descent of those who have come to earth for a single purpose: to seek and find the thread of contact with Almighty God and to demonstrate by their lives a living Truth. . . .

The Discipleship of Jesus

"I commend you to the seeking of the presence with you of the Holy Spirit. I commend you to a path of devotion. I commend you to the Path that has always worked for those who have truly and sincerely applied it just as Jesus taught it: prayer and fasting, sacrifice and devotions, prayers to God and service to the poor and the meek. This is the path of the balancing of karma, putting on the consciousness of God day by day, being the instrument of the flow of the mighty River of Life.

"This is the message of the discipleship of the teenager Jesus who went to find his teacher Maitreya, who went to sit at the feet of Buddha who had come and gone five hundred years before his journey. He came to sit at the feet of those Masters who had gone on before him. And he stopped at Luxor to be initiated in the first steps of the initiation temple, when he could have been accorded the full mantle of the Master of that temple.[11]

"Jesus gave obeisance and deference to the order of Hierarchy. And this you see well-recorded in scripture in the hour of his transfiguration—the Father and the Son ordaining the presence of the Ascended Master Moses, the presence of the Ascended Master Elijah. They talked with Jesus, they spoke with him! Ascended Masters spoke with the unascended Son of

God; and his disciples Peter, James, and John were witnesses and they wrote of it.[12] And it is set forth in the Gospels.[13]

"This is the example that is unmistakable of the chain of Hierarchy. It illustrates that there were some who ascended and were in heaven with God before Jesus—such as Enoch, who walked with God and was not, for God took him.[14]

"Thus, the ancients who went before were taken up by God. Thus you realize that the path Jesus followed was never an exception, was not something unique and exceptional where one life should atone for the sins of the many,[15] but the example of what had been done again and again and again— always the avatar coming to give to the disciples on earth the example that there is a way out of Death and Hell and the round of suffering. There is a way of self-transcendence. Death is not the end of life.

"And in the parting of the veil in that hour it is well to be prepared, to have woven the deathless solar body, which is referred to by Jesus as the wedding garment. And he said to that one who came into the marriage feast, 'Friend, how camest thou in without the wedding garment? Bind him, hand and foot, and cast him into outer darkness!'[16]

"The wedding garment is the spiritual body that you weave with the Word and the Work of God. It is the fiery aura of the saints, and it is the means of transporting the soul to those octaves of Light whence you descended into this lowly estate of flesh, as it is put—and to which you shall return.

"Beloved ones, the prayer 'Thy kingdom come on earth as it is in heaven' is the prayer of the saints who would bring that rarefied Light of the etheric octave into the physical, who would bring to this earth plane a Utopia perhaps—a new world, a New Atlantis, a way of life that can exceed this one, where people can be free from pain and terminal diseases caused not alone by their karma but caused by the chemicals, the impure foods, the substances they take in—a world free from war and the eruption of violence from the bowels of those whose free will has been used to commit them to a path of error.

"And error leads to unreality. And unreality leads to insanity. Thus, the insane stalk the earth taking innocent life. The insane take the life of the unborn and call it woman's right. Woman's right to murder her child! Is she liberated? No! She is enslaved to a pain that gnaws within her for the rest of her life and in future incarnations until it is resolved.

"Offering liberty, they sow corruption—corruption of the spirit and the soul and not of the body. And this is why the dangers of this age are so great. And this is why I say it is the greatest moment in all history for each and every one of you to make your statement and to establish that contact with God that all who have gone before you have made, and thereby become instruments of Light and spiritual power and healing and the holding of the balance of nations.

"The overwhelming proof is on the side of the path of discipleship. It has a consistency over tens and thousands of years. You will not find any difference, save perhaps in a slight manner of form or ritual, in the paths of the saints East or West. There is no difference in the Light of the eye or the shining of the aura or the power of the chakras or the beginning ability of transmutation and alchemy that comes into your life when you begin to invoke the violet flame.

"The consistency of this path, side by side with the absolute inconsistency of the factions of Protestantism, of Catholicism, of Judaism, or of the Moslems who argue perpetually one with the other and remain separated and divided because they cannot agree on the letter! And they have left off from the true Spirit. And even in that spirit of ecumenism, beloved ones, you find that they have not come to the resolution of their doctrine, nor have they given to their flocks the power of God to turn the tide of world conditions.

"One and all, understand the great joy as a child rejoices in his first step, the first word he can spell or read or identify on a sign, the first piece he can play on the piano, or a laurel wreath given at graduation. Understand that the path of achievement—striving, running in the race, winning the gold cup—is a path that mirrors the path of discipleship to all. It is the sense internally: 'I have worked, I have mastered—God with me and by his grace. And because I know who I AM and God is with me, I can do these things.'

"It's like having it in your pocket. It is something you have done. When and if it should ever be the case that a Master do for the disciple what the disciple can only do for himself, the disciple will be just like the child or any of you. The person for whom something is given without responsibility, without effort and work, without inner achievement resents the individual who gives to him that reward without effort.

"Thus, the false pastors who preach create, in fact, a servile relationship of sinners to a favorite son, and internally and subconsciously it is actually the hatred of Christ that is at work.... Realize this: that many pastors who are thus indoctrinated are not of an evil bent but have simply followed the party line they have been given and that has been carried on for generations."[17]

Developing the Christ Consciousness

The Tibetan Master Djwal Kul explains how the student of the mysteries can consciously develop the Christ consciousness through the practice of meditation and visualization: "Now as you read my words, sitting in meditation perhaps before the statue of the Buddha, the image of the Christ or the Chart of Your Divine Self, visualize concentric rings of Light emanating from the center of your heart, and realize that each successive attainment in cosmic consciousness anchors the Light of the Cosmic Christ as a permanent layer of Light within your aura.

"The layers of the aura that are filled with Light mark the levels of initiation—of the neophyte, the postulant, the acolyte, the disciple, the adept, and so on in the hierarchical scale. When each layer is filled with Light, and the soul moves in its expanding self-awareness to the point where it magnetizes more Light than the capacity of the layers, the aura is translated from the human to the Divine. And it is not long before the soul is elevated in its expression from the planes of Matter to the planes of Spirit—for the world can no longer contain it.

"As you increase the intensity of the aura through meditation and application of the sacred fire by giving mantras of the Spirit such as the Transfiguring Affirmations of Jesus the Christ,* which he taught to his disciples, you not only increase the dimensions of your aura in time and space, but you find that your aura becomes a means of communicating with new dimensions of the Spirit even while it transports your soul into higher frequencies of Matter.

"Whereas your communication with Beings and energies in the planes of Spirit may occur in periods of meditation and invocation, soul travel occurs most often while your body temple is at rest during the hours of sleep. For you see, the aura that you build as a reflection of your awareness of God in many planes surrounds not only the physical form, but also the etheric, mental and emotional vehicles.

"The aura, then, serves as the forcefield of Light that has been called the seamless garment. This garment adorns the etheric body as that body becomes the vehicle of the soul in its journeying in other octaves of Matter.

"To develop the aura, then, is to prepare the place of

*See page 252.

consciousness where, by the law of congruency, you can receive here and now in the planes of Mater* those Ascended Masters and Christed ones whose Light bodies will mesh with your own because your aura has taken on and become the frequency of the Holy Spirit that is individualized by various members of the Great White Brotherhood. To be sure, it is the dimensions of life with which you identify whereby the attainment of your cosmic consciousness is measured.

"The action of the law of congruency is indeed wondrous to behold! As the magnet of the heart in its rising action is the equilateral triangle that compels the descent of the triangle of Spirit, so that very six-pointed star will magnetize to your heart an identical momentum of Light that is held in the heart of one or more Ascended Beings.

"By your free will you can qualify the interlaced triangles of the heart with any of the frequencies of the seven rays or of the Holy Ghost that is the unifying Spirit of the Great White Brotherhood. When, for instance, you dedicate the fires of your heart to the Divine Mother and diligently give the salutations to Mary, your heart becomes an orifice of the Mother's love, your aura contains the very patterns that flow from the Virgin Queen to your own over the arc of your adoration.

"At a certain point in your devotions and in the evolution of your solar awareness of the Divine Mother, the magnet of the aura and the heart reaches, as it were, a critical mass—that is, an energy momentum sufficient to magnetize the very living Presence of the Divine Mother herself. And by the law of congruency, your aura then becomes the aura of the Virgin Mary.

"Then, as you recite the Hail Mary, you are giving the salutation to the flame of the Divine Mother that now burns

---

Mater is Latin for "mother." The term is used interchangeably with "Matter" to describe the planes of being that conform with the aspect of God as Mother—the physical, material universe.

within your own heart. And as you have called to become her hands and her feet, her body and her mind, so the call has compelled the answer. And the answer has come not as a miracle—not as an exception to natural law, but in fulfillment of that law.

"Thus, as you increase the intensity and the Light frequency of the heart, which in turn feeds energy to all of the chakras in Matter and expands the rings of the aura, you come to the place where, through the merging of the aura of the Ascended Masters with your own, you can proclaim the joy of God's geometry; 'Behold, I and my Father are one; I and my Mother are one!' And lo, the star Above has become the star below!

"Wherever you are in consciousness at this moment, know, O chela of the Light, that you are one with every other soul, whether in Matter or in Spirit, who is at this moment experiencing that level, that frequency, of God's Being. If you are meditating upon Jesus the Christ and his great life example, then you are one with all others who have an identical appreciation for his ministry. And if by your meditation upon Jesus you become that Christ, then you are also one with every other soul who has ever become the Christ—past, present and future." [18]

The Individualization of the God Flame

The early Christian Gnostics understood that to become the Christ was the goal of Jesus' teachings. We read in *The Secret Book of James* (also called *The Apocryphon of James*), a Gnostic text, that the Lord says to James: "If you are afflicted and persecuted by Satan, and do the Father's will, I say this: The Father will love you and make you my equal." [19]

How do you become the equal of Jesus Christ? The Christ Presence, the only begotten Son of the Father, is exactly your Holy Christ Self. If you will do the Father's will, the Father will enable you to become one with that Christ. When you become one with that Christ, you are equal to Jesus as he was one with that Christ. That does not make you an avatar in manifestation, but it restores you to your natural birthright and inheritance in Christ. It is an equal opportunity.

The great Truth of the Ascended Masters is that we have an equal right with Jesus to become the Christ. There is often a violent reaction among theologians today to anyone who will propose this, and that is why this teaching could not be brought through the churches. People are frightened to consider that there is more than one Son of God.

But is there more than one Son of God? We have to consider this great mystery. The only begotten of the Father, the Christ, the Second Person of the Trinity, is the principle of identity that is One. We have not departed from the Law of the One, from the teaching of Jesus: "Hear, O Israel; The Lord our God is one Lord."[20]

There is one Father, one Son and one Holy Spirit comprising the Trinity. The great mystery is that the manifestation of the Trinity as a flame, as a fire, can be multiplied, can be experienced again and again and again. Over and over and over again throughout cosmos, we can experience God. This does not detract from the essential oneness of God. It is in time and space that this one appears to be many.

Each of you has the Trinity as a flame burning within your heart. Does that mean that there are gods many? No, it just expresses the infinity of God to be himself wherever he wishes to be himself over and over and over and over again. And therefore, those who deny that essential element of the Godhead within deny God's ability to be infinite. They are circumscribing God with man-made laws.

We are joint heirs with Christ[21] because we have the inheritance of the Trinity as the threefold flame of life, which is the spark of Reality. When we understand this law, see how we are liberated to express our free will as a confirmation of that flame within. Therefore, the only begotten Son, the Christed One full of grace and truth, the Word that became flesh, is the Second Person of the Trinity that can be experienced anywhere and everywhere that God chooses. *And God has chosen to externalize that Christ within you.*

You can claim the totality of that Christ and that manifestation without ever depriving the person sitting next to you of it, without ever detracting from the splendor of the Saviour who is Jesus the Christ. Taking the Light that is God and becoming that Light will not deprive any avatar of it, will not detract from that glory, but enhance it. We enhance the life and the mission of Jesus Christ when we become the Christ.

There is no competition in God when you understand the great circle of the One. We are simply ones of the One—portions of the One adding to the great conflagration, the great sacred fire of all life that is Being itself. And the more we externalize that life and that fire, the more we add to the presence of Christ on earth.

The great lie of the ages is the lie that you are not, in reality, the Christ. That lie must be broken, because unless we break it, we cannot exercise free will. We cannot go beyond that point of the law of sin that says to us we are all sinners. If we accept that law, we are accepting our death, for the prophet said, The soul that sinneth, it shall die,[22] and Paul said, The wages of sin is death.[23] Because mankind have accepted this belief, we live in a society that is marked by the death cult.

The Return to the Great Central Sun

Sanat Kumara says: "I AM the Ancient of Days. I have spent my Light in earth, and it has returned to me. Now, I demand the multiplication of that Light, the fruit of the increase of my Tree of Life. Each one of you, that fruit, must come Home even as you left our star. You must come Home the victors over Death and Hell as Jesus is and was. As my Son told you, Except you become the Christ, you can in no wise enter in.

"Be fruitful and multiply thy Light, for all else is superfluity; all else is vanity. Let thy goings and thy comings, therefore, be for the increase of the flame."[24]

The birth in Mater must be the birthday when the soul decides to be free. Christians call it being reborn in Christ. It is the quickening and the awakening, the kindling of the soul, whereby the soul determines to return to the Great Central Sun. We have been electrons in orbit, planets in orbit. It is time for the great in-breath. It is time for our return. If your soul were not fully conscious of this one fact, you would not be reading this book. The rebirth, then, is that awakening and quickening of the soul that comes by the flame of the eternal Christ, the very personal Christ Jesus, your very personal Christ Self and the Cosmic Christ whose consciousness is focused for us by Lord Maitreya.

Sometimes the word *Christ* is a stumbling block. You don't have to use that term. You can call it your Real Self. Call it the fire, the Light, the spark.

The prophets of the Old Testament were every bit as much the Christ as Jesus was. And the great teachers of the East were also every bit the Christ as Jesus was. Christ is the Christ of all ages and always will be. There were Christs on Atlantis long before Jesus was born. Christ is the ageless Hierarchy of Light, the great Mediator.

And so, we have to realize that Jesus was the soul of the man who became the Christ. Speak your own name within your heart now and say, "I AM Mary—John, Bill, Bob or Tony—I AM that one whom God has designated to become the Christ." When the soul exercises right choice, it converges at the point of the Christ Self-awareness, and so, as this happened in the life of Jesus, he came to be called Jesus the Christ. The whole path of freedom, of initiation, the walk back to God, is based on the soul's communion with its own Inner Reality, with the Mediator—putting on and becoming Reality. This is what the Ascended Masters have come to show us.

Jesus and Our Own Christ Self

Serapis Bey explains the relationship between the Christ of Jesus and our own Christ Self: "O troubled one, let not your heart be troubled. For trouble and the grumbling over troubles must surely be because you think that all of the world's problems must be solved this very day. And when you demand it of the cosmos, the cosmos will not answer you; for cosmos knows that God has already solved every problem of the whole world, and he has set the mind of Christ for the cycling forth of the resolution.

"Yours it is not to solve problems, but to mount the spiral of the original problem-solver, the Cosmic Christ, and simply be in attunement with that mind that always knows everything to do and to say and to be, and to know to be active when it is time to be active and to know to be still when it is space for stillness.

"Listen, then. Problems will appear regularly like specters out of the astral deep in your life. They will parade across the screen of your mind, tempting you to become anxious and worrisome and burdened. But you see, God has already placed the image of the golden man of the heart across the very same screen. And these specters, by the magnet of Christ, are in the process of dissolution if you will only let them go and be dissolved! But if you energize them with your worrisomeness, they will be activated by a surge of energy that you release in states of emotional turmoil and disturbance.

"I said, *God has already solved every problem that will appear in your entire life!* And every problem is karma—yours or another's that you allow to get in your way. God has foreknown from the beginning the cycles of your karma, for he is the Lawgiver and the Lawtaker. Therefore, know there *is* a Christ. He liveth! He is the One Sent.[25]

"There is the Word. There is Maitreya. There is every Ascended Master you can name. But the most important name that you can name is your own! Therefore, name it and cry it out in this hour!

"That is the most important name you can pronounce, for to claim it as your own is to claim your opportunity to be Christ. The most important Christ that can become where you are is *your* Christ, you see. For you really cannot ultimately benefit from another's awareness and amazing self-mastery through that Christ.

"Now, they have taught you to believe that Jesus is the most important Christ. And sometimes you have believed that Saint Germain or Gautama Buddha or Maitreya or even Sanat Kumara is the most important Christ. When this lie of nonrecognition of God within came along, there also came along the great Teacher Gautama, who taught self-definition of Christhood and therefore has been condemned ever since by those indoctrinated with the orthodoxy of Rome and other materialistic ones.

"See, then, the God that is important is the God where you are. And because you are so trained to believe that Jesus is the one who is important, you forget to guard the Christ where you are.

"Jesus is compassionate. When you call him, he answers. But his answer is always the activation of Christ in you! Did you know that, beloved hearts? When Christians pray to him, he acts out of compassion to accelerate, by his own Light, their self-awareness of Christ. And many have seen the vision of

Christ, and they have said, 'I am well because Jesus did this to me,' when, in reality, they are well because Jesus connected the soul of their being to their own Christ Self. And in the moment of their receipt of the Light, every one has known and understood in the heart the relationship of the Christ Self....

"You are the living Christ. I come to show you how the living teaching, spoken to the waking consciousness and the conscious mind illumined by Christ, changes the whole world, the *whole world* of your being!"[26]

It Is Possible to Fail

Serapis also explains that even though Christhood is our destiny, it is our application to the Path that will determine the outcome. He says that there is only one way we can fail. "You can fail if you let go of the hand of the golden man of the heart, if you let go of love and forget your reason for winning and your reason for winning again. If you forget to look up to heaven before you bless and serve and heal all life, you may fail. And if you do not watch the earth—every footstep, where you carefully place it—you may fall into the trap, you may not notice the subtle plots along the way.

"There is only one person in the universe who can fail. It is *you*. There is only one person in the universe who can become the Christ. It is you. Gautama Buddha taught there is no one else but you in your universe. It is all up to you. No one can make you fail. *No one* can make you become the Christ!"[27]

And Jesus says, "Fear not to become thy Christ, but fear indeed to take the Light of Christ to improve the image of the not-self. Thus, perfect not the human. It is not perfectible. But let the soul be perfected through the shedding of unreality."[28]

"O my beloved, the essence of my teaching has been and ever shall be: You *can* become a Christ!"[29]

Section 5

The Path of Personal Christhood

THOSE WHO ENGAGE IN THE WORK OF
the LORD are those who have per-
ceived the path of karma yoga in the ethic of work. They have
seen work as a means of balancing karma and also a means to
spiritual attainment as they have developed mastery in the
physical octave that registers, records and magnifies the attainment at spiritual levels.

The danger of this path is that we engage in work for the
sake of work and lose the very goal and purpose of the work,
which is the victory of the ascension. Worse yet, we may think
that because we indeed work so very hard and make so many
sacrifices that these sacrifices will count for the balance of a
multitude of infractions of the Law or indulgences, or we may
consider that God will wink at other manifestations that must
have our attention.

In fact, this is not so. The reason we need a teacher and the
reason we need the Ascended Masters is that the things we need
to be taught are those things that we never see ourselves because

they represent the densities in our consciousness that blind us. When we are blinded to the condition of our density, we simply carry on in that density. The human may engage in human goodness or human badness, but yet it remains the human, and it has not the means of transcending itself. The soul that is in that temple is entirely bound, therefore, by the mortal and the mortal consciousness until it can make contact with its own Christ Self. But because of the great gulf that separates the soul from the Christ Self, this is difficult to do.

Therefore, God has sent teachers, avatars, great prophets, great ones from other planets and octaves to be on the earth, to state the message, to point the way by preaching and by example. Had it not been for all of these elder brothers and sisters, we would not know the way to go, and we would not understand the subtlety or the deadly nature of the unreality of maya, of illusion. We would not understand the subtlety of the antithesis of the Christ Self, which we call the carnal mind, or the synthetic image.

Self-Transcendence

Serapis Bey and the World Teachers have said that there comes a point on the Path when you are climbing the mountain, when all of a sudden you turn a right angle and you must go straight up. Your life changes entirely. All of your associations and past involvements change. Things happen in your life almost cataclysmically. If you accept this and you are willing to go forward, and if you can bear that period of adjustment of overcoming the old human habits of human association and involvement, you will meet the initiates and the Masters on that path. You will find yourself contacting the Brotherhood, station by station, and the personal experience the Great Ones have had will be yours.

This is not a collective experience, but an individual one,

and therefore each one must find the reckoning with his own Christ Self and I AM Presence. Each one must discover what is acceptable and what is not. This is not condemnation. God does not condemn us. But when we are sensitive, we know what we must do, and we know when we are not functioning at that level at which our Christ Self impels us to function. We realize it from within, and we must not let our own forcefield, our own atmosphere of self-condemnation interpret the LORD's rebuke or the LORD's chastening or his teaching as the LORD's condemnation.

The LORD does not condemn us. Morya does not condemn us, neither does Serapis Bey. But there is a very firm vibration of the Law that communicates to us, if we are willing to hear it, a certain sternness that says, "You cannot any longer indulge this specific vibration and fulfill your calling or win your victory." It ought not to be rationalized. It ought not to be feared. We should not get in a tailspin and feel that we are not loved or not praised, and so forth. But we should heed that call. Dismiss every vibration of condemnation, but go to the heart of love and realize that love is stern because it is concentrating upon you and me the energy necessary for us to come out of the cocoon, to shed the snakeskin, to always transcend ourselves day by day.

Beloved Helios once said, "I want to tell you that a million years from now you would not even shake your own hand, because you would not wish to contaminate yourselves."[1] Realize that there will always be the sense of dissatisfaction with one's former state. Even if there is nothing evil about it, nothing malintended, it is simply that the former state is more limited than the state we have with each new birth and each new day.

The Ascended Masters and the Elohim are standing before you personally. You are a beloved chela of the Ascended

Masters. If you would put yourself in the place of God, with his profound love for the disciples and the children of Light on earth, do you not think that, if you were able to by Law, you would not pour out upon the chela every possible blessing and gift of the whole universe? If you could see the Ascended Masters, you would realize that they have to hold back because they cannot extend the reward; they cannot extend the initiation because there is a nonfulfillment of the Law somewhere in your being.

The Fulfilling of the Law

Those who are orthodox Jews place a great weight on fulfilling the law of Moses and the law of the Talmud. They recognize that when God sends forth his Law as covenant, it is important that we obey, because obedience to the Law is the key to our liberation.

The apostles taught and Jesus taught that grace becomes the fulfilling of the Law and that there is a higher law of self-transcendence, that it is not necessary to observe in a materialistic sense all of the proscriptions and dietary laws of the Old Testament. Nevertheless, there is a basic, fundamental law whose thread runs through the law of Moses, of Sanat Kumara and of every religion. When we are in violation of that law, we suffer loss.

The fundamental law that we must obey is the law of harmony. This means harmony in all of our members. It also includes dietary harmony. Beginning from that premise, from that central sun of harmony, we go forth and we discover all of the other laws. Harmony is love; harmony is oneness.

We encourage you to consider yourself as one of the lonely ones, as an individual unique and apart from the group for the purpose of the exercise of determining your path—your path of individual self-mastery, your path of Christhood. And then come together again and feel the oneness of community. Do not allow any sense of collectivism or organization to dilute your intensity or your placing your emphasis where you have found that particular teaching or Master that you know you are answerable to, you know you must work on.

Do work on it. Become a star on that path. Become an expert. And by your example of Light and purity and love, let others also be inspired, not to follow your path but to find their path, to find their Master and their key of acceleration.

The Path of Christhood Portrayed by Isaiah

The Bible and the scriptures East and West portray the path of the Bodhisattva, of the disciple becoming the Christ. But unless you understand the progressive revelation of the Ascended Masters in this age, you do not savor the details and the wonderful gems that are there.

The path of your Christhood is beautifully outlined in the Book of Isaiah, and chapter 53 of Isaiah is a magnificent testament of the perception of the prophet of the coming Christ. We must read it with the realization that the most crucial event happening in our life today and on the planet as a whole is the individual becoming that Christ. Because the one soul who does embody that Christ in his temple, who does all things necessary that that Christ should be comfortable in his temple, is the one who, when raising up that Light, can hold the balance for the world.

This testament is Isaiah's understanding of the experience of everyone who has ever fulfilled the mission of the Word incarnate.

Who hath believed our report? and to whom is the arm of the LORD the mighty I AM Presence revealed?

For he shall grow up before him as a tender plant, and as

a root out of a dry ground: he hath no form nor comeliness; and when we shall see him, there is no beauty that we should desire him. This is the description of the soul becoming one with Christ.

He is despised and rejected of men; a man of sorrows, and acquainted with grief: and we hid as it were our faces from him; he was despised, and we esteemed him not. This is the one who has become the Christ in our midst.

Surely he hath borne our griefs, and carried our sorrows: yet we did esteem him stricken, smitten of God, and afflicted.

But he was wounded for our transgressions—this is Jesus, this is Gautama, this is the Son of man—he was bruised for our iniquities. He was burdened for our karma, for our failure to surrender, to transmute, to press on in becoming our own Christhood. The chastisement of our peace was upon him; and with his stripes we are healed. We allowed him, that Christ, to bear our burden, and in turn, we were healed by his very afflictions.

All we like sheep have gone astray from our own Christ Self, we have turned every one to his own way; and the LORD hath laid on him the iniquity of us all. The great teaching is that the Christ and the one who has become that Christ incarnate bears the karma of those who would not and will not, for it is every man's option so to do.

He was oppressed, and he was afflicted, yet he opened not his mouth: he is brought as a lamb to the slaughter, and as a sheep before her shearers is dumb, so he openeth not his mouth.

He was taken from prison and from judgment: and who shall declare his generation? Who shall declare that the Christic generation of the seed of Light shall be our generation with all of its burdens and woes? Who shall claim him for his own? For he was cut off out of the land of the living: for the transgression of my people was he stricken.

And he made his grave with the wicked, and with the rich in his death; because he had done no violence, neither was any deceit in his mouth.

Yet it pleased the LORD to bruise him. Allowing that Christ to be bruised is the testimony that we must see. We must see that Christ bruised in the homeless, the dispossessed, the oppressed people of every nation. We must look into the face of a Lightbearer in Afghanistan and say, "There is Christ. And he is bruised because I have not become that Christ." God uses all kinds of people on this earth to deliver the message that we cannot allow ourselves to become fattened in the spirituality and the spirit that is the free gift of God to us, that there are obligations and a price to be paid for this path. **He hath put him to grief: when thou shalt make his soul an offering for sin, he shall see his seed, he shall prolong his days, and the pleasure of the LORD shall prosper in his hand.**

He shall see of the travail of his soul, and shall be satisfied: by his knowledge shall my righteous servant justify many; for he shall bear their iniquities.

Therefore will I divide him a portion with the great, and he shall divide the spoil with the strong; because he hath poured out his soul unto death: and he was numbered with the transgressors; and he bare the sin of many, and made intercession for the transgressors.

Stages of the Path

This teaching helps us understand the nature of the Path and the psychology of the soul personality that is yet bound by certain cords of its own mortality and the laws of mortality that it has accepted.

When the soul first receives the teaching and the gladness

and the joy of the violet flame and the delight of the fruit of the tree of Maitreya, the experience is like a perennial childhood we have longed for, to be in the very presence of our Father-Mother God—those joyous days of light overflowing and the perpetual smile and the childlike heart. This is the newness of the contact with the teachings of the Ascended Masters. There is very little responsibility or obligation; yet our cups are full with the new wine, the wine of the Spirit. Our decrees afford us liberation from our greatest burdens.

Then, we pass into a stage of adolescence with the usual rebellions: "Well, I don't really want to have to tether to this law. I want to be apart from it for a while. I want to enjoy the universe without obligation." If we have wise parents, they don't let us get away with it. If we listen to our gurus, we know that they will tell us we cannot afford this indulgence.

Then there comes the point of spiritual maturity and adulthood, and it is marked by the hour when the Brotherhood determines that the individual disciple has received the full awareness, the full education, the knowledge, the opportunity and the gifts of the Spirit in abundance. There is a moment when, after the immense giving, there is a shift of the weight. Now the soul contains the momentum of God she* has received. Now, what will she do with it? Will she give it back to God by way of service to his own? Will she go out again with all of this light and energy and squander it in fun, in doing all those things she always wanted to do but never quite could because of the limitations of her karma, which is now being borne by this servant that bears our iniquities?

There comes a moment of full maturity where the adult stands at the "Y" and must choose the left-handed path or the right-handed path. The left-handed path is adeptship in the use

---

*The soul is the feminine counterpart of the masculine Spirit, and thus is referred to as "she".

of all of this energy and Light for self-aggrandizement, for the building of a temporal kingdom, moving with the false hierarchies of the centuries. The right-handed path is the path of adeptship where one goes on and, with that Light given, recognizes this principle: that each new day to receive more Light, which is necessary to simply maintain the new position, one must give up more.

Now, some have said in their hearts, "I will not choose the left-handed path, for I see the dangers," but in fact and in practice, neither have they chosen the right-handed path. They try to remain aloof from either choice, remove themselves from that place where they might receive some message of their own Master; or they will tune out the message of their own Christ Self that surely does tell them that they cannot simply stay at a certain niche. There are grave consequences to this choice, because one will go back. One may deceive oneself into believing that one can remain at a certain place, but one cannot.

The following episode drawn from Elizabeth's life illustrates a similar principle.

A Lesson from Life

I remember the great lesson I had when I was young. My father had a boatyard on a river in New Jersey that led out to the sea. I used to like to go down to the river and take a rowboat and row around the river, and on nice days I could row very far out and tie up to a buoy and sit back and read a book or go swimming off the boat. Sometimes I would take a picnic lunch.

One day I took a girlfriend with me and we two ventured forth in the rowboat, and we got out, far out into the river and a great storm came up, taking us farther and farther away from my father's dock. I was rowing, and I had to row with the full and total strength of my being, and in doing so, I could maintain the boat where it was. I could not get ahead, but I was not going back.

But then I thought to myself that I was getting weary, so I decided to turn over the oars to my girlfriend. She was not an experienced rower. She did not have the developed strength in rowing that I had from years of doing this. When she took the oars, I found that we were swiftly drifting further and further away, what seemed like miles down the river. So, as soon as I could, I got myself back in the seat and started rowing to make up for the distance that we had lost.

This was an amazing lesson to me, because I realized that in taking the raft over the sea of samsara, over the astral plane, that all would depend upon me. I could not rely on anyone. I would have to summon my own internal strength, my spiritual forces and my momentum gained in the physical plane. And if I should let go for one moment and trust anyone else with my life, my path, the work that I must do, I would lose that ground, because I would be abdicating my personal Christhood.

The next lesson I learned from this experience was that when one is giving all of one's strength against the storm of life and truly doing everything one can with all one's resources, the Divine Helper comes, and that in the person of the Guru.

I could not do any more, given the knowledge I had then. So, in the person of someone with a speedboat (a total stranger), the Divine Helper came along, tied a rope to our rowboat and towed us in, which is the only way we could have gotten back.

It somehow was a very archetypal lesson, because every now and then that picture comes back to me. El Morya holds up the scene and then shows me how to read the lesson from it. I was very young, and the lessons we learn when we are young go into the subconscious and they are there, and we make decisions based on many lessons we've learned in life.

The Path Requires Striving

Here we are on a similar path. It is no less strenuous. After all, God is about to transfer to you and reward you with the fullness of the I AM Presence, with that Godhood dwelling in you bodily. He will demand all of you and more, all that you can summon beyond yourself. Your Christ Self and your soul, one with that Christ Self, has a period of going through what is described in chapter 53 of Isaiah.

Serapis Bey has delivered the message that Jesus Christ is taken down from the cross and that we are also taken down from the cross.[2] We are no longer available for the crucifixion. This is true. But each one has to claim this for himself. And the freedom from the crucifixion is not the freedom from bearing personal and world karma. We are all called to bear it, and the more Christhood we put on, the greater the weight of karma we will carry.

You can allow the period of karma-bearing to be experienced as though it were the crucifixion or as heavy persecution. Or you can establish the mastery of it by that wondrous period on the path of the Bodhisattva that falls on the three-o'clock line* of the joyous one, the saint, the one who realizes the I AM THAT I AM. Not God, but you determine whether or not you experience life as a crucifixion, a burden, a persecution —or as the immensity of the Light.

There is a place where you do accelerate, you do charge forward, you do make the decision to enter that right-handed path with the full force of your being, and you begin to experience

---

*The Ascended Masters diagram the different manifestations of God on the lines of the cosmic clock. The three-o'clock line is the line where we realize God as the Christ, as the Person of the Son. Twelve is the line of God as Father, six of God as Mother, and nine is the line of the Holy Spirit. For further information about the cosmic clock, see *The Great White Brotherhood in the Culture, History and Religion of America,* chapter 15.

some of these symptoms that are described in Isaiah of that Christ—the Son of man.

There is a period where you strive. You have indeed dipped into and put on a certain momentum of your Christhood. And now come the burdens. Now come the greater requirements of the Law. Now comes the stress. And the soul whose psychology is programmed by the mortal mind and the law of mortality says, "This is too much for me. I am going to go backward a little bit. I am going to take it easy. I am not going to get involved with all these things that put all this pressure on me."

So, to avoid psychological tensions and stresses and things that we can allow ourselves to either indulge or overcome in a very practical way, we fall back. We taste our Christhood and we say, "I am not going to be a martyr. I am going to live my life sanely. I am not going to be a fanatic with the Path."

You have to realize that the Reality of your Christhood does not contain all that stress. It does not contain all that burden. If you take *all* of your Christhood, your Christhood has the Light to offset the burden. The part of us that suffers is the part that does not surrender, the part of us that holds back, the part of us that wants the best of both worlds.

If you want the best of the astral plane and the best of heaven, you will not be able to take it. It will drive you insane. And so, just before you go insane, you announce to everybody that "Instead of going insane I am going to put myself at a wide, wide distance from this situation. I can't take it. I am just not made that way. I can't do all these things." Well, that's the human will. That's the carnal mind. That's the mortal mind that's limiting that soul that really wants to be born in Christ. People will come up with the most complex, yet logical and seemingly practical reasons, why they cannot be in their intended place of service to God *now*, which means being in your Christhood and the fullness of the glory of God where you stand.

There is no reason for martyrdom. The Great White Brotherhood does *not* advocate that any of their chelas be a martyr. It went out with the Piscean age and the misinterpretation of Jesus' doctrine. Jesus was no martyr.

Nothing can stop you from realizing your Christhood except yourself. Nothing else in the world can keep you from that goal except yourself.

Discipleship and Christhood

El Morya's definition of a disciple, or chela, is "one who is striving to become the Christ."[3] The path of discipleship unto Christhood has been well marked by those who have walked it before us. They have outlined on this path the following steps of initiation unto the Living Word:

(1) **Student:** Under this phase the individual studies, becomes a student of the writings and the teachings of the Master. He is free to come and go and has declared no particular responsibility to the person of the Master. He has taken no vows, made no commitment, but may be studying to "show himself approved"[4] in order to be accepted as a servant (otherwise known as "chela") of the Master.

(2) **Servant or Chela, i.e., Disciple:** The individual desires to enter into a bond with the Master—to be taught directly by the Master rather than through his published writings alone. The servant, or chela, receives initiations in the course of his service to the Master. His heart, mind and soul have begun to unfold a greater love as appreciation and gratitude for the teachings received in the previous level of student. This love is translated into action as self-sacrifice, selflessness, service and surrender to the Christ. When this step has been accelerated to

the level of the "acceptable offering," and the chela is engaged in balancing his threefold flame and his karma, he may be considered for the next step.

(3) **Friend:** Those counted as friend of the Master enter by invitation—"Henceforth I call you no more servants but friends" (see John 15)—into a relationship as companion and co-worker on the path of world salvation. The friend bears the cross as well as the burden of Light of the Master; he demonstrates the qualities of friendship as in the life of Abraham and other chelas who have risen to a level of understanding the very heart and the experience of the Master—providing comfort, consolation, advice and support out of loyalty to both the purposes and the person of the Master.

(4) **Brother:** The degree of brother is the level where the oneness of the Guru-chela, Alpha-Omega relationship is complete through the horizontal figure-eight exchange heart-to-heart; the Guru has actually made his disciple a part of his own flesh and blood and offered to him the full momentum of his attainment and portions of his mantle and authority in preparation for the Master's ascension and the disciple's assuming part or whole of the Master's office. This is the love relationship exemplified between Jesus and John and perhaps his own flesh-and-blood brother (or cousin) James.

(5) **Christ:** The full incarnation of the Word.

The Hour of Christhood

"The hour of Christhood in you," says the Lord Sanat Kumara, "is more important than any other event taking place upon the planet."[5] When the Christ is born in the waiting chalice of the heart, that is when the Light of the Great Central Sun descends to illumine a world. If this is more important than any other event on the planet, then we must take this calling very seriously. We must realize that never can we do more for this world than on that day and date when we decide to walk in the footprints of our Lord and Saviour and to internalize the Word that he fed to us morsel by morsel, drop by drop of his precious blood.

Jesus has told us, "I have come to bring to you the Word of our Father, and it is this: The hour has come for you to understand that nothing less than becoming the Christ will suffice as fulfillment or requirement of the Law. This is the day that the path of thy Christhood must begin in earnest."[6]

You may have a number of goals in your life today and one central goal that is all-consuming. We urge you to pray as to how you can make all of your goals converge at the point of the path of Christhood. For you, becoming that Christ may be being a householder and having a family and children, or being a professional or doing all kinds of things that are necessary to fulfill positive momentums of karma and to balance negative karma.

All these things can converge. You don't have to let go of anything except it come under the heading of such things as incorrect livelihood or other activities that are not compatible with the Eightfold Path of the Buddha.

Whatever is lawful in the purity of the Christ and the Holy Christ Self, whatever is lawful for the Buddhic manifestation within you, which is love and joy and the givingness of self—whatever that is can become a part of your Christhood. And whatever else you are doing or you are that is not a part of your Christhood, let go of it. Just let it drop.

It is no sacrifice to be the Christ. It is the greatest joy and the greatest gift of God to us. It is the joy of divine love. When we talk about a path of surrender and sacrifice and selflessness and service, it is not a path of self-denial. It is a path of the affirmation of True Being and the letting go of all that is unreal about ourselves. Let go forever of those things that you keep looking back to and that you cannot let go of, when all of the things that are really important in life are yours in abundance, in joy, in happiness, in glory. The path of Christhood is not a path of the sorrowful way.

The Highest Calling

Archangel Gabriel says that the person "who will claim his Christhood and call forth the Father and the Son to take up their abode in his temple may displace the darkness of ten thousand–times–ten thousand individuals."[7]

Understand what is the greatest calling in life. Understand the power of Jesus Christ and what he is offering to you in the transmission of the momentum of his Christhood as you are willing to walk in the footsteps of the path he has outlined for us.

The definition of the Christ is the incarnation of the Word, the Word that was with Brahman in the Beginning. And that Word can be ignited in you, can be increased. The point of Christhood can start with the point of Light in the heart, and it can increase day by day by good works, by love, by prayer, by teaching, by giving of oneself until one has given the whole cup of one's life each day.

The Elohim of the Fifth Ray, Cyclopea, teaches that "one individual who knows his Christhood is more valuable in the earth in this hour than any other individual of any other capacity. You must place supreme value upon your emergent Christhood. Treat it as a diamond that must be cut and polished and treasured, beloved."[8] Cutting and polishing the diamond of your personal Christhood takes work, hard work. But doesn't anything else you strive for in this world take hard work?

The Ascended Lady Master Portia says, "Do not accept that it takes so many years or lifetimes to achieve your Christhood, neither entertain the folly that the achievement of Christhood is easily won. It is not easily won, beloved, or you should have long ago won it."[9]

The Imitation of Christ

El Morya says that before becoming the Christ, the disciple does become, on occasion or often, the vessel of his Christ Self.[10] So first, we are the vessel, and in the process of being the vessel for the love of Christ, the truth of Christ, the qualities of Christ, we are putting on that oil of truth and that oil of love. We are becoming saturated with it, and we begin to take on its characteristics. We begin to think as Jesus thinks. And when we ask, "What would Jesus do?" we know exactly what he would do—and therefore what we should do. It is a very gradual process. It does not happen overnight, and that is why you have to be attentive day by day, weaving the wedding garment.

Archangel Jophiel and Christine give us a key to assessing our progress on the path of Christhood: "When you hear yourself saying things that you know your Holy Christ Self would not say, then you know that that Holy Christ Self has ascended far above you and cannot enter in. When you say things with a tone of voice of condescension, with criticism, with burden or depression, sarcasm or the vibration of gossip, then you will know your Holy Christ Self cannot enter; for it is the Law of God.

"Therefore, pursue the path of the imitation of Christ. Speak as you know or believe Christ would speak, with love but firmness, sternness where required, mercy when it is due, soft-spoken when needed, in the intensity of the sacred fire when you would awake a soul who will not be awakened. Blessed ones, speak as Christ would speak, and Christ will speak through you....

"Think as Christ would think, and Christ will think

through you, and the mind of God will become congruent with the physical vessel.... When you think thoughts impure, unkind, critical, intolerant, the mind of Christ is not in you."[11] And when you catch yourself, make your calls to the violet flame, apologize if necessary, make things right and get right back into communion with God with ever more alertness to see to it that you are in control of thought, feeling and spoken word.

"When you have feelings that are not the feelings of the compassionate Christ, then you know Christ is not in you. Hasten, hasten to your altar! Call, then. Affirm. Replace. Practice sweet thoughts, sweet feelings, sweet words, and soon they will come naturally....

"Finally, beloved, perform deeds that you know Christ would perform and shun those that Christ would not engage in."[12]

Keys for the Path of Personal Christhood

Obedience

Obedience to the inner voice of God is the first precept of Christhood. Jesus told his apostles, "If you love me, keep my commandments."[13] The Ascended Master Jesus says, "Listen to the inner voice that does guide thee. Before thou speakest in an ungodly manner, the Presence does warn: 'Refrain thy speech; it is not pleasing unto the Lord.' Each act, each desiring, each contemplation of deceit or ambition as it does come from the tempter is rebuked by the Christ. Listen to the inner voice and obey, and all shall be well with thee."[14]

Trust

You really cannot be obedient to the inner voice of your Christ Self or the Master's commandments if you do not have trust. Where does trust come from? In this life and in previous lifetimes, we learned trust from our parents. If we could count on our parents, if they were there for us, we began to have the sense that we could give our trust to the most important people in our lives.

But what if you were abandoned as a child? What if you went from home to home and everyone who ever took care of you mistreated you? These things build a momentum of mistrust that is very difficult to overcome. Trust is not something that is automatic; it is either built into us, or it is not. And this is why we need to be very careful with people, and especially with children. If we give our word, then we must keep our word.

Trust even comes before faith. Trust is being able to say, "I can count on you, God. I can count on you, my parents. I can count on you, my friend, my priest, my pastor, my fellow chela on the Path." If you don't have that trust, it is truly a curse. If you have not learned to trust God in others, you do not have the trust in God that will be your anchor as you go through the storms of life.

Life brings good times and bad times. You have to know that neither good nor bad, in the human sense, is real. Human badness, human goodness is not ultimate Reality. On the path of personal Christhood, you have to trust God and the Guru and yourself.

Trustworthiness

The next most important quality on the Path after trust is trustworthiness—being worthy of being trusted yourself. If you have not had people around you that you could trust, the best way to balance that karma is to make a decision, "I'm going to be trustworthy even if my parents and the most significant people in my life were not."

Self-Knowledge

Self-knowledge is one of the keys to personal Christhood. Gautama explains that "the first self-knowledge you must have is that of your Reality." You have to know your God-Reality, your ultimate Reality. Whether you know it by meditation or you know it by sensing, you have to know that you are founded on the rock of Christ, you are embedded in the bedrock of Reality. You are part of what is Real and what is foundational to the universe. You are part of the Great Central Sun. You came forth from your Father-Mother God. You have that essence of God in you. The major part of you is Real; the very smallest part of you is not real.

Gautama Buddha says, "When you are grounded in the self-knowledge of your Reality, then you begin to study your unreal self. Your self-knowledge must then be of that unreal self and of that unreality. He who knows both and stands poised between the two, he who knows how to daily affirm his Reality that will swallow up his unreality, that one is a wise man, a wise woman, a wise child."[15]

Jesus teaches: "Seeing the causes, beloved, is most of the victory. First, is seeing the causes. Second, is the desiring to be rid of them and their effects. And third, is the will—the absolute God-will in you that says, 'I will do it! I will do it *now!* For nothing is impossible to me in God.'"[16]

The Word of the Master

Another tool for the path of personal Christhood is to recite the dictations of the Ascended Masters. Jesus says, "Our dictations are rituals in themselves. The worded release only serves to anchor in your heart the meaning of the great Light that does shower upon you. These dictations are rituals, they are services, they are rosaries—even to the point where you come to know them by heart and recite them. In our dictations you have precious cups of Light. Let these dictations become recitations. Let them become your psalms."[17]

Omri-Tas says, "Every Ascended Master dictation that has

ever gone forth through our Two Witnesses* upon earth does contain within it the power of Elohim for the re-creation of oneself." You are re-created by the power released in the cups that are the words. "It is not without forethought that we have released to you the *Only Mark*† series. It is not without consideration that we have made available to you year upon year the audio- and videotapes of our dictations."[18]

The Violet Flame

A most important key on the path of personal Christhood is the violet flame. Lady Master Leto says the violet flame facilitates your fusion with your Holy Christ Self.[19]

Omri-Tas says, "The violet flame can penetrate bone substance itself to render supple again all of thy body and Inner Being to be remolded in the fullness of the stature of Christ. You are not mere creatures, prisoners of habit, but you must know this. You must look at your momentums. You must study the teachings on momentum given to you in *The Lost Teachings of Jesus*[20] as well as the *Corona Class Lessons*[21] on the subject of habit. You must put down those untoward momentums and re-create the new momentum! When there is a groove in consciousness, fill it with Light and begin again as you would be, as your Christ Self is. Do not wait until the breaking of the mold of this lifetime to re-create yourself in God. It is a daily rejoicing to know that you are a co-creator with God and that with the violet flame all things are possible in God!"[22]

---

*Rev. 11:3–12. The Two Witnesses of Revelation are archetypal figures of twin flames who deliver the Word of the Lord in every age. In this dispensation of the release of the teachings of the Ascended Masters, the office of the Two Witnesses has been held by the Messengers Mark and Elizabeth Prophet.

†The *Only Mark* series of audiotapes was inaugurated to release in chronological order all of the dictations given through the Messenger Mark L. Prophet.

Jesus' Vigil of the Hours

In 1964, Jesus inaugurated a special service dedicated to the protection of the Christ consciousness of every Lightbearer on earth. It is called "Watch With Me, Jesus' Vigil of the Hours." It is a service of prayers, affirmations and hymns that students of the Ascended Masters give weekly all over the world.[23]

Jesus promises that he will be in your midst as you give this prayer service weekly and that he will place his Presence over you in the room where you pray for the entire duration of your service. He says, "I promise you that all who commit to be my disciple as a Keeper of the Flame shall have my Sacred Heart superimposed upon him or her throughout this Watch each week. The Watch is for the opening of the heart so that I might enter and release to the earth renewed Light and Presence. Through you I desire to increase the Christ consciousness on earth."[24]

Bearing Our Own Burden

The definition of Christhood is that you must bear your own burden of karma. Jesus has asked us to take back the karma that he has borne for us these two thousand years.[25] Jesus has borne the sins of the world, but he himself has not atoned for those sins. He has carried that karma, or that sin, for us until we should come of age and have this teaching, be on the path of personal Christhood, have the gift of the violet flame and transmute that karma. He says that by balancing this karma ourselves, we will grow in the stature of our Christhood, and he will then be free to help other souls who need him to bear their burdens. Jesus pointed out that we can also invoke the violet flame and call upon the Ascended Master Hercules to help us bear our karma.

Sometimes devotees on the Path feel that because they give

mantras or perform good deeds, their karma should not descend on them. Once people become accustomed to a benefit, they often begin to consider that it is their right, and the more they are given, the more demands they make. The carnal mind and the dweller-on-the-threshold become very demanding. And that carnal mind and those who entertain it may beat their fists and say to the Masters, "You have to do this for me!"

Chelas sometimes forget the basic principle that we must bear our own burden—karmic burden, financial burden, psychological burden. Paul wrote, "Let every man prove his own work, and then shall he have rejoicing in himself alone, and not in another. For every man shall bear his own burden."[26]

The Calls of Jesus

Over the years Jesus has delivered a series of dictations in which he has called us to fulfill specific requests. These Calls of Jesus outline a path of discipleship unto the Ascended Master Jesus Christ leading to the goal of personal Christhood.*

1. "Come, leave your nets! I will make you fishers of men." Called from their occupations and their preoccupations, the twelve decided that they would become extensions of Jesus. They would be his apostles. He would send them before him into every town and city where he would go. They would become fishers of men. You don't have to stop your business, your occupation or anything else to put in a certain amount of time giving the teachings you have to others.

2. "Take up the sword of the Spirit and fight for my sheep

---

*The Calls of Jesus, with extensive excerpts from the original dictations of Jesus and additional commentary and teaching by Elizabeth Clare Prophet and the staff of Summit University, can be studied in the book *Walking with the Master: Answering the Call of Jesus* (Corwin Springs, Mont.: The Summit Lighthouse Library, 2002).

ere they are lost to the clutches of the drug peddlers and the peddlers of deceit and annihilation." Defend the children.

3. The call to the path of the ascension.

4. "I call you to be world teachers."

5. Jesus called us to gather "ten thousand who will call themselves Keepers of the Flame of Life."

6. "I call you to be my disciples."

7. "I ask that you renew your commitment to giving my Watch, my 'Vigil of the Hours.'" Jesus said it is tremendously powerful; it has a great and powerful impact upon the world. And we are strengthened as a body even as we are strengthened individually as we give this vigil.

8. "This is the day that the path of thy Christhood must begin in earnest.... Become that Christ! ... It is time for you to be true shepherds and ministers."

9. The call to be true shepherds of the children of God. Shepherd them, go after them, care for them. When you are bringing someone in to the knowledge of the Path and the teachings of the Ascended Masters, go into your Christ Self and shepherd. Don't leave them alone. They need your help. They need your understanding. They need you to teach them.

10. "I call you to the House of the Lord, your mighty I AM Presence."

11. "I *command* you to allow that Christ to descend into your temple."

12. "Take back unto yourself the karma I have borne for you these two thousand years."

13. "I call you to a life of the Holy Ghost"—walking and talking with the Holy Spirit, seeking the initiations of the Holy Spirit.

14. "I call you to my temple of initiation." Jesus has an etheric retreat over the Holy Land. He will take you into his temple if you accept his call to be initiated by him.

15. "Above and beyond all to which I have called you, may you become all love."

16. "Become agents of the Cosmic Christ that the children of the Light might enter in to this sheepfold." Know the Cosmic Christ, Lord Maitreya, Jesus' Guru. Read the teachings of Maitreya. Know him well. Know the victory of the God flame and bring that victory into manifestation that the children of Light might enter in. Don't keep this knowledge under a bushel. Don't keep the Light under a bushel. Share it.

17. "I call you to the perfecting of the soul as my apostle."

18. "I have come to call you to be my shepherds."

19. "Drink this cup of my Christhood. Be the instruments of my Light to the youth of the entire world, to children bruised and battered."

20. "See the great calling to embody that Light, that I AM THAT I AM, that portion of Christos that is yours to claim."

21. "Save the homeless and the street people from that sense of abject self-negation. Be converted to serve those who sense they are the poor in spirit." Take a day out of your month or a day every two months and help people who are working with the homeless and the street people. Experience life at all levels and learn how to reach life at all levels. Recognize when you're dealing with street people, you're dealing with people with enormous depression and an absence of will to live in the mainstream.

To really help them, once you have physically gone to comfort them personally, you have to go home and go into your closet and pray and call to Astrea* to cut them free from entities of depression and the burdens that are on their souls. You can't save people with physical, human kindness alone. It

---

*Astrea, feminine Elohim of the Fourth Ray, is the Master we call to specifically for exorcism and for cutting people free from entities and malevolent forces. See decree 10.14 in *Prayer, Meditations and Dynamic Decrees for the Coming Revolution in Higher Consciousness*.

requires efficacious, fervent prayer.

22. Jesus calls us to "espouse the higher calling in God" and "to stand in defense of life."

23. "I call you to repentance"—repentance from all actions, thoughts, words and deeds that you do not want to be a part of you anymore.

24. "The Call of Love"—the "outreaching of your heart, your hand and your speaking of my Truth to all of those who have been a part of me and my life."

25. Jesus calls us to prepare for the initiation of the descent into hell—even as he descended into hell from the cross on Good Friday and Saturday. He went there to preach to the rebellious spirits. You don't have to look too far to find rebellious spirits in embodiment. Go and preach to them. Put on your armour and be determined that if God is going to save a soul, he will save that soul. Don't think you can ever save a soul. We can bring love and comfort and teaching, and if God wills that soul to be converted, the Holy Spirit will convert that soul.

26. "I call you to the heart of God." Having a right heart with God, there is no distance between you and God. You are not going anywhere at the hour of death or transition. You are already there in the heart of God.

27. "I call you to be those mighty electrodes of your Holy Christ Self and of your mighty I AM Presence that the earth might receive the Light."

28. The last call that Jesus has given us was on October 12, 1992, when he said, "I make known to you that when all is ready in your world and you feel the strength of balance in your body and in your spirit and you are ready for me to enter, the call that you may make to me—as the conclusion of the numerous calls and callings I have given to you—is the call to walk the earth as my twin."

"Walk the Earth as My Twin"

The concept of being Jesus' twin is found in the Gospel of Thomas, an early Christian writing that Church Fathers did not include in the Bible. This gospel speaks of the apostle Thomas as Jesus' twin. Some people have mistakenly interpreted this as meaning a physical twin brother. But the Gnostics understood that as we aspire to and become our Real Self, we are becoming one with that Christ Self.

The Christ Self of us is also the Christ of Jesus. They are one and the same. So when we become like, or the reflection of, our Holy Christ Self, we also become the twin of Jesus.

Jesus is our role model. When we fulfill his sayings and his Word and his Light, our vibration, our countenance, our love should be like him. We should understand and know what Jesus would do and, therefore, also do those same works.

Jesus said in this dictation, "Yes, beloved, your Christ/my Christ. There is indeed only one Christ, one begotten Son of the Father-Mother God, and it is the eternal Light personified and manifest wherever the ray of Light of a son or daughter of God has gone forth from the Central Sun. It is your calling, beloved.

"I have given to you in my dictations of past years the steps and stages whereby you might seek that attainment and that oneness with me as my twin. I withhold nothing from you, beloved, but sometimes you do withhold yourselves and therefore forfeit all that you might receive from me.

"It is my desire, with a deep desiring of God that fills all of my being—and my being that is manifest now, filling the Matter cosmos—it is my desire to walk and talk with you that your Christ might greet my Christ and we might embrace and that Presence in the twain might be as one heart: thy heart/my heart. . . .

"Beloved hearts, my call to you to walk the earth as my

twin is an open dispensation. It is the dispensation that you can call for, even as I have called you. I do suggest that you run over the calls that I have given in the past dictations so that you may implement those calls as a foundation. I suggest you take your time, if you will, to decide. But know, beloved, that you are preparing for the bonding to my heart, and I am preparing to receive you as my brides."[27]

Section 6

The Christ Flame in the Heart

SEALED IN THE SECRET CHAMBER OF your heart is the threefold flame of life. It is your divine spark, the gift of life, consciousness and free will from your beloved I AM Presence. Through the love, wisdom and power of the Godhead anchored in your threefold flame, your soul can fulfill her reason for being on earth. Also called the Christ flame and the liberty flame, or fleur-de-lis, the threefold flame is the spark of the soul's divinity, her potential for Christhood.

Saint Germain speaks of the importance of this Christ flame within us: "Your heart is indeed one of the choicest gifts of God. Within it there is a central chamber surrounded by such Light and protection as that which we call a 'cosmic interval.' It is a chamber separated from Matter, and no probing could ever discover it. It occupies simultaneously not only the third and fourth dimensions but also other dimensions unknown to man. It is thus the connecting point of the mighty silver cord of Light that descends from your divine God Presence to sustain the beating of your physical heart, giving you life, purpose and cosmic integration.

"I urge all men to treasure this point of contact that they have with life by paying conscious recognition to it. You do not need to understand by sophisticated language or scientific postulation the how, why and wherefore of this activity.

"Be content to know that God is there and that there is within you a point of contact with the Divine, a spark of fire from the Creator's own heart, which is called the threefold flame of life. There it burns as the triune essence of love, wisdom and power.

"Each acknowledgment paid daily to the flame within your heart will amplify the power and illumination of love within your being. Each such attention will produce a new sense of dimension for you, if not outwardly apparent, then subconsciously manifest within the folds of your inner thoughts.

"Neglect not, then, your heart as the altar of God. Neglect it not as the sun of your manifest being. Draw from God the power of love and amplify it within your heart. Then send it out into the world at large as the bulwark of that which shall overcome the darkness of the planet."[1]

The Flame upon the Altar

Jesus explains the importance of this divine spark: "The law of the threefold flame of love, wisdom and power must be understood. This flame is anchored within the Holy of holies, the temple of your heart. There, as in the ark of the covenant, the Shekinah* glory of the threefold flame blazes forth from

---

*Messenger's note: The definition of Shekinah given in *The Oxford Universal Dictionary* will be of interest to the student: "The visible manifestation of the Divine Majesty, especially when resting between the cherubim over the mercy-seat or in the temple of Solomon; a glory or refulgent light symbolizing the Divine Presence."

the midst of the cherubim of adoration and ministration. The blue plume of power majestically emphasizes that there is no power apart from God that can act in your world. The golden flame of illumination saturates your form and rises above the temple of your forehead in the fullness of Christly wisdom and discrimination. The wondrous pink flame of love manifests the comfort and beauty of life in action and completes the power of the three-times-three, enabling you to enter, as did the high priests of old, into the Holy of holies, thus fulfilling Jeremiah's vision of the new covenant.[2]

"You see, long ago in the wilderness tabernacle only the high priest could enter there; all others were excluded. Today the understanding is published abroad that each man, by the power of his Presence, becomes his own high priest. Within the tabernacle, the holy place of your heart, purified by the sacred fire, the immortal threefold flame rises and pulsates. Its effulgence blazes like a star through the silent night of the sleeping world consciousness, changing all into the illimitable Light of the Daystar from on high.

"Precious ones, I am radiantly aware of the meaning of the Holy Christ Flame, for I carried out my mission in Palestine in the constant blaze of its glory. What do you think made it possible for me to gain my victory, aside from the power of my own mighty I AM Presence, the prayers of my blessed Mother, the Lord Maha Chohan and others of the Brotherhood? Was it not the magnificence of my own Holy Christ Self?

"That which was done for me can be done for everyone who will make the necessary application and visualization. It takes only a few minutes each day to put your attention upon this spiritually tangible flame within your heart, to pour out your adoration to it and to call for its magnification. By visualizing it expanding as Saint Germain's fleur-de-lis—the triune flame flower, an immortelle—and feeling the power, wisdom and love emanating from that triune spiritual fountain, you can learn to bask in its radiance throughout the day, even as I did. You see, blessed ones, in time, after persistent application, it becomes somewhat automatic; and your mighty God Self will continue to sustain that which you have already magnetized by your attention.

"Many people have either misunderstood or not known the meaning of life and have thought, because of the public demonstration that I gave the world, that I am unique and the only Son of God, by whom everyone would automatically be lifted and saved from every vestige of discord or harm. Beloved ones, would to God this were so! Would to God this could be so!

"When I wept over Jerusalem, do you realize that this 'gathering feeling' filled my heart?[3] If it were possible, I would have drawn the world unto me as did Noah when he took the children two by two into the ark and gathered all into the very Holy of holies of God's great temple of life; yes, I would have taken all into the fullness of the salvation and victory that I knew even then. The Law did not permit this, however, even though I had been initiated into the High Priesthood of Melchizedek. It was thus the need of my heart to express itself in lamentation for those whom I longed to draw to God, to shorten the days of their travail. It is needful that all who would be free hear the truth of their own being and realize that the Christ of every man is the Light that brought him into the world, and that Light is the mighty illumination that will exalt him into the fullness of his Christ victory and ascension in the Light.[4]

"It is the I AM of every man, his own immortal God Being, that must be recognized as Father-Mother, not the mere physical being. If man recognizes the Father-Mother, he must also recognize his Holy Christ Self as the Son and his real Spirit as the Holy Spirit, the power of life whose cloven flame of duality makes him at all times a part of God—waking or sleeping, smiling or frowning, sinning or beginning. For although sin, sleep and frown may not be a part of God, they are the temporary illusions of the experience of that part of the duality that has entered the world of form. Man, having been made a little lower than the angels, will be crowned with more glory and honor as he ascends into the fullness of reunion with his mighty I AM Presence.[5] There the twain that were the duality are made one; the sensory delusions finally crucified, the Christ Man emerges in the resurrection of all that is good, pure and lovely and ascends to the heart of God to abide forever in the unity of the holy Tri-Unity (Trinity).

"The footstool creation of God is destined to become altogether heavenlike by the power of God's will. It is the destiny of men to harness their free will as I did in order to hold faith in the universal concepts of God-purity and progressively to go forward, using the flame of life to exalt faith, discover truth, pursue understanding and maintain victory!

"The assistance of the flame of life within the heart is given to everyone; but when the flame is consciously recognized, it is mightily amplified. In visualizing this flame, remember that the power portion is a beautiful pulsating blue radiance (to your left), the illumination segment is a rising glorious golden flame (in the center), and the love plume (at your right hand) is an all-pervading glorious pink radiance whose warmth flashes forth from heart to heart and sets the world aglow with grace and love for every man, every woman, every tree, every elemental, every flower and all life everywhere."[6]

The Mission of Jesus Christ:
Reigniting the Threefold Flame, the Christ Flame in the Heart

T HERE WAS A TIME IN EARTH'S HISTORY
when there was not a single, solitary
soul in embodiment who acknowledged or adored this threefold flame within the heart. It was the darkest point in earth's
history, as there was the total degradation of life almost to
the plane of the animal. At that moment Sanat Kumara, the
Ancient of Days, came to earth.

The Ancient of Days brought the Light to earth to rekindle the threefold flame in the hearts of her people. And so,
every year at Winter Solstice (the time of Christmas) for thousands of years the Ancient of Days would light the Yule log. In
primitive times that great fire that burned would be there as the
source of physical fire to the people, and they would journey
from all over to come to that flame and to carry that fire back.
It was one of the earliest rituals and celebrations of the Light.

The celebration of the Yule log is a very ancient tradition
that continues to this day in commemoration of the coming of
Sanat Kumara. Understanding its origin, we see that the real

Yule log is the flame that burns at Shamballa, the city that was
built by those who came with Sanat Kumara for the keeping of
that flame.

So the flame was enshrined, the retreat was built, and
Sanat Kumara became the first Keeper of the Flame after the
Fall of man and woman on Terra. Other souls and other Ascended Masters came also with Sanat Kumara to keep the
flame. Among them was Saint Germain, who carries the flame
of the Aquarian age and has come in this time to found an
order called the Keepers of the Flame Fraternity dedicated to
keeping the flame of freedom on behalf of mankind in memory
of the Ancient of Days.[1]

The Coming of the Mother Flame

Jesus unveils for us some of this ancient history of earth:
"O eternal Light of the Mother flame, I, Jesus, bow before the
Cosmic Virgin, my Mother, as the one who is the Mother of the
God flame within me.

"I salute the Light of the Mother burning in the dark night
of Mater. And yet, the Light is the All, the Supreme One, and
I AM Jesus the Christ—*because* the Mother flame burns
brightly in heaven and in the earth.

"Thus my beloved Father sent forth the Archangel, Mary the
Queen of Angels, to embody in the earth that the Omega Light
might be therefore framed in clay and in the vessel that we must
wear. Thus God in the earth, truly the incarnation of the Archeia,
gave to my heart the very pulsations of the Great Central Sun.

"Fortunate are ye, as I am, that the human mother who
bore me was also the Divine Mother veiled in flesh. Thus Alpha
as my Father in heaven, represented on earth by beloved
Joseph, and Omega as Mary became, therefore, truly the coor-
dinates of living fire whereby, O blessed hearts, heaven and

earth might once again be united in the gift of the Christ Child.

"Thus, the Trinity, the balance of cosmic forces, does provide for the reunion of spheres—the great joy to the world of the incarnation of the Word *where you are,* which does take place daily in the hour of the dawn, celebrated by angels of Light. This birth of Christ in you is the sign that once again God and man are one and no longer separated by the judgment that was the edict of Lord Maitreya, there in the mystery school [known as the Garden of Eden] when the early father and mother were sent forth, having compromised the Great Law of the path of initiation through the false teacher called Serpent.

"Thus, those thousands of years until my own birth provided the evolutions of many races who had gone after the admiration of the fallen angels, to experience life without the Great Mediator, without the person of your Christ Self—the one you have come to know and love as The Lord Our Righteousness.

"Therefore, understand, beloved ones, that the wedding of heaven and earth occurs through that point of Christ, and there is naught beneath that can commune with aught Above except by the mighty flame of the heart. And as you have understood, as you have been taught, it is the flame you now hold—the flame of Mother—whereby that Christ is born.*

"Christ as the Word, beloved, is also the Mother. The person of the Word embodying the flame of Mother is called the Christ because the Christ is the one *anointed* with the Mother flame or the Word of the Logos. The one so anointed—male or female—then is called the *Son* of God, and the true meaning of that 'Son' is the s-u-n. For the Son of God is the physical manifestation on earth of the Alpha-Omega of the Great Central Sun. And because the earth is Matter, therefore that portion of the Sun that is manifest is the Omega Light, while the Alpha

---

*Throughout this address by Jesus, each devotee held a candle lit from the flame upon the altar.

keeps the fullness of that Light in heaven.

"Thus, when you are Omega on earth, you also contain the Alpha. And when Alpha is in heaven, he contains the Omega. But the one contains the other according to the Spirit, the Matter—the plus, the minus—of the God force.

"Understand that the very physical fire itself, though it be the highest representation in Matter of the spiritual fire, is that fire in the feminine potential of being. And this fire is the sign of far-off worlds and the awakening of the memory of Sanat Kumara and the bearer of the ancient fire to the earth.

Dark Ages of Earth's History

"Now think upon those long, dark centuries, the dark night of the soul of earth—truly the dark ages when all had lost the contact with the mighty threefold flame and therefore became almost as the animal creation, without the divine spark, without conscience or consciousness. Beloved ones, that hour of darkness, where even the physical fire was no longer known or understood, was truly the darkest dark night preceding the coming once again of the Lord Sanat Kumara.

"Realize, then, that this darkness in the earth did even precede the era of the mystery school of Maitreya and of the experience of Adam and Eve. And this great, great darkness of the earth, of ancient days of long ago, this era no longer recorded in the history or the scriptures of the world, is a period, beloved ones, that also was corrupted by fallen angels and the Serpent and his seed who themselves had created that mechanization man without the God flame and the divine spark as an experimentation of an animal creation.

"Beloved ones, you can see how this mechanization man without the flame of the Mother went forth, therefore, to influence the children of Light who had that threefold flame.

And therefore, beloved hearts of Light, they imitated the ways, the loud and raucous ways, of those without the Holy Spirit in their temples.

"Thus, all was in great, great darkness. And the coming of the Lord Sanat Kumara, beloved hearts of infinite fire, was to rekindle the physical light and the spiritual Light—first to keep the flame for those until some, *one,* would respond to the keeping of the threefold flame of life. And therefore, one by one, the children of the Light once again had the opportunity for God consciousness and for the eventual appearance of the person of the Christ and the opportunity to experience the union with the Godhead and the union of the spheres of Matter with Spirit.

"Realize how long these ages have been—millions of years according to the annals of earth's history. And there is sparse understanding of this period because so much is left out of holy scripture; and what remains in East and West is not understood in terms of the centuries and the millennia that have passed.

"Thus, in pre-golden ages and in the dawn before those Golden Ages, ancient times, there were mighty beings of Light who never did embody in the physical dimensions where you are, yet were in the Matter spheres and did achieve an attainment of the Mother flame which did predate that cycle of early Lemuria.

"I come in the fullness, therefore, of the Universal Christ to give you a sense of the background of the original Light and the seed of Light and your soul cycling through the Great Causal Body—the eventual descent farther and farther into the densities of Matter, the loss of God consciousness and of the sun consciousness of the Great Central Sun, and finally, for some, the going out of the divine spark.

"Thus, when I came a mere two thousand years ago to restore that divine spark, some had wandered the earth without that flame for a half a million years, reincarnating again

and again the mere psyche, the soul consciousness and its physical and desire awareness, the mental body such as it was, and
a very small layer of the etheric body or divine memory.

The Light in the Earth Must Increase

"The necessity for the increase in the evolution of the children of the Light is very great. As you understand, it is an hour
when there is a demand of cosmos for the Christed ones to fan
the fire and expand it, lest in the turning of worlds there be that
upheaval and cataclysm that the LORD God would desire to
avert and does so desire—and would do so if it were permitted
by cosmic law.

"It is ordained from the beginning that the evolutions
upon earth in this hour, seeing that which has come to pass and
that which has been, must themselves therefore hold the Light.
For too many epochs have come and gone when avatars have
held the Light and brought again and renewed the divine spark;
and those who witnessed their coming have left off from their
worship of the Light in the absence of the One Sent. Thus, you
can understand how your evolution is at the end not of merely
the age of Pisces, but at the end of many ages and many dispensations whereby the Light has gone forth, been rejected and
spurned, and its bearers been crucified, denied and murdered.

"Thus, beloved hearts, God has said before the Four and
Twenty Elders and the councils of his Sons and before the
Great Silent Watchers that there is a record in those who are of
God in the earth in this hour of all that has gone before. The
Lightbearers know the voice of the true shepherd and they
know the voice of Serpent. Therefore, they may choose to live
in the everlasting Light of God and save the world, else the
world itself cannot be saved.

"Thus, all intercession by the LORD God—all interference,

as it were, with the Law—must be manifest through the individual Christ of every son of God, which Light and whose Light *is* that Mother Omega flame. By that flame that you bear, you stand between the Great Law of the Lawgiver, the Mighty One of the Great Central Sun, and evolving humanity. It is this Christ and this Christ alone that can save the world."[2]

Evolutions of Light and Darkness

Thus we see in the long millennia since darkness first came upon the planet that earth has been host to many different evolutions, and not all of these evolutions descended from God. Jesus makes this clear in the Gospels when he says of the Pharisees, "You are of the father, the devil. I am from above; you are from beneath."[3]

Jesus left a record of these different evolutions in the parable of the tares and the wheat. He explained to his disciples that the good seed were the children of God, and that the tares were sown by the enemy, the devil, and that these were the seed, the offspring of the evil one.[4] He gave only one lesson that is recorded but many lessons that are unrecorded concerning two separate evolutions that existed on earth and that exist to the present hour, side by side.

We see that fallen angels were cast down into the earth in judgment for their failure to bend the knee before Christ the Lord. There was war in heaven. Archangel Michael cast them out of heaven because they violated the Christ principle.[5] They took embodiment.

A class of these fallen angels is called Watchers, written about by Enoch.[6] Another group is known as the Nephilim.[7] These fallen angels and the laggard races[8] who came to this planet had great scientific knowledge. They knew the mysteries of creation, and through genetic engineering, they were able to create human bodies. And so their creation has multiplied. These are known as *mechanization man* (to distinguish from those who have the divine spark, who have an I AM Presence and who have a Holy Christ Self). There are also evolutions upon this planet that have come here in spacecraft from all over the universe. And these individuals, many of them, never originated in God, yet they are highly sophisticated and developed.

Thus, there is a whole order of beings who did not descend from God. There are also some who once *had* a threefold flame but lost it by continually misusing the flame—for instance, through lifetimes of uncontrolled anger and uncontrolled misuses of the sacred fire in their chakras. However, in this day and age the absence of a threefold flame does not disqualify anyone from the Path—as long as they meet the requirements of the Guru-chela relationship.

Any one of these beings—from the Watcher to the Nephilim to the laggard to the mechanization man to the child of God who has lost the threefold flame—has the opportunity, through Jesus Christ, to accept him as their Saviour, to bend the knee, to walk a path of discipleship, to take accountability for their karma and at some point on the Path to receive the gift of a threefold flame and also to have imparted to them the substance whereby the soul itself comes into that temple and reincarnates. It may take lifetimes for this to occur, or by heroic deeds for God and the Christed ones, by becoming a servant of God, an individual may receive that gift in a single lifetime.

The Rekindling of the Threefold Flame

In looking at all these evolutions on earth, it is not where someone has come from that determines the outcome; it is not from whom they have descended or what their evolution is. The open door of Jesus Christ throughout this Piscean age has been that anyone, no matter what their origin, could receive a divine spark and therefore the opportunity for eternal life.

The story of Pinocchio exemplifies the choice one must make to have or not to have a threefold flame. At first Pinocchio was very naughty. He willfully and deliberately did not listen to Jiminy Cricket, who represented Pinocchio's conscience. When Pinocchio finally decided to diligently follow the path of the imitation of Christ, the divine spark was restored. He had to prove himself brave, truthful and unselfish to become a real boy. He was rewarded with a real heart, symbolic of receiving a threefold flame and becoming a real son of God.

You shouldn't worry about whether or not you have a threefold flame. If you have lost it, you can get it back through daily sacrifice, daily surrender, daily selflessness and daily service. This is what brings us back to the feet of our Lord.

Since the coming of Jesus Christ, the Light and the option of Divine Sonship has been transmitted through the Messengers whom he has ordained through the Piscean dispensation. With the coming of our Lord came access to the Holy Christ Self as well as the opportunity to have the threefold flame rekindled and to be reendowed with the Holy Spirit.

Jesus has taught us that "to those who believe on the name of the Son of God Jesus Christ and the Sun behind that Son and the Messenger of that Son, there is given 'power to make them sons of God.'[9] There is given power to ignite in them the threefold flame. And this is what was given to Peter. The keys of the kingdom[10] are the keys to the Causal Body and the threefold flame"[11] of each and every Son and Daughter of God.

Life through the Son

John the Beloved, the apostle who was so close to Jesus, tells us of his ministry and mission: "Beloved, the teaching of the Son of God, Jesus Christ, concerning his mission is that he has come to reignite the threefold flame in those in whom it has gone out and to reconnect with their Holy Christ Self those who have become disconnected. This life of the Son is both the life of the Son Jesus and the life of the Holy Christ Self. Without this connection, there is no true life.

"Thus you see the immensity of the gift of God in sending that Son, Jesus Christ, into the world. For without Jesus as the initiator, as the Guru of the age of Pisces, the majority of those of this planet could not enter into their Holy Christ Self. This, then, is the great promise of the intercessor. And this is God's promise to you as you would be in the role of intercessor to many, that you receive Jesus Christ and thereby allow him to work through you in assisting many to come into the knowledge of their own threefold flame."[12]

"I AM the Resurrection and the Life"

Jesus gives the most profound affirmation of this mission of the Son of God in his statement: "I AM the resurrection and the life: he that believeth in me, though he were dead, yet shall he live."[13]

Those who are the dead are those who are dead to Christ, dead to their Holy Christ Self, dead to their I AM Presence because they give no adoration, no worship, no acknowledgment of God. They have no love in their hearts. Certainly the definition of life and death is not because we have a beating heart or because we are breathing or because we are thinking. We look out upon the world, and we see many who are the living dead.

There has been a long period when there was not the embodied Saviour, since the last ages when the Cosmic Christ could offer this gift (and that was Lord Maitreya). Jesus is saying to all those vast millions who have lived on earth since that time, to all those who lost their threefold flame, their divine spark, those in whom the Holy Spirit does not dwell, these dead, "though they were dead, yet shall they live." And they will live because they believe that Jesus is the incarnation of that Christ and are willing to bend the knee before him and acknowledge that God anointed him to save their soul, reignite the threefold flame, reendow them with the Holy Spirit, restore them to that place where they could even begin to be his disciple, begin on the pathway back to the Great Central Sun.

He said, "Whosoever liveth and believeth in me shall never die."[14] Once you have a threefold flame, there is no death. To reincarnate again and again is not to die. We do not die every time we lay aside this coat that we wear. It is merely set aside for the next episode. But those who pass from the screen of life without having that flame reignited may be cast into outer darkness, because all they are is the shell. There is nothing to endure beyond the four lower bodies.

Jesus, the Avatar of Pisces

What did Jesus do, then, in declaring himself to be the Son of God? Why did Jesus say, "No man cometh unto the Father, but by me"?[15] And why do we hear Christians say and why do we find it written in the Bible, "Believe on the Lord Jesus Christ, and thou shall be saved."[16] There is a specific reason: Jesus was the Avatar of the Piscean dispensation. He was the Avatar who came to deliver a single message: I AM the Son of God; because I AM the Son of God, you also can be the Son of God.

There is one person here, the person of God the Father, the Son, the Holy Spirit and the Mother, one flame—"Hear, O Israel: The LORD our God is one LORD"[17]—and out of the

One, many manifestations who return to the Source and yet retain the individual identity. This is the great mystery.

We, in our rebellion, had rejected that same Christ Presence in the mystery school of the Garden of Eden. We rejected our teachers, even when we saw them face to face. We were therefore put out of their presence to go forth and work out our karma by the sweat of the brow, tilling the soil in sorrow and travail, bringing forth children in pain and sorrow. Woman was made subject unto man. And this was our lot—not just the lot of Adam and Eve, but an entire lifewave of which we are yet a part.

We rejected the incarnation of the Word, the Christ in the Lord God, the Guru, to whom we had direct access. Could we then become the fullness of the Christ, having denied it in him? Karmic law, cosmic law then stated we would first go through a period of ignorance, to find out what it's like to live without this Word. And then, one day there would be the coming of that one for us, for our evolutions, who was the Word incarnate—Jesus Christ. He would be the fullness of that same Word made manifest. He would face the initiations that we had failed—the three temptations of the Serpent given to him as the three temptations of Satan in the wilderness. He passed where we failed.

And therefore, "No man cometh unto the Father, but by me" is a scientific statement of being. If you can look upon the Master Jesus Christ and say he is the Son of God, there is an arc of energy that flows from your heart as love, devotion, recognition to the Guru, the Master. Instantaneously it contacts the heart of Jesus. The arc of energy is returned, and the Son of God ignites in us our own Christ-potential that was sealed in the atom of being and that now comes forth as the living Presence of the Word.

This is Hierarchy. This is initiation. We are required to be humble enough to say that one son became the fullness of the Christ—and many sons have become the fullness of the Christ, whether in Krishna, whether the Christ understood as Buddha in Gautama, as Mother in Mary, in those who were before Jesus Christ (for he said of that Christ, "Before Abraham was, I AM"—the I AM had been coming forth again and again)—and those who were able to confess his name would, themselves, be saved by the same energy.

"Power to Become the Sons of God"

We find this truth distorted in the religion of today. Instead of understanding that without any detraction from the Lord and Saviour Jesus Christ, we also can become the fullness of that Christ, orthodoxy has taught that we are miserable sinners; that we can do nothing to save ourselves; that only through the vicarious atonement can we be saved; that works are not necessary; that we do not have to do anything but simply believe on Him, and somehow magically, miraculously we will arrive at the fullness of being. This is a distortion of the truth that he taught.

Jeremiah spoke out in the Word of the Lord, "Woe be unto the pastors that destroy and scatter the sheep of my pasture! saith the LORD."[18] Jeremiah spoke that Word of the LORD for the coming of this age. He said "I will gather the remnant of my flock out of all countries whither I have driven them. . . . And I will set up shepherds over them which shall feed them: and they shall fear no more, nor be dismayed, neither shall they be lacking, saith the LORD. . . . In his days Judah shall be saved, and Israel shall dwell safely: and this is his name whereby he shall be called, The Lord Our Righteousness."[19] This is the Second Coming of Christ in the incarnation of that Word in you and in me—quickened by the fact that we have the humility to

confess that in one son was the fullness of that Christ in manifestation.

It is written "But as many as received him, to them gave he
power to become the sons of God, even to them that believe on
his name."[20] That power is the unlocking of the seed atom of
being, which we ourselves in a million years cannot unlock
without the assistance, the intercession of this personal Christ
of Jesus Christ.

We find, then, that we can accept Jesus Christ as our Lord
and Saviour and still be true to our Christian faith, our Judaic
traditions, and even to the true path of Buddhism or Hinduism
and never depart from or compromise our essential faith.

The Problem of a False Doctrine

Even though this understanding of Jesus' mission is found
in the scriptures, it has become buried under layers of doctrine.
Jesus explains: "You can become a Christ! This is the true message of this revolution in higher consciousness, which is in the
now even as Maitreya is in the very chalice of the moment of
the beating of your heart.

"O my beloved, the essence of my teaching has always
been and ever shall be: You can become a Christ! . . .

"Free will must be tethered to the Christ mind, and that
leap must be assisted. The gap must be closed by embodied
teachers who will explain by the logic of the Logos these steps
of the Law and how they have gone astray from my original
teaching.

"I plead with you in this hour to make known the real
truth of my mission in Galilee and Judaea and all the words
that I spoke and the meaning of my parables and of the
prophets who went before and of John the Baptist.

"They do not understand the message; and therefore they

have determined that in order to update the message, they must now borrow from Karl Marx. . . .

"The message of the eternal God through my heart was and is complete for the Piscean dispensation. And that very message itself—not complete in the written word, but the totality of my message—is the foundation for transition into the seventh dispensation that is made known by Saint Germain.

"If they would but read what they have, they would find a way out from a dead doctrine and dogma! But they cannot even read the printed word without it being precolored, preconditioned. Their minds are preconditioned—their hearts, their souls. Therefore, when they hear a certain passage, beloved ones, that passage automatically means and has for them the conviction of a doctrine that has been taught since they were born.

"When a doctrine is sealed, such as the phrase 'Jesus died for your sins,' it becomes a law that no longer has an understanding, such as proper nouns that were originally taken from words, but the proper nouns no longer are thought of in the context of their original meaning because they are everyday words. Thus, everyday statements of the Bible no longer are thought through, and only those who have escaped that indoctrination freely think and understand and are receptive to the Holy Spirit—the Holy Ghost who will reveal unto them all truth and give the true interpretation of holy scripture to your hearts."[21]

Somehow or other, we've become confused about Jesus. We misunderstand his mission. We think that he came to this world to save people from their sins and take them straight to heaven. In reality, the purpose of the Christ was to awaken man to the realization that he should bear his own burden, that he has the strength of God inside of himself, that he was created by God to be a Son of God as Jesus was, that the purpose of life is to become a member of the Brotherhood and to understand the principles of the Brotherhood, to cleanse his consciousness, to learn how to govern his mind.

Jesus explains this misconception to us in his own words: "You may say, 'How could anyone misunderstand?'—and yet, offenses and misunderstandings have arisen again and again. When I declared, 'I AM the way, the truth and the life: no man cometh unto the Father, but by me,'[22] blessed people, it was to acknowledge the power of the God Presence, I AM, and never was it intended as a personal glorification of my mission. When a man approached me with the words, 'Good Master,' I repudiated him by saying, 'Why callest thou me good? there is none good but one, that is, God.'[23] Thus, I continue to serve to set human error and misapprehensions aright and trust that many are blessed thereby."[24]

Opportunity for Every Man

This Light by which all things were made dwells in abundance in Jesus the Christ because he nourished it, because he nurtured it, because he loved it. He revealed the Father to man because he *was* the Father in action, even as the Son and the Father are One in all who will accept it.

The mission and message of the Christ is made no less by this correct understanding of divine and universal Oneness, but rather it is strengthened immeasurably because it places opportunity within the realm of every man. He may attain the selfsame glories that Jesus knew with the Father before the world was, for he too was with the Father, in the Father's consciousness, as potential creation from the beginning. No longer must man, then, sulk in frustration and limitation and be destroyed by the concept of the Only Begotten, which, in reality, is God's gift to him, even as it is to the universe. Man, as the living Christ, is able to say, "All power is given unto me in heaven and in earth."[25] He is able to claim his divine Sonship and receive salvation through accepting this great Mediator of his Real Self made in the Divine Image.

This does not detract from the person of Jesus or from any man's person; rather it adds to each man's person and stature immeasurably, for it shows that God made Jesus like unto us all; that the Christ is in all, in embryo. Being found in fashion as a man, this Christ "humbled himself, and became obedient unto death, even the death of the cross."[26]

And those who may be angry because they feel that someone is trying to take away their Jesus, should understand that the highest compliment that can be paid to Jesus and his mission is the compliment of emulation—of walking in the Master's footsteps and of accepting all that he accepted of God.

The Redemption of Twin Flames

Lord Maitreya was Jesus' Guru and teacher in his Galilean embodiment. He gives a profound understanding of the mission of the Saviour: "My beloved, I welcome you as I welcomed to my heart long ago the youth Issa, your Jesus, when he came to the Himalayas and touched the fire of Tibet and knew the ancient lamas and found me.* For I was the one promised and known of him even before birth, as the entire drama of the mission of the Avatar of the Piscean age was, of course, premeditated by God and directed from above.

"Sweet Jesus, the strong, when he said to his parents at the age of twelve, 'Wist ye not that I must be about my Father's business?'[27] he spake of the Teacher, the eternal Guru he must go and find. He must go to the East, and as all such saints,

---

*In the Buddhist texts that describe Jesus' journey to the East (and in many legends of the region) he is known as Issa. See Elizabeth Clare Prophet, *The Lost Years of Jesus.*

receive the anointing from the lineage of his descent.

"Thus I unveil to you the real mission of the Saviour, so truly stated by the apostles, for the redemption of the twin flames who took up the path of the Tree of Life in the ancient mystery school and were turned aside by the cunning of the serpent philosophy, which was the philosophy of the fallen angels who were determined to subvert the Light of twin flames and misdirect the great gift of God to all generations who would come after them.

"The blame, of course, is not upon those two or any in particular, for we ascribe no blame but only the new cycle of opportunity once again to take up the flame of Alpha and Omega, twin flames of the One. Nary a soul gathered here nor any on earth this day has not in some form, mostly unbeknownst to him, succumbed to some subtlety of the lie of Serpent. Thus, all are in the process of either going forth from the ancient mystery school or returning thereto. . . .

"The mission of Jesus was to go back to Eden, yet the Motherland was long gone. Therefore, he came to Shamballa. And he came to the ancient repository of the tablets of Mu and the writings of Maitreya and Gautama and Sanat Kumara. He came for the redemption of those who had been turned aside from the Law of the Divine Mother and to restore to them the true path of discipleship under the Cosmic Christ.

"Such a perfect one was he that the Ancient of Days determined that as much of the path of the mystery school as the Great Law would allow should be demonstrated by example in his mission. The testing of that mission and his ability to sustain those initiations in the outer world were the subject of our training sessions during his eighteen years in the Orient.

"A student, yea, a scholar and a sage he became, passing through the schools of preparation and receiving from my heart the empowerment of Gautama and Sanat Kumara to return to the scene of the darkest karma on planet Earth, none other than Palestine, the crossroads of the Middle East, the place of the Mother and the place of grave darkness and movements of many lifewaves and evolutions who had been pitted against the living Word on their own home stars and so continued that momentum in that era and time.

"Thus, the greatest Light is sent to the darkest corner to expose, to accuse by way of isolating error that all may choose the right, the left, north or south, east or west. You know direction is everything, beloved, and the all.

"Jesus, the Master, love of my heart! Indeed, I am the Teacher who lived to see the pupil exceed his own teaching. It must always be so. For this is the purpose of the conveyance of the mantle, that the Light of the pupil multiplied by the Guru should exceed the former as well as the latter. And greater works by the living Word should be the new fruit of the Tree of Life that increases in power and wisdom and love with each succeeding two-thousand-year dispensation....

"Indeed, indeed, you must acknowledge him the Saviour of your life, for he is! He restored to you the contact with your own Christ Self, and he is here today to increase that spark or even ignite it again if, by your words and your works, you may be rotated one hundred and eighty degrees to face the living Son of God. If you cannot see the Saviour in him, I cannot teach you; there is nothing else. He has taught my teaching. I would take you from that level and beyond. You can never save so much as a bumblebee if you do not see the glory of that life.

"Come now. Let the fears and rationalizations, let the materialistic ideas of God, let all of the complaining concerning the mission and life of Jesus cease! For he was and is God incarnate, truly in the unique sense that God raised him up as the example but never in the exclusive sense that all could not follow in his footsteps...."

"I and My Father Are One"

"'I and my Father are one' is the mantra of the protection of the Guru-chela relationship that I gave to him, the Son of man. I and my Father are one! When you speak these words, the lineage of your Ascended Masters is with you, the Electronic Presence of Jesus is upon you, your own I AM Presence and Christ Self are there, and I AM instantly there. For Jesus would have you call him 'Brother' and me 'Father.' And I agree, for it is a reminder that he is not so far above you but at your side, even though many of you have known him as Father.

"Thus you see, the 'I and my Father are one' mantra is actually a call. It is a call you may give in time of danger, chaos, confusion or accident or illness or any need, as long as you have the perception that the call cannot and will not fail and as long as you have the understanding of who is Father. The LORD God Almighty is Father, and his emissaries to whom he has given the mantle of his I AM Presence to teach mankind are Father. Thus, the 'I and my Father are one' mantra uses the I AM name to confirm the bond of our oneness.

"By cosmic law I cannot fail to answer the call of this mantra. The only variation in my answer is in your vibration. For though I may be with you, you may not feel it until you have quelled the turbulence of your emotions. Thus our oneness becomes ever closer as you put on the likeness of the image of the Father that I would bequeath to you."28

Section 8

The Cosmic Christ

IN THE FIRST CHAPTER OF JOHN, VERSES 1–3, we read:

In the beginning was the Word, and the Word was with God, and the Word was God.

The same was in the beginning with God.

All things were made by him; and without him was not any thing made that was made.

This is an exact translation from the ancient Vedas, where we read:

In the beginning was the Word and the Word was with Brahman. And the Word was Brahman.

The same was in the beginning with Brahman.[1]

The creation is wrought by the Word, or the Cosmic Christ Principle, which, being one with God, is God. And by that Cosmic Christ all things are created. Nothing was created without that Word.

We have found the one whom God sent to us in this time
to be the incarnation of the Word. That is the closest approach
we can make to the Word that was in the Beginning with Brahman, out of which our twin flames were created by Elohim.*
They have created us by the agency or mediatorship of the
Word, the Cosmic Christ. Through Jesus we can shoot as a ray
of light back to the heart of Brahman and the Word.

That is the great mystery. John was given this teaching by
Jesus, who spent eighteen years in the East and studied all the
ancient texts. It is no coincidence that John the Beloved, the
closest disciple to Jesus, opens his Gospel with the affirmation
of the Word in these first three verses.

In the following verses he speaks of this Word being made
flesh in the person of Jesus Christ:

> In him was life; and the life was the light of men.
>
> And the light shineth in darkness; and the dark-
> ness comprehended it not.
>
> There was a man sent from God, whose name
> was John.
>
> The same came for a witness, to bear witness of
> the Light, that all men through him might believe.
>
> He was not that Light, but was sent to bear wit-
> ness of that Light.
>
> That was the true Light, which lighteth every man
> that cometh into the world.
>
> He was in the world, and the world was made by

*Elohim: plural of Heb. *Eloah* "God." One of the Hebrew names of God;
used in the Old Testament about 2,500 times, meaning "Mighty One" or
"Strong One." Elohim is a uniplural noun referring to the twin flames of the
Godhead that comprise the "Divine Us." The Seven Mighty Elohim and
their feminine counterparts are the builders of form; hence, Elohim is the
name of God used in the first verse of the Bible: "In the beginning God
[Elohim] created the heaven and the earth." They are twin flames of God, the
Divine Us on each of the seven rays.

him, and the world knew him not.

He came unto his own, and his own received him not.

But as many as received him, to them gave he power to become the sons of God, even to them that believe on his name:

Which were born, not of blood, nor of the will of the flesh, nor of the will of man, but of God.

And the Word was made flesh, and dwelt among us, (and we beheld his glory, the glory as of the only begotten of the Father,) full of grace and truth.

John bare witness of him, and cried, saying, This was he of whom I spake, He that cometh after me is preferred before me: for he was before me.

And of his fullness have all we received, and grace for grace.

For the law was given by Moses, but grace and truth came by Jesus Christ.

No man hath seen God at any time; the only begotten Son, which is in the bosom of the Father, he hath declared him.[2]

Jesus–Lord and Saviour

When you believe in Jesus Christ, you are connected to the Cosmic Christ and to the I AM Presence. As long as you sustain that belief and that tie, you have everlasting life. It does not mean at the end of this lifetime you are going to heaven. It does not mean you are perfect. It does not mean that you don't have to balance your karma, atone for your sin, pay all your debts, do everything that God requires of you. What it does mean is that you have a tie to everlasting life in the person of Jesus. And Jesus is bypassing the karma, the electronic belt, the

Crown Chakra

Third-Eye Chakra

Throat Chakra

Heart Chakra

Solar-Plexus Chakra

Seat-of-the-Soul Chakra

Base-of-the-Spine Chakra

substance that is between your soul and your Holy Christ Self.

You may ask, "Well, if I have a mighty I AM Presence and a Holy Christ Self, why do I have to go through Jesus to have eternal life?" It is because you are in the karmic condition. Your soul is lodged in your body in the seat-of-the-soul chakra. Between that chakra and your heart chakra (the place of the threefold flame and your Christ Self) are all the layers of thousands, if not millions, of years of karma. Your soul does not have the attainment to bypass that karma and sustain a direct tie to your Holy Christ Self. That tie is sustained through Jesus Christ, and that is why you need a Saviour.

Once you have accepted him as your Lord and Saviour, he occupies that unique position in your life. Through him you may be blest with having the Guru El Morya, Maitreya, Gautama, Serapis Bey or any one of the other Masters. Because you have acknowledged that the Christ is in Jesus and that that Cosmic Christ has the power to save you, you now gain entrée into the entire Spirit of the Great White Brotherhood, and you do have communion with your Holy Christ Self. The voice of the Son of God speaks in your heart, and you hear that voice. The scriptures say, "And they that hear the voice shall live."[3] This is what Jesus has done for you.

We know there is a Hierarchy of Light. We know that Jesus had Maitreya for his Guru. We know that Gautama was Maitreya's Guru. We know that Sanat Kumara was Gautama's Guru. This does not in any way displace the pivotal position that Jesus Christ holds in our lives. What we must understand is that we, who are yet unascended, in order to get to Lord Maitreya, Gautama and Sanat Kumara, must go through the heart of Jesus. We cannot skip Jesus. We cannot say, "Well, I don't have in my background much interest in Jesus. El Morya is more important to me or Paul the Venetian, or I like to commune with Lao Tzu or some other Master."

You may gain great assistance on the Path. You may increase your Light. You may do a lot of things. But you cannot continually bypass Jesus. For you to have the power in you to convey the conversion of the Holy Spirit to those whom you meet, you must have established your heart-tie with Jesus, hence, opened the door for your Holy Christ Self to descend into your temple, because this is the way the Father has ordered it.

Jesus also submitted to the order of Hierarchy out of which he descended in that life. And therefore, he had the testimony of the Cosmic Christ, his Guru Maitreya, in his heart. He has submitted to that order of Hierarchy, even though he had great attainment in past ages of earth's history. Jesus has always humbled himself before the chain of Hierarchy into which God placed him for his service.

We have the dictations of the Ascended Master Jesus Christ. We hear his Word, we hear his teaching and we testify that it is true, not because it is spoken from the altar but because we hear it simultaneously spoken in our hearts. We feel the vibration of it. We bear witness, and the Spirit testifies with us that we know we are hearing the Word of the Lord Jesus Christ when we are in the midst of that dictation.

Jesus and the Father

Jesus speaks of Lord Maitreya as the one who sent him in the lineage of the ancient Gurus: "I, then, came into this world sent by the One who has sent me, and when I said, 'I and my Father are one,' I spake of the All-Father and the living I AM Presence and of his representative, the One who should wear the mantle of Guru. Thus, the One who did send me in the chain of Hierarchy of the ancients was none other than Maitreya. . . .

"Blessed hearts, the continuity of the message of Maitreya come again is in this hour in you, not in one individual chosen apart, but through you and through that Holy Christ Flame. . . .

"Come unto my heart and know me, then, as the Son, the 'Sonshine' of Maitreya. Know, then, that my mission, going before him, even as John the Baptist went before me, was to clear the way for the coming of this Universal Christ in all sons of God upon earth."[4]

As recorded in the New Testament, Jesus often spoke of the Father who had sent him. Jesus wanted his apostles to know the one he called Father as the Ascended Master Maitreya, who had overshadowed him as his Guru throughout his final incarnation. And he wanted them to know himself as the One Sent by Maitreya. For thereby they would not worship his flesh and blood, but they would worship the continuity of the Word incarnate, which was in the Beginning with God and had been in Lord Maitreya and his predecessors, the Lord Gautama Buddha and the Lord Sanat Kumara, as it was now in Christ Jesus.

Furthermore, the Master wanted his own to know the Word incarnate in him as the same "Light" that, he told John, "was the true Light, which lighteth every man that cometh into the world."[5]

Jesus wanted his disciples to walk in the Light of their own Christhood while they had the Light of the Great Ones with them through his personal Messengership of the Word, lest the darkness of the untransmuted self come upon them.

For did he not say, "He that walketh in [the] darkness [of

his own karmic condition and of his own dweller-on-the-threshold] knoweth not whither he goeth [without the Guru, who embodies the Light of the I AM THAT I AM]?"⁶

In response to Jesus' uncompromising declaration of his oneness with the Father, "My Father worketh hitherto, and I work"—which you, beloved, must also declare—"the Jews sought the more to kill him."⁷ For not only had the Master broken their law by healing on the Sabbath, but he had also said that God was his Father, making himself equal with God.

Jesus' answer rebukes their denial of his Christhood as well as their ignorance of the law of the succession of the Buddhas. He states in unequivocal terms his oneness with his mighty I AM Presence and his oneness with his Father Maitreya, establishing the mantle and the empowerment that is upon him through the Hierarchy of the Ancient of Days.

> Verily, verily, I say unto you, The Son can do nothing of himself, but what he seeth the Father do: for what things soever he doeth, these also doeth the Son likewise.
>
> For the Father loveth the Son, and sheweth him all things that himself doeth: and he will shew him greater works than these, that ye may marvel.
>
> For as the Father raiseth up the dead, and quickeneth them; even so the Son quickeneth whom he will.
>
> For the Father judgeth no man, but hath committed all judgment unto the Son:
>
> That all men should honour the Son, even as they honour the Father. He that honoureth not the Son honoureth not the Father which hath sent him.
>
> Verily, verily, I say unto you, He that heareth my word, and believeth on him that sent me, hath everlasting life, and shall not come into condemnation; but is passed from death unto life.⁸

And when at the Last Supper Philip said to him, "Lord, shew us the Father, and it sufficeth us," Jesus answered him:

> Have I been so long time with you, and yet hast thou not known me, Philip? he that hath seen me hath seen the Father; and how sayest thou then, Shew us the Father?
>
> Believest thou not that I AM in the Father, and the Father in me? the words that I speak unto you I speak not of myself: but the Father that dwelleth in me, he doeth the works.
>
> Believe me that I AM in the Father, and the Father in me: or else believe me for the very works' sake.
>
> Verily, verily, I say unto you, He that believeth on me, the works that I do shall he do also; and greater works than these shall he do; because I go unto my Father.
>
> And whatsoever ye shall ask in my name, that will I do, that the Father may be glorified in the Son.
>
> If ye shall ask any thing in my name, I will do it.
>
> If ye love me, keep my commandments.[9]

Here again Jesus reveals to his disciples his desire to be known as the Christ, the Avatar of the Piscean age, the present link to the past and the future in the chain of Hierarchy of the Buddhas and the Cosmic Christ.

Thus the Master would have said to his own: "If you have seen me, you have seen Lord Maitreya, you have seen Gautama Buddha, you have seen Sanat Kumara—for each one in his turn and time has embodied the Father. And not only have you seen the personages of the Father in those who have sponsored my Christhood and my mission, but you have also seen the Father as the mighty I AM Presence overshadowing me and entering my temple:

"For I and my Father are one.[10]

"The indwelling Father—as the I AM Presence and the living Guru—dictates the words that I speak and the works that I do.

"If you don't believe that I am in the mighty I AM Presence and the mighty I AM Presence is in me—if you don't believe that I am in Maitreya and Maitreya is in me—then accept as proof the works that I do. For I of mine own self can do nothing; it is the Father in me, the Guru (the Buddha) in me, the Word in me, and the Christ (the Light) in me that doeth the work![11]

"Moreover, he that believeth on me as the Messenger of the Father, the Guru, the Word and the Christ shall do the works that I do and greater works. Because, by his affirmation of (his belief in) the Law of the One by which I live, he, through his own Holy Christ Self and mighty I AM Presence, will also become the herald of God in this chain of Hierarchy.

"And because 'I ascend unto my Father and your Father, and to my God and your God,'[12] I will sponsor you on this path of the disciples of the Cosmic Christ becoming the Bodhisattvas of the Buddha Maitreya. As I AM, so you may also become. If you do not choose this calling sent to you from your Father and your God through my Messengership, then I will have failed in my mission, and you will have failed in yours."

Jesus then explained to his disciples the all-power of the Father that is vested in his name. He promised to transfer this power to his disciples by doing "whatsoever ye shall ask in my name," that the Father may be glorified in the Son.

Indeed, the only way the Son can glorify the Father on earth is by his Word and Work being manifest and multiplied through his sons and daughters. *And the name Jesus Christ is that way.* He has taught us that when we invoke the power of Almighty God "in the name I AM THAT I AM Jesus Christ," the Light of his Causal Body is made accessible to us as his disciples. Since Jesus Christ is the foremost sponsoring Ascended Master of all who follow the Christic and Buddhic paths, it is through his name I AM THAT I AM Jesus Christ that his disciples may also invoke the powerful intercession of Lord Maitreya, Gautama Buddha and Sanat Kumara.

Therefore, when calling upon the name of the Lord, chelas of the Word incarnate who desire to achieve oneness and communion with the sponsoring Gurus of the ages of Taurus, Aries, Pisces and Aquarius always preface their prayers with the pronouncement of his sacred name in the full acclaim of his sponsors, saying: "In the name I AM THAT I AM Jesus Christ/Lord Maitreya/Gautama Buddha/Sanat Kumara." And in so doing, these chelas establish the thread of contact with Hierarchy, as Above, so below.

The all-power that God gave, in heaven and earth,[13] to his only begotten Son in Jesus Christ at the conclusion of his Galilean ministry, he makes accessible to you through your mighty I AM Presence and Holy Christ Self because you confess that Jesus is Lord.[14] This confession is your acceptance, not only that Jesus is the incarnation of the Christ, the Son of God, which should come into the world,[15] but also that he is the incarnation of the Word, which was *with* God and which *was* God in the beginning.[16] That Word is the I AM THAT I AM. Thus, when you confess and you accept that Jesus Christ is your Lord and Saviour, you are affirming that he is actually the embodiment of the mighty I AM Presence.

Maitreya's Mystery School

The teaching of Jesus Christ parallels that of Gautama Buddha, that of the indwelling God flame, the indwelling Christ, the indwelling Buddha. Although Lord Maitreya was Jesus' Guru, he comes to us out of the historical setting of Buddhism. He is not only the Coming Buddha who has come but also the representative of the Universal Christ, and he holds the office in Hierarchy, at present, of Cosmic Christ and Planetary Buddha. According to the traditions of Buddhism, Gautama Buddha prophesied to his disciples that after the planet had been steeped in a period of darkness, Lord Maitreya would descend to earth to preside over an age of enlightenment. Buddhists today await Maitreya's coming much in the same way that Christians await Jesus' Second Coming.

But whereas Buddhists believe that Maitreya is coming at some future date, we affirm that the Ascended Master Maitreya *has* come and is here today to initiate all who qualify themselves to be his students. His chief disciple, Jesus Christ, announced the founding of Maitreya's Mystery School on May 31, 1984:

"We are sheltered in the heart of Lord Maitreya. And he desires me, as his pupil, to announce to you that he is dedicating this Heart of the Inner Retreat and this entire property as the Mystery School of Maitreya in this age....*

"You realize that the first Mystery School of Maitreya was called the Garden of Eden. All of the Ascended Masters' endeavors and the schools of the Himalayas of the centuries have been to the end that this might occur [i.e., that the Mystery School might be lowered] from the etheric octave into the physical—that the Mystery School might once again receive the souls of Light who have gone forth therefrom and who are now ready to return, to submit, to bend the knee before the Cosmic Christ—my own blessed Father, Guru, Teacher and Friend.

"Beloved hearts, the realization of this God-goal and the willingness of Maitreya to accept this activity and Messenger

---

*The Heart of the Inner Retreat is the spiritual center of the Royal Teton Ranch, a wilderness retreat in North America's Rocky Mountains, on the northern border of Yellowstone Park.

and students in sacred trust to keep the flame of the Mystery School does therefore gain for planet Earth and her evolutions a dispensation from the Hierarchies of the Central Sun. For you see, when there is about to become physical through the dispensation of the Cosmic Christ the renewal of the open door to the etheric retreats of the Great White Brotherhood whereby souls—as students of Light who apprentice themselves to the Cosmic Christ—may come and go from the planes of earth to the planes of heaven and back again, this is the open door of the coming of the Golden Age. Maitreya's Mystery School reestablished in the physical octave is the open door of the pathway of East and West to the Bodhisattvas and the disciples.

"This being so, the planetary body has therefore gained a new status midst all of the planetary bodies, midst all of the evolutionary homes. For once again it may be said that Maitreya is physically present, not as it was in the first Eden but by the extension of ourselves in form through the Messenger and the Keepers of the Flame. And as you have been told, this mighty phenomenon of the ages does precede the stepping through the veil of the Ascended Masters—seeing face to face their students and their students beholding them....

"See, then, that Maitreya truly is more physical today than ever before since the Garden of Eden. For his withdrawal into higher octaves was due to the betrayal of the fallen angels and the acts of the fallen angels against Adam and Eve and others who were a part of that Mystery School.

"Thus, the long scenario of the fallen angels and their devilish practices against the pure and the innocent have ensued. And one by one, each must come to the divine conclusion of the Return. Each one is accountable for leaving the Mystery School, and each one is responsible for his own return and his making use of that which is available and accessible as the divine Word.

"Thus, Maitreya is truly with us."[17]

The Coming Buddha

Therefore, through the Sacred Heart of Jesus the Christ, the foremost disciple of Maitreya in the Piscean age, let us enter the path of the Coming Buddha.

As the Ascended Master who holds the office of Cosmic Christ and Planetary Buddha, Maitreya teaches us the same path of individual Christhood leading to the attainment of Buddhahood that he taught Jesus more than two thousand years ago.

The instruction we receive from the Ascended Masters for the perfecting of our souls in the disciplines given by the avatars of the ages of Taurus, Aries, Pisces and Aquarius come to us under the banners of Lord Maitreya and the World Mother.

The dictations of the Ascended Masters embody the mysteries of the Universal Christ spoken by Gautama as long as he walked the earth in the Light of his God unto the hour of his ascension from Shamballa after his passing in Kushinagara, India, circa 483 B.C.; and by Maitreya as long as he walked the earth in the Light of his God unto the hour of his ascension in 531 B.C.; and by Jesus Christ as long as he walked the earth in the Light of his God unto the hour of his ascension.

Jesus exemplified the path of the Buddha, right while he was in Galilee. He came in the tradition of the Christed ones, the avatars out of the East. He went to Kashmir after his mission in Palestine and Galilee, lived a full life there, continuing his mission as the Christ. He passed on in Kashmir at the age of 81, and he took his ascension through the etheric retreat, Shamballa. Jesus and his disciple Kuthumi have attained to the level of Buddhahood. And so, both of them are Buddhas. Jesus was the outpicturing of the Lord of the World and the Cosmic Christ. He was the perfect balance of East and West, the Christ and the Buddha.

In the ages of Pisces and Aquarius, the disciples and Bodhisattvas who do realize the Universal Christ individualized in
the person of their beloved Holy Christ Self mirror the archetypal Christhood of the Avatar Jesus or Maitreya in their individualization of the Word. And we believe and we are witnesses that the only begotten Son of the Father has indeed
come to us "full of grace and truth,"[18] first in the person of
Jesus Christ or Lord Maitreya and second in the person of our
beloved Holy Christ Self.

Maitreya's Presence with Us

In studying the elements of historical Buddhism, we should
remember that Maitreya is not so relevant to us as a past Bodhisattva or a future Buddha as he is gloriously relevant to us as a
very present Ascended Master in our midst having full Buddhic
powers and attainment, which he may transmit to us through
teachings and initiations.

In truth, as the records of akasha reveal, Maitreya has
worn the mantle of the Buddha since the hour of his ascension
in 531 B.C. In a holy, holy ceremony at Shamballa, attended by
a multitude of Ascended Masters and Heavenly Hosts, the
Blessed Maitreya was crowned Buddha by the Lord of the
World, Sanat Kumara. Maitreya's ascended twin flame, who
had been waiting for him in octaves of Light until he should
complete his incarnations on earth, stood to the right of Sanat
Kumara during the sacred ritual while Lady Master Venus
stood to Sanat Kumara's left.

The Light that poured forth from the Great Central Sun on
that never-to-be-forgotten occasion opened the very heavens
and anchored in the earth the glory and praise of the entire
Spirit of the Great White Brotherhood upon the birthday of
"the Coming Buddha who has come" to earth from Venus for

the salvation and enlightenment of many. And the Light of that day and hour remains at Shamballa as a testimony to the victory of our Lord in our behalf. For the Law attests: What one Son of Light can do, all Sons of Light can do. And so the Light of Maitreya's Buddhahood has been multiplied by the Causal Bodies of all the Buddhas and Bodhisattvas who have since received their initiations at the City of Light.*

We are living in the eternal Now at a very crucial moment in the planetary cycles; and in this slice of eternity we have determined to make our mark in time, in space. And so *today* we accept the fusion of our beings with the Christ who is Jesus, the Christ who is Maitreya. "*Now is* the accepted time; *now* is the day of salvation," Paul cried.[19] Because we don't have any other time but now! We don't live yesterday, we don't live tomorrow; we only live today.

Maitreya's Many Roles

Maitreya, the Coming Buddha, the Future Buddha, plays many roles in the various Buddhist traditions throughout the Far East. Not only is he the guardian of the dharma but he is also an intercessor and protector, a guru who personally initiates his devotees, a messenger sent by the Eternal Mother to rescue her children, a Messiah who descends when the world is in turmoil to judge the wicked and save the righteous, and last but not least, he is the Laughing Buddha.

All these descriptions are the many faces of your Holy Christ Self. When you visualize your Holy Christ Self, visualize the appropriate personification of Maitreya as the Guru above you. For instance, Maitreya, as well as Jesus, serves you in the role of confessor, as does your Holy Christ Self.

*Shamballa, etheric retreat of the Lord of the World, is also known as the City of Light.

Professor Jan Nattier writes that in Central Asian texts "Maitreya is explicitly involved in the process of the confession and expiation of sins."[20] Why should he be? Because he desires to shorten the distance between your soul and your mighty I AM Presence. This is likewise the function of the Divine Mediator, your Advocate before the Father, your Holy Christ Self.

Thus, when the day is over, do not neglect to confess your sins (whatever you believe to be a sin) to your Holy Christ Self or to Maitreya. Call on the law of forgiveness, repent, i.e., go and sin no more, and be willing to give to your beloved I AM Presence a violet-flame penance for the alchemy of world transmutation in the form of dynamic decrees; then actively render service to the Sangha* to balance whatever wrongs you may have inflicted on any part of life.

Go to sleep with the peace in your heart that comes from acknowledging to your Lord the error of your ways and your desire to make amends. Sign off from this waking world with a prayer of profound regret in having offended God in anyone, in having hurt or burdened any part of life, determined that the Light of God shall infill you and strengthen your resolve not to repeat the mistake. And lastly, accept the overshadowing of your guardian angel, who will help you to "go and sin no more." Then have a sweet and peaceful sleep, knowing you have at least begun the process of resolution and resolve. We need such resolution before we go to sleep each night.

Sangha [Sanskrit]: Buddhist religious community or monastic order.

Section 9

The Second Coming

TWO THOUSAND YEARS AGO LUKE GAVE us his beautiful description of the birth of Jesus in Bethlehem, the First Coming.

And there were in the same country shepherds abiding in the field, keeping watch over their flock by night.

And, lo, the angel of the Lord came upon them, and the glory of the Lord shone round about them: and they were sore afraid.

And the angel said unto them, Fear not: for, behold, I bring you good tidings of great joy, which shall be to all people.

For unto you is born this day in the city of David a Saviour, which is Christ the Lord.

And this shall be a sign unto you; Ye shall find the babe wrapped in swaddling clothes, lying in a manger.

And suddenly there was with the angel a multitude of the heavenly host praising God, and saying,

Glory to God in the highest, and on earth peace, good will toward men.[1]

And many centuries before the birth in Bethlehem, Isaiah foretold the coming of the Christ: "For unto us a child is born, unto us a son is given: and the government shall be upon his shoulder: and his name shall be called Wonderful, Counsellor, The Mighty God, The Everlasting Father, The Prince of Peace."[2]

And more recently, we can hear ringing in our hearts the words of the song, "The Birthday of a King."

> In the little village of Bethlehem
> There lay a child one day
> And the sky was bright with a holy light
> O'er the place where Jesus lay.
>
> Alleluia! O how the angels sang
> Alleluia! how it rang
> And the sky was bright with a holy light
> 'Twas the birthday of a King.
>
> 'Twas a humble birthplace, but O how much
> God gave to us that day
> From the manger bed, what a path has led
> What a perfect holy way.
>
> Alleluia! O how the angels sang
> Alleluia! how it rang
> And the sky was bright with a holy light
> 'Twas the birthday of a King.[3]

The coming of Jesus Christ in the Second Coming has been long awaited by Christians. It is a very real event, but it is also a mystical one. As we await for him to descend in clouds of glory, we must look again and realize that he is already come. He is come to our hearts as we have acknowledged the Christ in Jesus, in Saint Germain, in the Ascended Hosts.

The First Coming of Christ is the manifestation of the Word incarnate in the Guru, in the Teacher, in the Hierarch. The Second Coming is the igniting of that flame incarnate in the chela, in the disciple, in the one who acknowledges "I am nothing, Lord, you are my Allness; be within me that Allness."

Jesus Christ, in the Second Coming, has come to quicken our own Christ consciousness. This is the Second Coming. And therefore, it can come at any hour in any age. We are not waiting for an outer millennium, but we are pursuing diligently the inner millennium, that moment of alchemy when suddenly we realize, "Why, I AM the Mystical Body of God, Christ lives in me, Buddha lives in me, and I am judged of my Lord."

Jesus teaches us that the Second Coming of Christ is when he comes to you as your Bridegroom, when you are able to receive him because you have walked a path of personal sainthood, you have your wedding garment. The Second Coming of Jesus Christ is the descent of Christ into your temple when you, yourself, become one with him, and you are that Christ Presence in manifestation.

The First Coming of Jesus Christ was his coming to set the example and to show what is the life, the Path, the works, the teaching, the example of one who has internalized the only begotten Son of God. Jesus did that for us, and the saints who followed him, who have led exemplary lives, who have made their ascension, have also demonstrated that path.

The Second Coming is the Ascended Master who comes to us and restores to our memory by the Holy Spirit all the things that he has taught us. Jesus has already come in his Second Coming as the Ascended Master. He is with us. He is teaching us. That is not to say that some will not experience him and see him coming in clouds of glory on a certain day. But we have to understand that revelation becomes very personal, and it comes to each one individually.

The true Second Coming may come at any time. It is not a one-time event of the centuries, but an hourly event. It came for John the Beloved prior to his ascension in his embodiment as the apostle who wrote the Book of Revelation. It may have come to some of us when we walked and talked with Jesus. It may come to us two thousand years later.

The Second Coming of Christ may very well come with clouds and great glory and the sound of trumpets and Jesus appearing in the heavens. That may be happening every day, but the world may not perceive it. Jesus is here with us now and always with us. And when we receive him in that Second Coming and the Word is internalized where we are, that is truly the Second Coming of Christ.

Recognizing the Christ

As disciples of the Word incarnate, we are meant to mirror the archetypal Christhood of the Avatar Jesus or Maitreya in our own individualization of the Word. This we can do every day. *The Imitation of Christ* by Thomas à Kempis is important for us to read, for it shows how to gather the virtues of the Christ and to live them and outpicture them in our life.

When we have attained to this level of the realization of the Christ within, we may also recognize the Ascended Master Jesus or Maitreya, or both, standing before us in their Second Coming. The Second Coming is not a function of the times, nor of time and space, but of the readiness of the soul. It is written: "When the pupil is ready, the Teacher appears."

There are two aspects to the Second Coming. The first is your receiving of Christ in your heart. When enough of mankind have accepted him, then they will see him coming in clouds of glory. They will be able to see him in the air because they already have him in their hearts and they have something with which to identify him.

In a time of wickedness of the people, many do not recognize the Christ. They did not recognize Jesus when he came because they themselves had not yet received the Christ in their hearts. John the Baptist tried to prepare the people for the coming of Jesus by calling them to repent of their sins and be baptized so that they could be washed of their impurities. They did not respond. And therefore, they did not recognize the Christ in Jesus. They denied him, they persecuted him.

Paul said that no man could confess that Jesus is Lord without the Holy Ghost.[4] This means that in order to perceive the Christ in anyone, we have to receive the Holy Spirit. When we have that Spirit, we can confess the Christ as being the true identity of every son and daughter of God, the real spark of life. When we can begin to acknowledge that, then we will see the Master Jesus descending in a cloud.

The appearances of Mother Mary to thousands of people all over the world are an example of this. The Christ in Mary was recognizable by many people because they had Christ in their hearts.

In the Second Coming, we will not only see Jesus coming in clouds of glory, but all of the saints, all of the Masters who have gone before us of whom the Book of Revelation speaks, "they who overcame by the blood of the Lamb."[5] And these are the ones who are robed in white and who stand before the throne of God. These are the ones who have gone before us in the Christ consciousness.

The Rapture

The rapture is an awareness by mankind, perhaps a simultaneous awareness, of the Heavenly Hosts; and we believe that the coming of the Masters in their dictations is a preliminary to that event. First, we hear them by their Word, and when we hear the Word and become the Christ, our vision will be purified, and then we will see.

And therefore, if we see the Christ descending out of heaven, there is no reason why we cannot also ascend to meet that consciousness. Those who see with the consciousness of knowing and being will become that which they see. And they are the ones who are received into the Presence of the Ascended Masters. But they can enter that Presence through the same ritual whereby Jesus entered: through the ascension.

We are at the end of an age. It is a time when there are many advanced souls who have lived before, taken the initiations in other lives, and who are purified and standing ready for the Second Coming, for the rapture. There will come a time when they will be quickened. And when they ascend in these mass ascensions from the hillsides that have been prophesied, we are certain that Jesus Christ will be in their midst; and so it will be a literal fulfillment of the prophesy of the Christ descending and some among mankind ascending to his Presence.

The Everlasting Gospel

The Bible prophesies the coming of the Everlasting Gospel in the Book of Revelation. There flies in the midst of heaven an angel that has the Everlasting Gospel to preach to the men of earth.[6] This event is thought to precede the Second Coming.

We understand that this Everlasting Gospel is here now. It is a thoughtform and a matrix of the mind of God like a swaddling garment, like a sphere of yellow fire that surrounds the earth. It imparts to all people the sense of the universality of religion, the oneness of all religion and the universality of the Christ. People are very much aware that this Christ who was in

Jesus is a Universal Presence who is also with them—that Presence prophesied in Jeremiah as the coming of The Lord Our Righteousness.

We believe that the Second Coming of Jesus Christ *has* taken place, that he *has* descended in clouds of glory, that this Ascended Master has descended to earth, has delivered his message of the Everlasting Gospel, is continuing to do so. And the prophecy that every eye shall see him applies to every eye that is in that vibration and wavelength where he is caught up by the Spirit of his resurrection to the plane of perception. This does not occur simultaneously; but it occurs not according to time and space, but according to the individual soul's capacity to receive him.

The Fulfillment of the Age

The great significance of the Second Coming is that in the First Coming Jesus is the great exemplar at the beginning of the age of Pisces. In the ending when he comes, it is to inaugurate the universal age of the coming of Christ into all of our temples. And that is the finale, the grand finale of the Piscean age.

The Ascended Master Hilarion, who in a previous embodiment was the great apostle Paul, teaches: "Do you not understand that those Christians who have waited two thousand years for the Second Coming of the Lord have not realized that the Second Coming is the coming into the heart of the fullness of their own Christ awareness? In the fullness of the stature and measure of Christ Jesus, your own Christ Self comes. This *is* the Second Coming; and when you receive Christ as your own Real Self, then that Christ will welcome Jesus the Lord, who will dwell with you and live in you and be in you the Saviour of the world.

"Let us be up and doing! Let us be filled with the Holy

Ghost! Let us be up and doing as those who have appropriated the Word, whom God has appropriated to be servants."⁷

Procrastination of the Second Coming

As we enter the New Era with the teachings of the Ascended Masters as our guide to the individualization of the God flame, we see a most unfortunate resistance to change on the part of the orthodox hierarchies of both Christianity and Buddhism as well as the other world religions. Nowhere is this resistance more evident than in the attitudes toward the Coming of Christ or Buddha.

For example, as Christianity carries forward the two-thousand-year prophecy of the Second Coming of Christ, so Buddhism adheres to a lore and a history that has been recited for twenty-five hundred years concerning the coming of Maitreya. This waiting for the future Coming of the Christ Jesus or the Buddha Maitreya with their disciples and Bodhisattvas has created a vacuum of spiritual ignorance.

"No Christ or Buddha is in embodiment," they say, "therefore darkness covers the land." But this darkness is circumstantial: it occurs not because Christ or Buddha has not yet come, but because people are either too dense to be aware of the indwelling Presence of Christ or Buddha, or out of Self-ignorance, they deny the present possibility of God coming into their temple.

Paul queried Christ's followers at Corinth, "Know ye not that ye are the temple of God, and that the Spirit of God dwelleth in you?"⁸ Evidently they didn't! But they were no less informed than are some Christians and Buddhists today.

Gautama and Maitreya likewise affirmed the indwelling Spirit of God when they taught: "The indwelling Buddha . . . is by nature bright and pure, unspotted, . . . hidden in the body of

every being like a gem of great value that is wrapped in a dirty garment, ... and soiled with the dirt of greed, anger, folly and false imagination.... All beings are potentially Tathagatas.*
... The road to Buddhahood is open to all. At all times have all living beings the germ of Buddhahood in them."[9]

The great cataclysm of spiritual darkness that has come upon earth in ages past and present is, in fact, the result of the acceptance of the false prophecy that the seed of Light is not planted in the soul, that the divine spark is not kindled, that God has not entered the temple of man, that the Spirit of God does not dwell in his offspring and that the Christ or the Buddha has not yet come to quicken the spirits of the dead.[10]

This procrastination of the incarnation of the Word is a lie that is sown throughout the world's religions. Judaism, in rejecting the Christ of Jesus, has denied Christ's incarnation in world Jewry today and postponed Messiah's coming any time soon. Islam reveres Jesus as a true prophet along with Abraham, Moses and Mohammed but denies that any of these four were "incarnations of God."

Most Muslims place their hopes in the coming of a *mahdi,* or "divinely guided one," who will usher in a short period of justice and peace. They say that this Golden Age will be followed by a decline leading to the Day of Judgment and the end of the world. Zoroastrianism also awaits a saviour *(saoshyant)* who will lead the forces of Good in a final battle against evil during the end times.

---

*Tathagata: a title for Gautama Buddha used by his followers and by Gautama when he is speaking of himself. Literally translated as "thus come one" or "thus gone one," the word is variously taken to mean a perfectly enlightened one; one who has come and gone as other Buddhas, teaching the same truths and following the same path; or one who has attained "suchness" *(tathata)* or become one with the Dharmakaya (which corresponds to the Causal Body and I AM Presence), hence he neither comes from anywhere nor goes anywhere.

Where is the religion that proclaims that the Second Coming of Christ has already taken place? That religion is right here. And it is the religion of the Ascended Masters.

The Second Coming Has Occurred

In his 1989 Thanksgiving Address Jesus explained that "the so-called Second Coming has occurred and recurred" and that from November 23, 1989, unto the end of the age of Pisces, "I shall have appeared to everyone on every plane of this Matter house. . . .

"I come, then, in the appearance prophesied,[11] and I come again and again and again, my beloved, for the so-called Second Coming has occurred and recurred. So understand, beloved, that I am in the earth as foretold, and I am here to fulfill the prophecy that every eye shall see me.[12]

"Blessed hearts, I have called you to be my own, my disciples, my apostles. I have called to you to be the Christ.[13] I have called, beloved, that the multiplication of my Body, which is broken for you,[14] might be that my Electronic Presence should move in the earth through you and that my Sacred Heart upon your sacred heart might amplify that threefold flame and that open door of the heart whereby through us, one upon one, my Self superimposed upon your self, the souls of earth might enter into the path of discipleship unto the same fulfillment of the Law that you yourselves are realizing and have realized in some measure."[15]

The Coming of Maitreya

As we have said, Buddhists today await Maitreya's coming much in the same way that Christians await Jesus' Second Coming. Most Buddhists believe Maitreya's coming will be thousands, millions or even billions of years from now. This is procrastination.

But Maitreya refutes this doctrine of procrastination as he proclaims his coming in this age. "Being the Coming Buddha, then, I am come into your temple. Just as there is prophesied in the West the Second Coming of Christ, so there is prophesied in the East the coming of Maitreya. The significance is the descent of the Buddha who is the Cosmic Christ into your heart. It is not delayed. It is ready.

"I AM here, beloved. I would enter. As the chamber is emptied and then filled again, emptied and then filled again by the fire breath of illumination's flame, know that in your process of processioning through the inner canyons of being, mounting, then, the spiral staircase to the heart, I am with you, and in a moment of recognition, we experience the divine awareness of we two in the heart of hearts communing."[16]

The moment we postpone Maitreya's coming or his presence with us because we're preoccupied with our human existence—even if we only postpone it for five minutes—we have engaged in the lie of procrastination that displaces the Planetary Buddha and the Cosmic Christ where we are.

Jesus explains what the dispensation of Maitreya's advent in the dawn of the Aquarian age means to each one of us: "When I was in embodiment, I was the presence of Maitreya. As much of Maitreya as could be delivered to the people, he delivered through me. And it was a mighty work and a mighty delivery that has sustained millions these two thousand years.

"In this hour, because of my ascension and the acceleration of Lightbearers, 'He that believeth on me, the works that I do shall he do also, and greater works than these—*greater works than these*—shall he do!'[17]

"Thus, in the dispensation of the presence of Maitreya as the Coming Buddha who has come at the dawn of the Aquarian age, you realize that the greater works expected also means that the Law expects a greater portion of Maitreya and myself to be delivered in this age through this Messenger and through the many disciples worldwide who keep the flame and, in some cases, are empowered beyond that power that was held by the apostles. This, beloved ones, is due to the turning of worlds and the turning of cycles. Thus, not necessarily by achievement but by the wind of the Holy Spirit in your sails, by the momentum of the Great White Brotherhood with you, do you deliver the presence of Maitreya to the world."[18]

Inasmuch as cosmic law has allowed exceptions to the rule that Ascended Masters do not reembody, it is possible that the Ascended Master Maitreya may reincarnate with his Bodhisattvas in the future as the Coming Buddha who will embody and propagate the dharma of the New Age. According to the Ascended Master El Morya, if the world enters a Golden Age, Maitreya may decide to incarnate five hundred years after its commencement.

But we also know that a Buddha, whether ascended or unascended, may choose to appear in a tangible form to selected lifestreams. Thus, without reincarnating, Maitreya might be seen walking and talking with his disciples in his Ascended Master Light Body, which he may precipitate to the etheric level for those who can see him at that level, yet whose karma binds them to the physical octave.

Preach the Word of the Second Coming

The Ascended Master El Morya gives his vision for what the Second Coming can mean for all, not only the few: "Let us, then, summon from the holy energies of the elect the power that will cause mankind to correct the distortions upon the screen of life and awaken the masses of mankind to the mighty power of the resurgent Christ image—that the Second Coming of Christ come not only to the few but to the many, that the elect be summoned from the four corners of the earth, and that the world itself no longer dwell in shadow and blight but in the abundant life envisioned by the Master Jesus, the abundant image envisioned by every Master of the Great White Brotherhood, the piercing white Light of the sacred fire."[19]

"And I say unto you: if you know not what to do, then pause and seek the flame of God's holy will, and then move forward and continue the race. Follow the star and arrive at the place where you will be the full outpicturing of the Christ in manifestation for all mankind to see and behold the only begotten of the Father come forth again in the Second Appearing and the third appearing and the millionth appearing, after each lifestream shall have also manifested likewise, until the entire earth shall become a diadem of stars—stars in such number that the entire universe shall see and know that the holy will of God, the will of the Christ, is come in each man into manifestation.

"To this end do we serve in Darjeeling. To this end do we stand with the evolutions of this planet. Will you stand with me this day?"[20]

Sanat Kumara also speaks of the necessity of taking the message of the Second Coming to the nations: "Behold, now is the accepted time, now is the day of the Lord's salvation as Messiah comes into your temple! And the mission of his Second Coming is to ignite your own threefold flame into the full expansion of the presence of your Christ Self dwelling in you bodily.

"This is the good news of your Saviour that I, Sanat Kumara, call upon you to preach. But some of you have seemed to think over the years that you may choose to be or not to be the living preacher. But I say unto you, until you take up the mantle of your Master, as Elisha took up the mantle of Elijah and smote the waters of the human consciousness, you will not receive from the Holy Ghost the signs that follow them that believe."[21]

The Doctrine of Original Sin

IN ORDER TO SUPPORT THEIR OFFICIAL decrees raising Jesus to his unique stature as God, the Church Hierarchy developed several corollary doctrines. One of these is the doctrine of original sin. This doctrine as it has been taught in the Roman Catholic Church states that as a result of the Fall of Adam, every member of the human race is born with a hereditary moral defect and is subject to death.

The Catholic Encyclopedia says that the term original sin designates "a condition of guilt, weakness, or debility found in human beings historically, prior to their own free option for good or evil. This is a state of being rather than a human act or its consequence."[1]

Because of this inherited stain of sin, no man is capable of achieving either his decency or destiny without a saving act of God. This is accomplished, according to the Roman Church, through the death and resurrection of Jesus Christ.

We must challenge this doctrine of original sin that is

believed by so many millions on earth. Let us disabuse Light-bearers of the notion that they were born in sin and can rise no higher. For until we challenge this lie, we are subject to the burden of this condemnation.

History of the Doctrine

For the most part, there is barely a trace of the concept of original sin among the early apostolic fathers, who believed that no sin could prevent man from choosing good over evil by his own free will.

In the fifth century, original sin became the center of a controversy that was eventually settled in A.D. 529 by the Synod of Orange. The synod decreed that Adam's sin corrupted the body and soul of the whole human race; sin and death are a result of Adam's disobedience. The synod also declared that because of sin, man's free will is so weakened that "no one is able to love God as he ought, or believe in God, or do anything for God which is good, except the grace of divine mercy comes first to him."[2] Thus, grace and not human merit was primary to salvation.

There was much at stake in the outcome of the debate on original sin. The controversy threatened to undermine the role of the Church in the life of the communicant. The Church taught that baptism was the way in which the faithful were initiated into the Church and introduced to grace, and that a life of grace was sustained by the sacraments. If the sacrament of baptism was no longer necessary to wash away original sin and to attain salvation, then the Church and its clergy would be expendable.

What the Roman Church did with their doctrine of original sin is to doom the entire human race to failure except through the saving grace of Jesus Christ, which is a law that is not a law of God and cannot be fulfilled as they have so declared it.

The Intercession of the Christ

We believe that without the Holy Christ Self as intercessor and the soul responding to the call of God, the soul will be set upon by the powers of hell of this world and the fallen angels to compromise her Light, to squander that Light—in other words, to sin and to make karma. We believe in the necessary intercession of that Christ and in the Christ of Jesus working with us.

Jesus speaks to us of baptism as the sacrament that does deliver us and set us on the path of fulfilling the will of God. Baptism, then, becomes the very first sacrament. It is the consecration of the soul to the will of God. He says, "Yea, they are baptized once in a lifetime, dipped in water. The ceremony then is complete. I tell you, I would baptize you daily in the Water of Life, in the living Word, in that which flows from the I AM Presence, beloved, that crystal-clear stream. I would be the instrument to you. Come unto me, all ye who labor, all ye who are weary: I shall give you rest[3] as restoration and re-creation and a re-infiring of the cells and the molecules of life and life-force within you."[4]

Jesus is saying that the once-in-a-lifetime baptism is not sufficient to take the sons and daughters of God all the way to their ascension. He affirms that we must be anointed daily by the Water of Life and he, as our living Guru, would come to us and give us this daily.

As we accept this daily anointing by grace, we must also refute the belief in man's state of sinfulness. This belief is something that we see reinforced even in the Catholic prayer of the Hail Mary: "Hail Mary, full of grace, the Lord is with thee. Blessed art thou among women and blessed is the fruit of thy womb, Jesus. Holy Mary, Mother of God, pray for us sinners now and at the hour of our death. Amen." Each time that is repeated, the individual confirms himself as a sinner, unable to escape that cage or that mold.

Mother Mary has given us a new version of the Hail Mary, which overturns the doctrine of original sin. The New Age rosary gives us the ending that Mother Mary taught us: "Pray for us, sons and daughters of God, now and at the hour of our victory over sin, disease, and death."

> Hail, Mary, full of grace,
>   The Lord is with thee.
> Blessed art thou among women
>   And blessed is the fruit of thy womb, Jesus.
>
> Holy Mary, Mother of God,
> Pray for us, sons and daughters of God,
> Now and at the hour of our victory
> Over sin, disease and death.

The Real "Original Sin"

The Ascended Masters teach that the fallen angels are the original sinners, who committed the original sin against God by challenging the Divine Mother and the Divine Manchild. They have led the children of God into paths of sinfulness in order to convince them that they are "sinners" and, hence, unworthy to follow in the footsteps of Jesus Christ. The fallen angels have kept from the children of God the true understanding that God has endowed each of them with the Divine Image; instead they have taught them that they are forever stained by "original sin" and can never become Christlike or realize their own Christ-potential. The fallen angels have thus promulgated the false doctrine that because the children of God are sinners, they can only be saved by grace, thereby denying the necessity for each one to "work the works of him that sent me," as Jesus declared of his own mission.[5]

God has called us to forsake the sinful life of the fallen angels and to put behind us the sense of forever being sinners. We must accept forgiveness through Jesus Christ for our past transgressions and accept him as our Saviour. We must walk the true course set before us by the Lord. This is made possible by the grace of Jesus Christ, which restores our oneness with him and with our own inner Christ-potential. This grace affords us the opportunity to atone for our misdeeds and mistakes and pursue our own path of individual Christhood.

A Burden of Condemnation

Jesus explains how the lie of original sin burdens all mankind with a weight of condemnation: "I look upon the burdens of humanity, and I think of the story of Eden and the curse of sin and the test failed by those who heeded the voice of the Serpent. Ever since Augustine, the churches have preached that 'ye are conceived in sin and born in sin,' et cetera, et cetera.

"Consider, too, the words of David: 'In sin did my mother conceive me.'[6] Even he was the victim of planetary condemnation. This condemnation is subtle, and most of you are completely unaware of how it is directed against you and others who have descended into mortality to be on earth but for a little while only to enter again into the realms of glory.

"As you pray for your families and your children, I ask you to recognize that the root cause of discontent in each soul and lifestream (which is shared by families and communities and nations) is the belief sealed in the unconscious that the soul is stained according to the doctrine of original sin. It is the belief that the soul has sinned and that that sin is somehow linked to procreation; and thus the most wondrous act of creation, the giving of life on earth to naked souls who require physical bodies for the journey, becomes compromised by the so-called 'stain of sin.'

"The blessing of holy matrimony, the blessing of father and mother and child in the glory of the angels must be your first order of business as you serve God on earth. For you do not realize what condemnation of Death and Hell is upon you in this matter.

"That condemnation is imprinted in the darkest recesses of the unconscious. It is difficult to unleash. For, beloved ones, all have a sense of profound pain, irreparable pain, that they have compromised the sacred fire and the fruit of the Tree of Life. And it is as though nothing could possibly blot out that stain of sin.

"Blessed ones, Mother Mary came to your Messenger many years ago and told her that her assignment was to remove the stain of sin imprinted in people's minds by fallen angels and to impart to their consciousness through the Holy Spirit a sense of the sacredness of the union of man and woman in holy matrimony and in the conception of children. I ask you to take up this cause and to include it in your calls, especially in your calls to Astrea. For Elohim have created you in the Beginning, and Elohim will bring you back to the level of their being in the Ending."[7]

Let Us Affirm Our Origin in God

Many years ago, the Goddess of Liberty pronounced the fiat that original sin has no ultimate reality, since its origin is not in God: "You have heard, beloved ones, of the doctrine of original sin. I am the spokesman for the Karmic Board, and I tell you, beloved ones, there is no such thing as original sin; for God did not create it, the Cosmic Masters did not create it, and I think that it never has been created. Original sin, beloved ones, is a figment of the human imagination. That which is original is purity, it is the law of life, it is the law of eternal perfection, and it is that which was intended to act in the world of man as it acts in the universe."[8]

And Mother Mary brings the vision of our origin as not being in sin, but in God: "O beloved ones, it does not matter when the moment comes as long as it comes swiftly for you to declare, 'Behold, I am begotten of the Lord!' Let that statement cancel out the record of condemnation of original sin upon your soul, and know that the origin of your being is in the immaculate conception of Alpha and Omega. This is your original life, this is your original virtue, this is your original love; and God loves you with that purity that he loved you with in the hour of your soul's conception in the heart of the Great Central Sun."[9]

The Virgin Birth and the Immaculate Conception

THE FACT THAT ALL THINGS ARE POS-
sible with God is not in question in
our consideration of the conception of Jesus. Anything is possible. First, we must explore whether or not there is any reason
for God to make an exception to those laws he had sound reason for framing. Second, if we deem any phenomenon or miracle an exception to cosmic law, we must be certain that it is not
the fulfillment of a higher law of which we as yet are unaware.

The doctrine of the virgin birth is based partly upon the
salutation of Gabriel written in the Book of Luke. According to
the gospel account, at that time Mary was espoused, or promised in marriage, to Joseph. Her surprise at the annunciation is
expressed in the words, "How shall this be, seeing I know not
a man?"[1] The Messenger of the Most High then assured her
that the Holy Ghost would come upon her and the power of
the Highest would overshadow her. But he does not say
whether the Spirit would be imparted to her through her husband or directly from God. The question we must ask, then, is

whether there was any reason for God to make an exception to the normal birth process. And does that necessity arise out of man's preconceived notions about original sin, or out of the logic of the Godhead?

Conception in the Golden Ages

Before the Fall of man, conception took place as father and mother directed Light rays from their heart chakras that merged at a point in space and formed the body for the incoming child. As the result of man's original sin (which was not sex but disobedience to the laws of God), man descended into duality and eventually no longer had the mastery to create by direct precipitation. Thus, another method of birth was evolved by the Solar Lords, and the current method of procreation came into being, sanctified by God.

Sanat Kumara describes the process of childbearing as it occurred in those ancient Golden Ages and as it is destined to take place in the Golden Age to come: "The rising power of the Lords of the Flame from Venus is to become manifest within men and women upon this earth so that there may be restored once again the secret power of creation anchored in beloved Cosmos' two secret rays. This will make possible a birth upon this planet by those means of the power of the spoken Word whereby a man and woman, as they do upon Venus, may face each other before the sacred altar and call forth the mighty Light rays from the heart of their Presence that shall unite and blend before the altar of God in holy union and bring into manifestation on the instant the full-grown body of a Manchild.

"This release, when it first manifests upon this planet, will free the women of the earth, in time, from the burden of childbearing and remove the thorns (which were never a part of the divine intent) from the birth process, enabling both life and death to take on new aspects in human consciousness. This will mean that the terminus of an individual life not yet destined to ascend at the close of its embodiment will be one whereby the individual may come to the temples of the solar fire upon earth and stand before the priests of the sacred fire and step into the Flame to become absorbed by its purified essences while the loved ones of his own family gaze at his conscious exit from the screen of life without a tear, without a sigh, knowing that that individual will once again find a holy renewal in the vows of a *man*ifestation and a *womb-man*ifestation—a man and a woman—standing together before the holy altars of God to once again bring him into the form world from the formless.

"Thus, individuals will no longer suffer the pangs of the birth and death process as it is now known upon this planet, but the glory of the New Age will be shed forth and partaken of by advanced men and women who love and admire the culture of the divine Light."[2]

Making Jesus an Exception

Let it be clear that sexual intercourse was not the original sin. Let it also be clear that all men are not conceived in sin. However, all are tainted with the original sin of disobedience, else they would not be evolving upon this planet.

Somewhere, some time long ago, all human beings entered into original sin through their first act of disobedience to God. And through the Christ within each man, this sin can be atoned for. Sex, which simply means "sacred energy in action," is not of itself impure. It is the misuse of this sacred energy that is sinful, and this misuse may range all the way from gossip and hatred to lust in the sex act itself. Sexual intercourse, properly employed by those bound in holy matrimony, is the God-ordained method of procreation, and there is nothing impure in it except in the sinful consciousness of man.

We must ask ourselves, since the prevalent theories regarding original sin are incorrect (since man is not conceived in sin, but conceived himself in sin through his first act of disobedience), why would it become necessary for God to make an exception to the established birth process in order to bring forth his only begotten Son—the Christ, who is born and lives in every son and daughter of the Most High?

We perceive that inherent in this concept is not only the belief that sex is sinful, but the belief that Matter itself is not a suitable vehicle for the Spirit of God. Was Joseph any less holy than Mary? If her body was consecrated to bear the child Jesus, might not Joseph also have been consecrated by the Holy Spirit to bear the divine seed? If there were something inherently ungodly in the birth process, why would God use it in any form? If he could dispense with Joseph's function, why could he not have dispensed with Mary's and simply sent forth the Manchild direct from heaven?

It is precisely because the Luciferians desired to keep all mankind in the consciousness of sin, acknowledging themselves as sinners, that they conceived of the idea of making Jesus the exception to the rule, thus making him so far above everyone else that no one could possibly hope to approximate his goodness. Thus, the goal of Christhood ordained by God for every manifestation of himself becomes unattainable if we accept the doctrine of the virgin birth. For if this is a condition of holiness, man is defeated before he even begins.

We must ask ourselves if God would make an exception to his Law that would result in the exclusion from grace of all of his children save one. If Jesus were not fashioned like all other men, his mission would be pointless, for he came to teach men the way, not to win their salvation for them. He was the great exemplar, and he left a perfect example that can and must be followed in every respect if man is to reunite with God. Jesus came to show the only way man can find reunion, and his purpose in coming has been aborted because he has been worshipped and not imitated.

The Evidence from the Bible

As we examine the doctrine of the virgin birth, let us look first at the evidence from the Bible.

It is recorded in scripture that Mary and Joseph lived as husband and wife and raised a family after Jesus was born.[3] The Bible also records that at the time of Jesus' conception they were betrothed, but not yet married. In biblical times, marriage and betrothal carried very similar rights and responsibilities,[4] and it is entirely possible that Mary and Joseph had consummated their union before the conception of Jesus.

The biblical foundation for the doctrine of the virginal conception rests on a few key passages. The most significant of these is a few verses in the first chapter of Matthew: "Now the birth of Jesus Christ was on this wise: When as his mother Mary was espoused to Joseph, before they came together, she was found with child of the Holy Ghost," which occurred in fulfillment of that "which was spoken of the Lord by the prophet, saying, Behold, a virgin shall be with child, and shall bring forth a son, and they shall call his name Emmanuel, which being interpreted is, God with us."[5]

It is likely that the author of this part of Matthew[6] had a "Messianic proof text"—that is, a list of passages lifted from the Old Testament to demonstrate that Jesus was the Messiah, used as a preaching aid by early Christians—and took from it a mistranslated version of Isaiah 7:14 and incorporated it into the infancy narrative. The passage in Isaiah reads in the King James Version: "Therefore the Lord himself shall give you a sign; Behold, a virgin shall conceive, and bear a son, and shall call his name Immanuel."

However, some versions of the Old Testament use the words "a young woman" (RSV) or "maiden" (JB) rather than "virgin." The text of the Isaiah scroll found at Qumran library has made it clear that the original Hebrew word used to describe the woman was *almâ,* which means "young woman."

When the Hebrew Masoretic text of the Old Testament was translated into Greek in the Septuagint, the word *almâ* was translated (for reasons that are not clear) into the word *parthenos,* which means "virgin," rather than *neanis,* literally "a young woman." In any event, the Greek translation *parthenos* (virgin) still would have meant that a woman who is now a virgin will, by natural means, once she has united with her husband, conceive the child Immanuel. There was nothing in the Jewish understanding of the verse that would give rise either to the idea of conception through the Holy Spirit or to the Christian belief in the virginal conception of Jesus.

The Messiah was anticipated as the fulfillment of Jewish history. Nevertheless, there was no expectation of a virgin birth in Israel, nor was there any indication in the New Testament literature (outside of the infancy narratives) that anyone was aware that Jesus was born without the agency of a human father. The Gospels were preached for years without any mention of the virginal conception, and it is never touched upon in the writings of Paul.

Matthew is concerned only with showing Mary's virginity before Jesus' birth so that the Isaiahan prophecy will be fulfilled. As time passed, however, the notion of the virginal conception grew, and by the second century, traditions of the virgin birth developed, followed by the idea that Joseph and Mary never had normal sexual relations, finally concluding that Joseph, too, was a virgin!

Jesus' brothers and sisters are sometimes held to be children of Joseph by a previous marriage. "In antiquity there were debates whether these were half-brothers of Jesus (sons of Joseph by a previous marriage—*Protevangelium of James;* Epiphanius), or cousins (sons of either Joseph's brother or of Mary's sister—Jerome), or blood brothers (children of Joseph and Mary—Helvidius)."[7]

The other primary biblical foundation for the doctrine of the virginal conception of Jesus is based upon two Greek words in Luke 3 and four words in Luke 1. Some Bible scholars conclude that these words were probably not in the original gospel texts, but were added by a scribe who misunderstood the Hebrew doctrine of dual paternity.

For some time prior to the birth of Jesus, the Hebrews assumed that God was active in the generation of each individual—that Yahweh creates when parents procreate—something that biblical scholar William E. Phipps says might be called a theory of dual paternity: "This double sonship outlook became established in Jewish tradition. One ancient rabbi said that human creation occurs in this manner: 'Neither man without woman nor woman without man, and neither of them without the Divine Spirit.'

"In the first birth account of the Bible, Eve exclaims: 'I have brought a child into being with the help of YHWH.' ['I have gotten a man from the LORD.'] This was interpreted by a rabbi: 'There are three partners in the production of a man: the Holy One, blessed be he, the father, and the mother.' In that talmudic assertion 'the rabbinic theory of marital intercourse is summed up.'"[8] Therefore the statement of Gabriel that "he shall be called the Son of God" (Luke 1:35) is not inconsistent, according to Hebrew doctrine, with Joseph also being the father.

Luke 3:23 contains an obvious scribal insertion: "And Jesus himself began to be about thirty years of age, being (as was supposed) the son of Joseph, which was the son of Heli." Phipps proposes that the words "as was supposed" render irrelevant the aim that the genealogical compiler had in mind, which was to trace Jesus' descent through Joseph.

Luke 1:34 contains a less obvious scribal insertion. "Then said Mary unto the angel, How shall this be, seeing I know not a man?" The statement is incongruous when the words "seeing I know not a man" remain in the text. Phipps points out that an intelligent bride would hardly be puzzled by the means by which she would become pregnant. But if "seeing I know not a man" is deleted, then Mary's puzzlement refers to the magnificent destiny for a carpenter's son prophesied by Gabriel in the preceding verses, not the method of conception. Some scholars suggest that an old Latin version of this passage, without reference to the virginal conception, may be the way Luke wrote it.[9]

Effects of the Doctrine

There is no way to prove or disprove that the original texts of Matthew and Luke were tampered with, because the earliest existing manuscripts are several centuries later than the lost originals. However, it was in the second and third centuries that the virginal conception became exalted among Gentile Christians as the only fitting way for the Divine Logos to have become enfleshed.[10] Today it is the position of the Roman Catholic Church, the Eastern Orthodox Church and the Coptic Church that Jesus was the product of a virginal conception.

We do not believe that the conception of Jesus by his father Joseph, as the agent of the Holy Spirit, in any way detracts from the divinity of his soul or the magnitude of the incarnate Word within him; rather does it enhance the availability of the fullness of God through his chosen and anointed human instruments.

Every man and woman is the son of God (the Christ Self)

whose seed is transmitted by God (the Holy Spirit). Every man and woman is the son of man (the four lower bodies, the vehicles that are conceived through Matter and evolving soul consciousness).

The necessity for the condition of virginity in order to conceive Christbearers is a condemnation of all other sons and daughters of God who are in the karmic condition. The doctrine of the perpetual virginity of the Mother Mary is one that declares the unworthiness of all others upon earth: only Mary can bear the Son of God; we can do nothing to bring in the Golden Age.

It is also a condemnation of the Father and the Father Principle: he is not worthy to bear the seed of Alpha that can ignite and bring to life a living soul who is a Christed one. By this faulty logic, we cannot bring in the Cosmic Christs and the Buddhas and the seventh root race—because we are all stained by original sin.

The Immaculate Conception

The doctrine of the Immaculate Conception, which was elevated to the status of dogma by Pope Pius IX in 1854, goes one step further. This doctrine designates that Mary, by a unique grace, was free from the stain of original sin from the moment of *her* conception. In the eyes of Catholic theologians, this special grace—a privilege that no other human being has ever received—qualified Mary to be a suitable mother for Christ.*

The New Testament does not state that Mary was

---

*The conclusion that would be drawn from this doctrine is that Mary was karma-free—free from sin. There is truth in this, in that Mother Mary and Jesus descended in their final incarnations bearing only a very small percentage of karma unbalanced, in order to play their roles and to make their ascension. The concern with this doctrine is that it makes Mary unique and apart from all others, and therefore, no one else may attain to that same status.

immaculately conceived, and Origen and other early Church Fathers assumed the mother of Jesus was like other human beings. They thought that she was holy but not sinless, that is, not karma-free. Moreover, there is no comment anywhere in scripture about Mary's perpetual virginity, and nothing is heard from Christians of the first century on this topic.

But by the time the Council of Ephesus ratified the title "Mother of God" for Mary in A.D. 431, there existed a strong belief that her purity was flawless and her holiness incomparable, thus elevating her to the level of an idol, someone out of reach, someone we can never be like.

Much scholarly material has been written on this subject, pro and con, but the basic effect of this doctrine—which was never preached by Jesus himself—is to first put Jesus and then his Mother on a pedestal and therefore to deny us the opportunity of realizing that we, too, can sponsor avatars, souls of Light, through diligent preparation in the holiness of the marriage union.

Mary, the Cosmic Virgin

In fact, the blessed Mary is Archeia of the Fifth Ray and divine complement of Archangel Raphael; and the feminine Archangels, the Archeiai, are called Virgins. They are the heavenly Virgins. Mother Mary bore their virgin consciousness, their divine wholeness to earth. This is why an Archangel was chosen to descend into form to give birth to Jesus—it was her consciousness, her high estate, the great magnitude of her aura and her attainment.

Mother Mary is the Cosmic Virgin who took a form like ours in every respect, and by her immaculate concept of our souls does restore us, with Jesus, to salvation in God. Conceiving sons of God by Saint Joseph never compromised either

Mother Mary's virginity or Saint Joseph's virginity. *Because true virginity is not of the flesh, but of the mind, the heart and the soul.*

As Moses came that we might raise up the sacred fire once again, as Jesus came to represent our Christhood, so Jesus received his mother; and his mother was sent by God to hold the immaculate concept for his birth and mission, and for the restoration of our individual souls to our virginity, our original state of innocence in the heart of God.

Mother Mary tells us, "Let us begin, then, with the immaculate concept. Let us begin with the immaculate conception. Let all called to be conceived this day in the mind of God, to be reborn in the Light of the All-Seeing Eye of the Cosmic Virgin, let the conception of each identity be reenacted in this moment, as the love fires of Alpha and Omega flow from the heart of the Great Central Sun. Let there be a reenactment of the ritual of the conception for your soul.... And let that conception be because you have now reinforced the concept immaculate that you hold in your third eye of that which is to come as the fullness of the perfection of life."[11]

"I place my hand then upon your foreheads this morning to seal within the focus there of the All-Seeing Eye of God the immaculate conception of your own divinity; and I say, let that image of the cosmic City Foursquare, the temple beautiful of your own individuality, your own individed identity, appear now for the victory, parting the way, parting the Red Sea of your own human consciousness and providing the pathway into the Promised Land of the Golden Age and the new heaven and the new earth."[12]

The Vicarious Atonement:
The Body and Blood of Christ

J ESUS CAME AS THE WAY-SHOWER, AS the Mediator between our God and ourselves. This is the function of the Christ. We attribute it to Jesus because he became one with the Christ, but what he did, we all must do. This is the difference between the teachings of the Ascended Masters and the teachings of the Churches today. It is clear and simple.

Those who wish to follow the teachings of the Masters must realize that they have a responsibility: as they sow, they reap. We have a responsibility to become the Christ, to be joint heirs with Christ if we would have our freedom. We have the responsibility for all of our actions, all of the energy we use.

Many of the people in this world do not wish to take that responsibility. It's very easy to say, "I'll do what I want, and then I will proclaim my faith in Jesus, because he died for my sins; and by his death, my sins have been atoned for." But how could a man two thousand years ago atone for the sins we commit today? The very idea of it is illogical. It would not even appeal to a five-year-old child, and yet we have heard it so often that we don't even question it.

If, with the sin of Adam all men fell, then why were not all men resurrected the moment that Jesus died on the cross or the moment that he rose from the dead? If that was the propitiation for man's sins, why did they all not become sinless? Why was not the entire earth perfected? This would have to be the logic of a promise that we are saved through Jesus, through his death and through the shedding of this blood.

There would be no errors in the world if all of this were exactly so. For the error of Adam would have been canceled out by the death of Christ if God required a blood sacrifice. The only sacrifice that God requires is the surrender of man's carnal mind and the wrong attitudes that he has developed in his carnal mindedness toward God and toward man and the recognition of his own Christ identity, which Jesus proclaimed.

And so, we find that the theory of a vicarious atonement, that Jesus' sacrifice atoned for all men's sins throughout all of history, does not make sense for anyone who remembers his own inheritance, who can think for himself, who knows where he came from and where he is going.

The Concept of Sacrifice

Man considers God in the same manner as Abraham considered God when he received the command to sacrifice his son Isaac upon the altar. The son of promise, then, becomes a symbol to man of the concept of sacrifice. But the voice of the angel clearly declared, "Abraham, Abraham ... Lay not thine hand upon the lad, neither do thou any thing unto him," and advised him not to make the sacrifice of his only begotten son. The statement that had been made by Abraham, that the LORD would provide a sacrifice, was fulfilled, and it came to pass that the ram caught in the thicket became the sacrifice.[1]

Just as God did not ask for the sacrifice of Abraham's son as a propitiation for sin, so he would not ask for the death of Jesus as a propitiation for the sins of men; for God is not a tyrant nor one who desires sacrifice, but rather he seeks obedience, which he has declared is better than sacrifice,[2] thus showing the real truth of the Law.

Orthodox religion has amplified the sacrificial aspects of the crucifixion of Christ upon the cross. This is not done out of insincerity, but as tradition. This tradition has all but destroyed the true meaning of the cross, for the cross itself is the symbol of the meeting of two lines of force. The vertical, or descending, bar of the cross represents the energy of God, the holy energies that come down from on high—the infinite Spirit. The horizontal bar of the cross is symbolic of the plane of man's own creation, the finite—Mother. And the cross itself is formed at the juncture of these two lines where God and man meet.

The carrying of the cross, then, is, in truth, the living on the mortal plane of the life that is the Reality of the Immortal, of the Law that is love in action. This requires no other sacrifice than the giving of one's attention and whole being to the eternal purpose: "Present your bodies a living sacrifice to God, which is your reasonable service."[3]

In fulfillment of the immortal plan that God already has, and in effect is, the ram caught in the thicket is symbolic of man's unredeemed and misqualified energy, which like a scapegoat, is caught in the wilderness of form, of time and space, and is symbolic of his need to periodically transmute undesirable conditions into the original divine intent. This is divine fulfillment. It is sacrificial only in the sense that the old must be replaced by the new. It is sacrificial only in the sense that one must give up that which has not produced happiness and perfection for that which will. Flesh and blood cannot inherit the kingdom. Only the magnificence of the Spirit that is alive forevermore can inherit the kingdom. This is Reality. It replaces error by its Truth, and it is life replacing death.

This is the manifestation of the Christ, of the only begotten of the Father, of the universal Light and intelligence of Almighty God. Intelligent men and women, and even the consciousness of a child, can accept this—not the idea of bloody sacrifice as required by God, not the idea of vicarious atonement, where one man has the sins of the whole world laid upon himself. If this were so, then man would long ago have been freed from sin, for the penalty was paid two thousand years ago, according to man's concepts.

The Dangers of a False Doctrine

The Maha Chohan, the representative of the Holy Spirit to the earth, warns of the dangers to the spiritual seeker of accepting the idea of a vicarious atonement in place of the disciplines of the Path: "Ponder the fact that much of your present fund of objective knowledge about life was received through tradition from your parents, teachers and associates. In addition, the hand of error-prone bigots, well versed in their own conceit, has offered its instruction to the world quite readily. While the blind continue to lead the blind, we direct mankind's attention toward harmony and unity as more important than the doctrine of the vicarious atonement, which is predicated upon the appeasement of the wrath of an angry deity. Such erroneous concepts are in direct contrast to the truth concerning divine love, whose radiant, Edenic purity holds only the best and highest vision for every child of Light. Behold, this is the love of God that enables each one to atone for the sins of the past through the intercession of his own Christ Self.

"Yield not, then, to the lure and false promises of those

human apostles of ease who teach what is pleasing to man rather than the Truth of God and the instruction of the Ascended Masters. While some, steeped in the errors of orthodoxy, have promised mankind salvation through the sacrifice of another, others have suggested that in a few easy lessons one could gain enough spiritual knowledge to lead a charmed existence forever after without any effort—just letting God do all the work.

"Those who are looking for the easy way out and are not willing to exercise self-discipline in overcoming the momentums of their own past errors as well as those inherent within civilization may glory in such promises. However, when such individuals near the end of their life span, they see that there is no forthcoming fruit for labors left undone or half-done—no divine victory, no realization of the ever-present love of God or the hearing of his voice declaring, 'This is my beloved Son, in whom I AM well pleased.'⁴ Too late they will know that the ripe apple of promise has turned to ashes; and their wasted lives and blighted hopes will be proof enough, delivering in bitter terms the stern mandate that a change in course must be pursued."⁵

Saint Germain also speaks on this subject and explains how grace operates within the framework of the law of karma: "The law that states that every man shall bear his own burden,⁶ that is to say, the burden of his own karma, cannot be set aside, even by grace itself. Yet grace can provide the blessed assistance for which the aspirant longs, and this he will utilize as the unguent of his striving to win his own immortal victory. No one can ever win another's immortal victory for him. Yet, as in the case of Sir Walter Raleigh and Elizabeth the Queen, an Ascended or an unascended being can remove his own cloak to provide a pathway over a difficult spot, together with the energies from the storehouse of his own love and grace, for one whom he loves. This Christ Jesus did for a world, and his service will remain forever as a brilliant star adorning the firmament of the many sons and daughters of God....

"When one truly knows the life and work of Jesus, one's admiration for the Master knows no bounds. But this admiration must be great enough to inspire the soul to the imitation of Christ. To walk in the illumined footsteps of the Master, to relive his life by working his works, by entering into and participating in his passion and by drinking the whole cup of communion with the Lord—the cup of joys and the cup of sorrows—this is the way of the advancing path of the disciple who first admires and adores his Master and then, as the initiate, emulates his actions and his consciousness.

"*This is the only way one can accept the doctrine of the vicarious atonement* whereby it is believed that God and man are reconciled through the death of Jesus Christ. I underline these words in letters of living fire; for they are the effective repudiation of mortal man's misconceptions, which continually expound upon the sinful nature of man, reducing all mankind to the level of sinners who are helpless without the sacrifice of Jesus the Christ. Thus, with a mere twist of doctrine, the Christ-potential that God has bequeathed to every son and daughter is nullified, and the blessed children of the Father-Mother God must look to one man to make a sacrifice that they, through the Christ Self, are capable of making for themselves.

"There is no justice in the sacrificial shedding of the blood of one for the sins of the many. Jesus' supreme sacrifice on the cross whereby he laid down his life for his friends was an outworking of the Great Law that states that he who has attained to the Christ consciousness and passed the initiations of the sacred fire may hold the balance for world and individual karma. Any initiate of the stature of Jesus, by the weight of the Light that he bears within the heart as a concentrated focus of the sacred fires of the Holy Ghost, may carry the weight of mankind's sin and their sinful sense until they, themselves, are able to bear that burden and to say with their Lord, 'Behold, my burden is light.'[7]

"It is through the fiery baptism of the Holy Spirit that each one can, in the name of Christ, be the recipient of the flame of forgiveness by invoking the law of forgiveness. The violet flame is the seventh-ray action of the Holy Spirit and of its baptismal fires that transmutes darkness into Light, error into Truth, and is the means whereby the sinner is made whole. Thus, when Jesus spoke the words of the Christ 'Thy sins be forgiven thee, be thou made whole,'[8] he issued forth the command whereby the energies of the Holy Spirit were transferred from his heart flame to the being and consciousness of the supplicant for the consuming of that portion of his karma that the Law would allow."[9]

Jesus' Mission in Terms of Karma

The true understanding of Jesus' bearing the sins of the world is that when mankind make a karma that is so grave that it could not be balanced and therefore they would have to go through the second death, God has periodically taken mercy upon mankind and sent a Son of Light who is virtually karma free or has just enough karma to keep him on earth. That individual, by his attainment and his adeptship, will take on the planetary karma and bear the sins of the world; and by doing this he renews opportunity for those who sinned to correctly qualify energy and return to God.

However, the misinterpretation of this teaching has resulted in people ignoring the law of karma. The fallen ones have distorted the law of karma and distorted this concept of the Saviour taking on the sins of the world to mean that people need only confess their sins, and they can have salvation.

The karma that Jesus took upon himself is the original karma involving the fall of Lemuria through disobedience to the Law of God and the lowering of the energies in misuse of the sacred fire. Jesus did not take upon himself all future misdeeds of the race. He took upon himself that basic karma of the Fall, or the descent of consciousness, so that people could, in effect, from the point of grace that he had attained to and on the momentum of his consciousness, return to the state of grace in order to balance the karma of their electronic belts and thereby bring themselves to the place where they could bear the karma of their fall. And when they get to the place of bearing the karma of their fall, they are at the place of meeting their own dweller-on-the-threshold and the totality of the spirals that occurred through the Fall—the negative spirals of the fall of consciousness from the upper chakras to the lower chakras.

There is a difference between balancing the karma of day-to-day sins and the balancing of the karma of the original Fall. Since we have to function from the level of the consciousness of the planet, which is in the state of this fallen consciousness, we are functioning in a certain plane that almost of necessity involves sin on a day-to-day basis. Since that is a way of life on the planet, the Masters have developed a code of ethics by which people may live until they evolve out of this state of consciousness. People will be dealing with karma until they can come to grips with the mastery of the sacred fire.

Unfortunately, instead of doing this, people place the whole of their responsibility for all of their involvements on Jesus and think that thereby they have no responsibility. This is the scapegoat consciousness, the inherent desire of the carnal mind to place the responsibility for its failures, its inequities upon the Christ and upon the sons and daughters of God who have the Christ consciousness.

Sacrifice and Atonement

In his *Corona Class Lessons,* Jesus has written extensively on the concepts of sin and the vicarious atonement. Here he explains the true meaning of sacrifice: "Biblical writers, saints, prophets and holy men have written and taught about the idea of appeasing an angry God through the blood sacrifice of his Son. Although these have acted with great sincerity, they have nevertheless been influenced by the strictly pagan practice handed down from distant days when men departed from the ancient religions of Atlantis wherein true communion with God was taught and experienced as the interchange (sacrificial emission) of Light between the soul and the Spirit.

"Subsequently, the true art of sacrifice (self-giving unto God) degenerated into the sinister and perverted uses of the sacred fire in sexual rites performed at the altar. As a substitute for the ritual of self-sacrifice of the synthetic image (shedding the snakeskin of the serpent mind), the false priests offered temple virgins (in place of themselves) in sacrifices of appeasement to the gods. (It came to pass prior to the Flood that young men were offered in place of women.) The malpracticing priesthood encouraged the bizarre and sensual in their subjects, and magnetizing the denizens of the astral world through nefarious incantations, cooperated with the black magicians who created the conditions that led to the Noachian deluge and the sinking of Atlantis.[10]

"The Canaanite idea of child sacrifice, 'burning their sons and daughters in the fire,'[11] temple prostitution and burnt offerings and sacrifices to Baal, imitated by the Israelites, recalled the last days of a decadent Atlantis. These abominations, of Nephilim origin, were denounced by Jeremiah and Ezekiel, as well as by Isaiah, Amos and Micah.[12] By and by, the substitution of the blood of sheep and other animals for that of human beings was deemed preferable in the rites of atonement practiced in the cultures of the Fertile Crescent. Yet, to this day, human as well as animal sacrifice can be found on the continent of Africa.

"In the knowledge of the foregoing historical facts and self-evident spiritual truths, consider how unreasonable it is that a formula for human or animal sacrifice or the shedding of blood could have been required or ordained by God for the propitiation (atonement, expiation, balance) of sin (i.e., karma).

"If, then, sacrifice is *not* required for the remission of sins, what *does* life demand in order to balance humanity's debts? I am happy to clear up this point for all who adore the Truth that will make them free from such smoldering error that blind theology has kept active, thereby mutilating both the human and the Divine Image in man, which would otherwise have been universally outpictured upon earth long ago.

"Let us together examine the mystery of the blood of the Lamb as the acceptable sacrifice that, we are told, meets with the divine approval in remitting the sins of mankind.[13]

"*Life* and *God* are synonymous terms and denote interdependence in the interchange between the divine and the human, for the life of man is God, and God's life flows in man's veins. The term *life* is equivalent to blood in the scriptural sense and is preferred to *blood* by the spiritual student, who rejects the idea of the shedding of blood as abhorrent and inconsistent with true humanity and certainly with divinity.

"The scriptures declare that 'without shedding of blood there is no remission' of sins.[14] I am declaring to you and to all men forever the truth concerning this biblical statement, herein quite simply revealed: without the shedding (casting off) of that life, or life-force, that has been misqualified with human foolishness, the sins of man can never be remitted (requalified with the love plan of God). Moreover, without the release of the life-essence (i.e., 'blood') of the Lamb, who is your Holy Christ Self, you cannot balance your karma.

"Hence, it is by a continual requalifying, mastering, governing and controlling of energy through the Ascended Master Light of the individualized Holy Christ Self that men and women shall rise to the point where their former sins, which are solely error recorded in memory, are blotted out[15] by the Holy Spirit. This ritual of true sacrifice takes place as they invoke the violet fire of forgiveness, the white radiance of God-purity and the comforting assurance that as they put off the old man with his deeds, the new man—the firstborn Son made in the image of God—comes into manifestation in the glory of Reality.[16]

"The idea that God, your beloved I AM Presence, favors one child and rejects another is totally inconsistent with divine law. My own life was offered to God to epitomize the Cosmic Christ, to prove that man and woman in physical embodiment can ascend out of Matter and remain close by in octaves of Light (invisible, yet co-occupying the physical plane at a higher frequency) to mightily assist the earth and its evolutions in returning to the original divine plan of the abundant life.

"This I am doing to the present day. Well may it be spoken of me—as it should be of every soul who is destined, whether one knows it or not, to be a Christ—I AM (the I AM Presence in me *is*) the way, the truth and the life: no man cometh unto the Father but by the same path of personal Christhood that all who have embodied the Word have demonstrated.[17]

"In the purified state, man 'sheds the Light' of the I AM Presence through his sanctified (sacred) heart and other spiritual centers (chakras) for the transmutation of world sin (karma). In this release of Light, the initiate discovers the true meaning of the remission of sin by the 'shedding of blood,' noted by the mystic writer of Hebrews. However, the full force of this initiation is not experienced until after the records of personal *sin* (violations of the law of grace) are consumed by love, nor until personal karma (the obligations to life incurred through disobedience to God's laws) is balanced by sacrificial service (words and works, including dynamic decrees for world transmutation).

" 'Without *shedding of blood...*' is then seen to be the flow of life from God through the purified soul and temple of man. The pure life-essence of the Holy Christ Flame is released in 'rivers of living water' from the 'belly'[18]—and this refers to the solar plexus, or 'place of the sun'—which becomes the fount (chakra) of Christ-peace in all who also believe in the Christ of me as the God-power in themselves.

"Yes, without the shedding of this 'blood', there is no world remission of sin by the Son of God incarnate in you! And for this cause you and I came into the world—to take upon the office of our Christhood the burden of world karma so that the lost sheep gone astray from the house of Reality[19] might experience a deferment of their karma and a certain relief from suffering while they learn of me and my true burden, which is Light.[20] This Light, when internalized by themselves, will enable them in their turn to take full responsibility for their own burden of karma as they, too, follow the selfsame path of discipleship you are on: personal transformation through integration with Christ, the Light of your world."[21]

Holy Communion

Saint Germain explains the *Body* and *Blood* of Christ as it pertains to the statement of Holy Communion: "Precious communicants at the altar of the Lord, understand that the Blood of Christ contained the Light and the essence of the sacred fire that he focused even physically and tangibly within his heart. His blood contained the essence of that fire that is the very life and Spirit of God himself. His body was transfigured with that Light on the Mount of Transfiguration when he passed through this initiation before Peter, James and John in the presence of the Ascended Masters Moses and Elias.

"Thus, by the saturation of his form and consciousness with the Christic Light, Jesus' body had become the body of God, and specifically of the feminine aspect of God, as it was the focus of life in the plane of Matter. And thus, when Jesus made the statement 'Except ye eat the flesh of the Son of man, and drink his blood, ye have no life in you,'[22] it was the setting forth of the ritual of the mystical union of the disciples with the Body and the Essence of the Christ, which was undoubtedly perfectly manifest in Jesus. The actual drinking of the Blood and the eating of the flesh of Jesus is not the intent of this admonishment, nor is it the requirement of the Infinite Spirit whom Jesus called Father.

"Participation in the ritual of Holy Communion whereby Christians have partaken of the Last Supper of the Lord with his disciples is the means whereby they may spiritually enter into the drinking of the Blood and the eating of the flesh of Jesus. Through the alchemy of transubstantiation, the grape juice is charged with the Essence, the very Light of the Christ, and the bread assumes the frequency of his body consciousness. When the communicant partakes of the host, this charge and this frequency are transferred not only to his body but also to his mind and soul.

"The term *transubstantiation* means the changing of substance. Actually, the juice and the bread are not visibly changed in their form into the flesh and Blood of Jesus; but rather the Holy Spirit, who administers the communion through the minister or priest, focuses the energy spirals of Alpha (Spirit or life-essence) and Omega (the body consciousness) in the juice and the bread. Although the nonessential properties of the grape juice and the bread remain, such as taste, color, shape and smell, the essential properties are changed as the molecules of substance take on and are imbued with the Alpha and Omega spirals of the Holy Spirit.

"This taking-in of the energies of wholeness through Holy Communion is a means whereby devotees of Christ may put on the life-essence and the body consciousness of their Lord as they approach the throne of grace step by step, initiation by initiation. Each time they call upon the law of forgiveness, invoke the violet transmuting flame and accept the purging fires of the Holy Spirit for the transmutation of past sins, they are preparing to partake of the Sacred Eucharist in each succeeding Communion Service....

Sin and Redemption

"Please understand that had the death of Jesus on the cross served to atone for the sins of all mankind—past, present and future—as it is claimed by Christian theologians, the so-called original sin of Adam, which has not been correctly understood in the first place, would have been instantaneously canceled out. Thus, the sin, the disobedience and the death consciousness of Adam would have been immediately revoked for all mankind, and all would have been returned to the estate of Eden and to the consciousness of immortal life, the original gift of God to man. But this did not happen.

"Nevertheless, the statement of Paul to the Romans is correct when it is correctly interpreted: 'For if by one man's offence death reigned by one; much more they which receive abundance of grace and of the gift of righteousness shall reign in life by one, Jesus Christ. Therefore, as by the offence of one judgment came upon all men to condemnation; even so by the righteousness of one the free gift came upon all men unto justification of life. For as by one man's disobedience many were made sinners, so by the obedience of one shall many be made righteous.'[23]

"First of all, let it be explained that the Fall of man, which is explained in the allegory of Adam and Eve, was the gradual descent of the consciousness of many sons and daughters of God from a level of God Self-awareness through the immaculate vision of the All-Seeing Eye to the plane of duality and the relative awareness of good and evil. Gradually mankind's energies descended from the upper chakras to the lower charkas, and thus, Adam and Eve were typical of the evolutions living in the last days of Lemuria who had compromised the sacredness of the altar of God and begun the misuse of the sacred fire for the gratification of the senses and carnal desire. In this manner, consciousness of death and sin entered the race. Therefore, it was first by the few and then by the many that paradise was lost; and indeed, it is through the Christ, the one and only begotten of God outpictured in the life and work of Jesus, that all mankind regained the opportunity to return to wholeness.

"By his demonstration of the Law, Jesus restored on behalf of all mankind the knowledge of the gift of opportunity. Because he lived and made his supreme sacrifice, every son and daughter of God now has the opportunity to prove the selfsame laws that he demonstrated and thereby to inherit immortal life. Every son and daughter must make the same sacrifices that he made by sacrificing the human consciousness for the divine. Though all mankind may pay the price for the disobedience of those who first partook of the fruit of the tree of the knowledge of good and evil,[24] even so all mankind can know that because one overcame the sin of duality and the lie of separation from God, all can through the same Christ, individualized in the Christ Self, return to the oneness of God through the All-Seeing Eye."[25]

Section 13

The Crucifixion

I N THIS SECTION, WE WOULD LIKE TO put in order certain misconceptions in the world about the nature of the cross. We would also like to show you the wonderful peace that can come to you today and always through a proper understanding of the cross.

Saint Germain explains that "the cross is a very old symbol. And while it is unfortunate that crucifixion became the mode of execution for slaves and the worst criminals in the Roman Empire (Roman citizens exempted), it was no accident that Jesus was crucified. For the powerful symbol of the cross had long been defined as the meeting place of God and man. Here, where Alpha and Omega give birth to the Christ, Jesus must prove that the Christ, the I AM, is alive forevermore. (The vertical bar of the cross symbolizes the plane of Alpha, or Spirit; and the horizontal bar symbolizes the plane of Omega, or Matter. At the nexus where the two planes meet, the Christ consciousness is born when the ego dies.)"[1]

Taking Up the Cross

We read the words of Jesus: "If any man will come after me, let him deny himself, and take up his cross daily, and follow me."[2] Saint Paul also showed in his statement, "I die daily,"[3] that the crucifixion on the cross of Matter involves the yielding of control by the lower self to the Higher Self each day.

In the case of Jesus' death upon the cross, we see clearly that the power of God that was revealed through him, was also within him. This is why, when he hung upon the cross and for a moment was forsaken of this blessed inner contact, he cried out, "Eloi, Eloi, lama sabachthani"—that is to say, "My God, my God, why hast thou forsaken me?"[4] The great sun face of Almighty God, which was as familiar to Jesus as his own face (in fact perhaps more so), was for a moment eclipsed by the clouds of human density that surrounded Golgotha's hill. At that moment he was forsaken of that Presence in which he always dwelt.

Man, then, must understand that in the true revelation of the mystery of Christ, there is a great buttressing of strength, which comes to all who can accept it. Those who feel that forgiveness of sins is necessary through death and through suffering must understand that it is God in man who suffers, never man in God. Man in God could never suffer, for the moment that man becomes God, all suffering ceases. But God, the Infinite One, coming into manifestation in a state of limitation, in his great givingness would be the one to suffer the limitations imposed upon him by the manifestation of man who, holding wrong thought, would limit the infinite power of God to flow and would dam up that universal energy in a time constant, thus producing unhappiness, frustration and suffering through limitation.

An Example for Every Son and Daughter of God

The crucifixion of Jesus is the example of an initiation on the path of Christhood that all of the sons and daughters of God can take. Jesus set the example for this initiation, and he did not intend that he would be the only one who would ever pass through it. He made this clear when he said, as he was carrying his cross to Golgotha, "Daughters of Jerusalem, weep not for me, but weep for yourselves, and for your children."[5]

He comforted the women of Jerusalem with that statement because he knew that their crucifixion would come in the age of the testing of the mastery of the feminine ray, even as he lived to demonstrate the mastery of the masculine ray of Christhood.

Every son and daughter passes through the initiations that Jesus demonstrated in his entire three-year ministry, and even in the years that were not recorded in scripture, from his birth to the age of thirty. Knowing Jesus and knowing the intense life that he lived for three years, we cannot imagine that he was simply waiting around for his mission to begin for these thirty years of his life. We read from scripture that he was concerned, even as a child, to be about his Father's business.[6] He was very serious in his study of the Law, and we read in the Apocrypha that he had great power as a child, as the Christ. In those years of preparation, we find him studying in the retreats of the Brotherhood in the Near and Far East. We find him preparing for the most notable mission of a Son of God that has ever been portrayed for us, that has ever been set forth in the historical record.

Jesus realized the importance of that mission, even as we realize today, perhaps, some of the importance of our mission. He realized that if public records were not left of the crucifixion, if we did not have recorded his sermons on what would be taking place in the end of this two-thousand year dispensation, if we did not have the Book of Revelation, which he gave to

John, sent and signified by his angel, we would not know the way to go—we would not know what to expect.

The question that faced Jesus was not whether or not to be crucified, but it was whether or not to be crucified publicly. His agony in the Garden of Gethsemane, his being seized in the early morning hours, his trial before Pilate and Herod, represent the accusation, the trial, the judgment, that is leveled in every age against the son, the daughter of God who has the courage to elevate the Christ and to become the fullness of the Christ consciousness.

The Separation of Light and Darkness

When Jesus said, "And I, if I be lifted up, will draw all men unto me,"[7] he was telling us, "If I lift up the Light of the Christ, the energy of the sacred fire of God, it will become a magnet of the only begotten Son, and it will draw all mankind unto the Christ consciousness." Not only will it draw the souls of Light, but it will draw the souls of darkness. There will be some who will ratify the Light, confirm it, enter into it and become the Light. And there will be others who will deny it, vilify it, persecute it and seek to destroy it.

We notice during the days and weeks building up to this final episode that Jesus stood in the midst of the temple. He preached, he declared whereof his authority had come, and he did not fear to speak and to speak with a tremendous authority to those who questioned his right to call himself the Son of God. Today, there are some who will still argue whether we should call ourselves sons and daughters of God. And yet, John writes in his epistle, "Beloved, now are we the sons of God."[8]

The only begotten Son is the eternal Christ, whose consciousness, whose flame, whose Light, the very presence of the Word, becomes incarnate in us as we are willing to receive him, to be converted by him and to find ourselves in the new birth of Christ. When this takes place, when we receive Jesus Christ in our hearts, then we must count ourselves also worthy to pass through the same initiations that he passed through. We are then, in effect, his hands and his feet, his heart and his head and his body on earth as he reenacts the passion yearly and daily on earth.

There is a need for this passion to be reenacted, because it is the eternal overcoming by the power of the Word of all manifestation of darkness on earth. Jesus spoke to those who would crucify him and said, "This is your hour, and the power of darkness."[9] Jesus came into the world to release the Light of the Christ that the souls of God might be saved and that the ones whom he called the wicked and the seed of the wicked might be judged. Until the Christ should come and give them the opportunity, by their free will, to choose Light or darkness, the judgment could not come. The judgment of the wrongdoer comes when he seeks to destroy the Light of the Christ—not only in Jesus, but in all who follow him, in the little children, in every part of life on earth.

We find, then, that Jesus was not, in reality, crucified by the Jews but by the leaders of the Jews. And there is a vast difference. Those who persecuted Jesus were the same ones whom he accused and to whom John the Baptist spoke with the great intensity of the fire of Almighty God, rebuking them and telling them to repent and to be baptized.[10]

We come to understand, then, that along with this seed of darkness, many sons and daughters of God were embodied at that time as Jews. We also find that many of the seed of the wicked were embodied among the Gentiles, the Christians and every other nation on earth; and these same things are true today. Those whom Jesus rebuked among the Jews were a certain class of a godless generation who would not listen to the Truth or accept the true religion of the prophets. Had they done so, they would have seen the passing of the torch from Moses through all of the prophets to Jesus, for Jesus was the Messiah incarnate.

This coming of Christ was seized and attacked by Sadducees and Pharisees, those who were the seed of the wicked in the nation of Israel. And this persecution of Christ has come from the fallen ones not only in the camp of the Jews but also in the Gentile nations and also ultimately in the churches established in the name of Christ. For those who were not able to put down Christ from outside of the Church joined the Church and began his persecution from within that Church. And there, they were no longer persecuting Jesus; they were persecuting those who received the torch from him for the initiation of the crucifixion, the resurrection and the ascension.

Jesus came to show the Jews the way out from under these elders of the people, and there were many who followed him. And when the dispensation of his teaching and of Christhood was extended to all nations, everywhere the fallen ones followed to try to ensure that the people themselves would not realize the immense power of the Trinity that lay within their very own heart.

This is what has caused the degeneration of Western civilization. When people accept that they are sinners or that they are human beings simply following a scientific humanism, they have lost the source of their power. And that power that is God is the only power by which we can move the nations back into the consciousness of God.

The King of the Jews

Jesus was the one who brought this power to the people of Israel. And therefore, he was rightly called "King of the Jews." He spoke of the kingdom of his Father, and he said, "My kingdom is not of this world." And yet, when Pilate commanded that he be given the title "King of the Jews" as he hung on the cross, it was a most accurate statement. For we understand in the sacred mysteries that the word *king* means the one who holds the *k*ey to the *in*carnation of God.

Long ago, when earth had her Golden Ages, before the Fall of man and woman, those who had the right to rule were those who had elevated the Christ consciousness, who had magnified the sacred-fire flame within the heart. And that sacred fire became the intense manifestation of God as the flame that burns on the altar. It was the initiates, the sons and daughters of God who had the greatest attainment in cosmic consciousness, who had the right to rule in these Golden Ages —long lost ages of Lemuria and Atlantis, ages far beyond the Incas in South America, of which the Incas were simply the descendants; so long ago that these eras escape recorded history.

The concept of the divine right of kings, the divine right of the sons and daughters of God to rule, has come down to us from these Golden Ages. The degeneration of those in whom this rulership was vested occurred century after century, culminating in the last several hundred years when we have had the shift from the monarchy to the republican or the democratic form of government.

We see, then, that Pilate would not withdraw his statement that Jesus was the King of the Jews. He recognized the righteousness of the man, even as he felt the intimidation of the elders who were blackmailing him with political threats: "If you free this man, you are not Caesar's friend."[11] How often we have seen political leaders compromise because they have feared the Truth and the witness of the Truth.

We find, then, that these elders of the people, the chief priests who have gained positions of leadership in government and in the churches as well as in the economies of the nations, will persecute those who say, "I am the son of God and I will bear witness of the Truth." And they will say that Jesus was the only son of God, that there is no other son of God, and therefore they will deprive the people of the understanding that this one Universal Son, this only begotten of the Father-Mother God, is the Christ, the same Christ that lives in us all—the same flame, the one flame of the one God that burns in the heart of each one of us.

When we lose our right to Sonship, we lose our authority to speak the Truth, we lose our authority to be free. When we disclaim our heritage as sons and daughters of God, we no longer claim the authority of our Father and the backing of our Father, and then we lose the courage and the very platform for our taking the stand for Truth. Thus Jesus' declaration of his divine Sonship is the key in every initiation that will follow concerning the sons and daughters of God.

If we can be the example of those who will stand for the truth of our real identity and the real identity of all people of God in Christ, including all Jews, we will be able to say that Jesus is the only Son of God. And we will be able to affirm that the Christ that he brought forth is the Real Self of every Christian, every Jew, every Moslem, every Buddhist, every Hindu. Everyone on earth has that real identity in God through Christ. This overcomes the exclusivity that is not understandable to many who know within their hearts that they have that personal tie to God.

Christ, the High Priest

It is very important when we consider the true mystery of Good Friday that we understand the meaning of this public demonstration of the Son of God. It was very important for Jesus to pass through these experiences publicly, for by that demonstration, he would not only bear the sins of the world or save our souls by carrying that burden, but he would also impart the greater and more important lesson of the revelation of the personal Christ.

In the Temple of Jerusalem there was a veil that divided the Holy of holies, which only the high priest could enter, from the holy place, where other priests served, and the outer courts that were open to the people. It is written that in the moment when the murderous intent of the fallen ones became physical and death was upon him, that Jesus cried out with a loud voice and gave up the ghost. At that moment "the veil of the temple was rent in twain from the top to the bottom,"[12] therefore revealing the Holy of holies as the place where Christ the Lord himself officiates as the High Priest in the temple of man.

Thus we see that the crucifixion of Christ is for the judgment of all those who occupy the position of the authority of Christ and yet exercise it not as the Christ but as the Antichrist; and at the same time, the crucifixion is for the revelation that Christ is every man's Real Self. And if the soul is to unite with that Real Self, that one must pass through this hour of the crucifixion.

Their intent was to kill the Christ, not the man, for they recognized his power to be the eternal Christ in him. It is the Son of God in Jesus and in us all who experiences the crucifixion, and our souls experience this in the hour when, by the path of initiation, we are truly one in that Christ. The soul of Jesus, the Son of man, was one with that Christ; and therefore effectively, it was the integrated personality in God that was crucified.

The Personal Crucifixion

John the Beloved, the apostle who was so close to Jesus and who remained at the foot of the cross during the crucifixion, was the one to whom Jesus entrusted his mother, Mary.

John explains that at the turning of an age, there is the requirement for some to enter into the fullness of this initiation: "I come in the flow of the mystic Light. I come to commemorate the translation of each one whereby the soul as living potential is fired in the baptism of the Holy Spirit to become one forevermore with the permanent atom of being. As I witnessed the translation of our Lord, as I kept the vigil at the cross with Mary the Mother, with Jesus, so I come in this age to keep the vigil of the cross, to attend the new birth of each one.

"You have applied in your souls to the Lords of Karma to bear the weight of the sins of the world. You have reached out, yes, you have cried out in the night, 'O Lord, what can I do to help mankind?' And your souls have seen in the temples of the Masters that the way of salvation is the realization that life is one.

"If, therefore, one cell in the body of God desires to make that sacrifice of which Jesus spoke when he said, 'Except a corn of wheat fall to the ground and die, it abideth alone: but if it die, it bringeth forth much fruit'[13]—if, then, one cell in the body of God desires to become that corn of wheat that dies that the many cells might live, then the Lords of Karma and Maitreya, the Initiator, come nigh to give the initiation of the crucifixion.

"Do you understand that you can pass through this initiation without surrendering the four lower bodies? Do you understand that the atonement that you can make is an atonement of energy factor whereby through the surrender of all energy that God has ever given to you into the flame of the sacred fire, you can hold the balance for the planet by the weight of light. ('My burden is light!'[14]) The burden of light that you carry comes from the transmuted efforts of the sacrifice of all that is less than perfection.

"The day will come when God will claim the four lower

bodies also. But you can be a living witness to the purging of the cells and of many cells in the Body of God upon earth that these lively stones in the temple might be the electrodes that keep the whole consciousness of humanity intact, preserved for the coming of the great glory of the law of love.

"There are some in every age who elect to become stars in the firmament of being. And as one age is concluded and another begins, there must be those who make the arc, carrying energy spirals from one dispensation to the next, from one level of consciousness to the next. These form the bridge over which all of humanity pass into a Golden Age of enlightenment and peace.

"We would build a strong bridge, firm as a golden gate through which the masses might pass. To become pillars in the temple, pillars in the bridge is a goal indeed. To fulfill it you must come apart and be a separate people, elect unto God.[15] The pillars in the bridge must be without alloy, without impurities, without ties to the mass consciousness, yet they must also have four lower bodies intact, for the plane of Mater requires the support of vehicles for evolving souls."[16]

The Descent into Hell

John the Beloved describes an element of the initiation of the crucifixion that is not well understood: "You are living in the time when the drama, the reenactment of the sacred ritual of Good Friday of the descent of Jesus into the planes where those departed spirits dwelled is to be reenacted by the many and by the few on behalf of the many. The initiation of the crucifixion involves the descent of the soul to the darkest levels of the planet where there are those rebellious ones who have refused to acknowledge the Christ as the 'Light which lighteth every man who cometh into the world.'[17]

"Therefore, you see, while the body of Jesus lay in the tomb, his soul, his higher mind was active in the depths of the astral, in the place that has been called purgatory, where the souls of the departed ones from the days of Noah (the days of the sinking of Atlantis) were held because they refused to submit to the Law of God. Therefore they had been denied rebirth and entrance to the screen of life."[18]

This initiation of Jesus is described in the Apostle's Creed, a statement of orthodox Christian doctrine, which says that Jesus "was crucified, died, and was buried. He descended into hell; the third day he arose again from the dead."

Jesus himself has told what his preaching was to the souls confined to these levels: "And so tonight I exhort you, as I exhorted the rebellious spirits that in the days of Noah were disobedient unto God. The three days and three nights while I was absent from the body temple I did exhort them, as I shall now exhort you.

"O my brethren, the LORD God of Hosts is he! He is the Father of us all. The passion of his love is not known to thee, for it is too great and thy consciousness cannot contain it now. In thy present state, thou art unable to awaken within thyself the means to create the resurgent chalice of consciousness that would contain him, for the heavens and the earth cannot contain him nor can they contain his love.

"O my brethren, repent of all your acts of discord and of jangle, of darkness and of tangle—all that has involved you in a web. Repent, repent, repent! And turn unto God once again. Take his vows of holiness, of renewal, of the divine intent, of cosmic purpose of the Law.

"For he is the LORD, and there is none like unto him in the heavens and the earth. He is the LORD that raiseth mankind from the dead, that setteth before them their immortal destiny. By his hand they are fed. All are clothed in white raiment by his mind. He deifies the soul. He, the LORD, is ever kind. His mercy endureth forever.

"I AM the Good Shepherd. I have walked in many climes and many lands. I have descended through the air. I have seen the atmosphere of planetary body after planetary body. I have roamed the universe with my being, and everywhere I have seen the LORD, and I have seen him in action. I have seen his power and his Presence. I have felt his love, and I am a witness of that love.

"I urge upon you, then, my brethren, separated now by acts of disobedience, a return to the fold of his infinite compassion. Cast yourselves upon Him, the mighty Rock, and let not that rock fall upon thee and grind thee to powder. For the action of his love is great, and he is magnified within thy soul. And the power of his flame can free every soul, and the power of his love can make everyone every whit whole.

"My brethren, my brethren, my brethren, in memory of those moments when I myself felt forsaken of Him, I repeat the cry, 'Eloi, Eloi, lama sabachthani? My God, my God, why hast thou forsaken me?'

"Do you feel that moment, then, as I did? Oh, return to him and clasp him to your heart forever. For he is sweet and full of truth and the demons of despair and haughty intellect that have led you to this state are not able to do that which he can do. Nor can they confer upon you the vestments of immortality or bring to view the wonders of his love. I urge upon you now, then, a spirit of sweet acceptance of his grace that you may, then, by that grace leave this place for higher worlds, for octaves beyond compare.

"This, my brethren, was the sermon in essence that I preached and repreached and spoke again and again to each soul that I could find there who was in chains of bondage and despair. Many gazed upon me with dullness in their eyes—the dullness of despair, the centuries of timeworn care and fear and doubt. The very Light of God seemed to them put out, and I sought to rekindle it then as I do today to rekindle it in you God's way.

"*I AM the resurrection and the life! He that believeth in me, though he were dead, yet shall he live!*

"*I AM the Way! I AM the Truth! And I AM the Life! No man cometh unto the Father but by me!*

"Accept, then, your Holy Christ Selves and be free."[19]

The Assignment to Preach in the Dark Places

John the Beloved continues: "It was the assignment of Jesus (and it is the assignment of every man and woman who would follow through in the ritual of the crucifixion) to go to the darkest places of the earth and to preach the Light, to compel the spirits to come into alignment with the Presence of God. At the moment, then, just before the quickening of the body cells with the resurrection fire, it is necessary to bear witness of the Truth to the mass consciousness. Thus you will see how you will find yourselves teaching the Word of Truth in places you had not expected to be. You will understand that this is part of a sacred ritual and that you cannot partake to the fullness of the resurrection spiral until you have accomplished this mission.

"It is necessary that in the hour of trial these rebellious ones see the glory, see the sacrifice and the victory upon your brow. It is necessary that they come in contact with those who are willing to make the final sacrifice on their behalf. When the contact is made and the Word as the sacred bread of life has been broken, then you can return for the celebration of the resurrection spiral. And then the quickening of the body temple, the soul, the heart and the mind will also be for those to whom you have preached.

"For in their subconscious and in the inner awareness of the soul, they will have the ability to see that transforming power of the Light. By making the personal contact, they will retain the record of your Christ-identity as a pattern and a chalice within that subconscious. And whatever happens to you in the glory of the resurrection following that contact, they will also witness. By the very fact of the oneness of God, the oneness of all life, the currents that flow through you will also flow, albeit in lesser measure, through every cell in the Body of God evolving upon earth.

"You have heard that it is a requirement of the Great Law for the sustaining of the planet, for the justification of its reason for being, that one soul ascend back to the heart of God in each twelve-month cycle. Now I show you the mystery of this law. It is necessary that one receive the currents of the ascension flame each year so that, by the process of the electric energy flowing from cell to cell, each year there might be impressed upon the consciousness of evolving humanity the awareness of the flow of ascension currents—thus the very power of victory.

The Power of the Ascension Flame

"Behold how the fire of the ascension flowing through and magnetizing one soul to God can create tremors throughout the body of the earth and even the need for the adjustment in nature that manifests as storm, as cataclysm. You remember the lightning and the thunder in the hour of the crucifixion. How well I remember it, for I have heard that sound and felt that current each time a son of God has passed the test of the crucifixion and each time a son of God returns in the ritual of the ascension.

"All of nature must adjust to the influx of Light, humanity also. If this requirement of the Law is not fulfilled, then the reason for being of any world ceases to exist. As long as there are those, then, who are willing to submit to the disciplines of the Hierarch of the Ascension Temple, the world will remain as a place of opportunity for evolving souls. And as long as there be one who ascends, there will always be progress in human evolution. For even science and invention, education, the fields of medicine and healing are quickened and propelled forward by the action of the ascension of one life.

"And so you can see, when progress is meager, when earth has gone through the dark ages, there have been times when only one made the ascension. At other periods of great enlightenment and progress, many souls have ascended each year. And so, progress on the planet is directly proportionate to the evolution of the individual.

"How can we convey to those of you who have not experienced the influx of the great current of the ascension spiral what this energy is? Shall we say that it is like the splitting of a thousand or ten thousand atoms, and man himself being in the center? Shall we say that it is like the explosion of worlds or sun centers? Or shall we say that it is like the unfolding of a lily or a rose?

"Perhaps the poetry of the ascension ought to be written by you as you experience that great ritual—perhaps at the close of this life. For as you have been taught, the doors are open to all who will make the call and give the service and apply for each test. For line upon line, precept upon precept the victory is won.

"You are ascending daily. You are ascending the spirals of your own being and your own consciousness. You are not as you were yesterday or last week, and if you are giving daily devotions to the Most High you are light-years beyond your former self. Thus the days are shortened for the elect."[20]

The Crucifixion of the Nations

The Ascended Lady Master Thérèse of Lisieux reveals that the crucifixion is an initiation that is faced not only by the individual, but also by the nations: "I come to tell you that the way of discipleship can be seen by you as a thousand stairs upon a thousand-tiered golden spiral and that step by step there is an orderly path of discipline....

"Know, then, that each individual in his time passes through the initiations through which Jesus passed. There is a crucifixion, therefore, that is of this world as fallen angels attempt to preempt the day and the hour of the true sign of the cross in the life of the individual wherein the soul is fastened to the cosmic cross of white fire and angels gathering round celebrate the alchemical marriage—'Father, into thine arms I commend my spirit.'[21] Into the heart of the living Christ the soul, then, is assumed.

"The true crucifixion is in this hour, then, a path of initiation. And the transfiguration does precede that crucifixion, and prior to that a life of works, good works and healing, joy and teaching. Therefore, take care to study in order that thy teaching be true and just, rightly dividing the word of Truth.

"Blessed ones, I speak now not only of the individual initiation but to tell you that the hour is come that the nations themselves as tribes, ancient tribes of a karmic group, are also facing the initiation of the crucifixion. And because they have not responded to their ancient teachers and therefore have had a karma of vulnerability to the denial of the Truth to them by their current leaders, they come ill-prepared to this magnificent moment when, though the world condemnation and the trial of the world and the fallen ones be upon them, those nations could rally in defense of the living Christ and their own opportunity to give birth to that Christ.

"Therefore, you will see that the crucifixion, which is a divine initiation, is preempted by fallen angels who would desire to utterly crucify and destroy those souls who have not yet been wed to Christ, as Jesus was thoroughly wed to the Light in the initiation of the transfiguration on the Mount of Transfiguration.[22] That filling of his body with the fullness and intensity of the white Light was an experience whereby he was also empowered to move on and to face the courts of hell who put the Son of God on trial....

"Therefore, know, beloved, that there does come a time, as my Father in heaven has asked me to tell you this evening, when the walking of the individual path of the thirty-three steps of the Son of God, which are multiplied over those thousand stairs, does become the most important event in the life of the individual and the nations and the planet. Because the Light is so great and the victory of such cosmic import to all life upon a planet, the hour does come when their ministrations to life must be translated and must be raised to the point where the fulfillment of their individual Christhood along that path does become more expedient to the entire Great White Brotherhood and the World Mother than any other service that they might possibly render....

"Take heed, then; for those who accelerate on the path of Jesus' life all the way to the hour of their resurrection, they shall be ready when their nations undergo the trial and crucifixion, and they shall keep a flame in the mountain of God that the threefold flame of the nations be not extinguished but live and endure to be rekindled again when new generations of Lightbearers can be born once the earth has been purged of a karma of the seed of the wicked and of a neglect of the children of God. These things must come to pass.

"Know, then, that you may receive the initiation of the resurrection and yet retain physical life and form. To walk about

endued with the Spirit of the Resurrection, let this be thy goal. For remember, 'the Light shone in the darkness and the darkness comprehended it not, but we beheld his glory, the glory as of the only begotten Son of God,' in the profile, in the Presence of our brother Jesus."[23]

"It Is Finished"

It is recorded in the Bible that the last words of Jesus on the cross were, "It is finished." He then "gave up the ghost."[24] These words were not alone for Jesus, for we too can say, "It is finished." We can say we are finished with the round of making karma and the entanglements of the world. We can take our stand and affirm our identity with Christ today.

"It is finished" means that the human consciousness with all of its struggle, with its crucifixions and its trials, is finished. We can declare that that struggle is over at this very moment. We can determine that the entire turmoil of the human consciousness is finished. We need only to declare it.

It Is Finished!
By Jesus the Christ

It is finished!
Done with this episode in strife,
I AM made one with immortal life.
Calmly I AM resurrecting my spiritual energies
From the great treasure house of immortal knowing.
The days I knew with thee, O Father,
Before the world was—the days of triumph,
When all of the thoughts of thy being
Soared over the ageless hills of cosmic memory;
Come again as I meditate upon thee.
Each day as I call forth thy memories

From the scroll of immortal love,
I AM thrilled anew.
Patterns wondrous to behold enthrall me
With the wisdom of thy creative scheme.
So fearfully and wonderfully am I made
That none can mar thy design,
None can despoil the beauty of thy holiness,
None can discourage the beating of my heart
In almost wild anticipation
Of thy fullness made manifest within me.

O great and glorious Father,
How shall a tiny bird created in hierarchical bliss
Elude thy compassionate attention?
I AM of greater value than many birds
And therefore do I know that thy loving thoughts
Reach out to me each day
To console me in seeming aloneness,
To raise my courage,
Elevate my concepts,
Exalt my character,
Flood my being with virtue and power,
Sustain thy cup of life flowing over within me,
And abide within me forever
In the nearness of thy heavenly presence.

I cannot fail,
Because I AM thyself in action everywhere.
I ride with thee
Upon the mantle of the clouds.
I walk with thee
Upon the waves and crests of water's abundance.
I move with thee
In the undulations of thy currents

Passing over the thousands of hills composing earth's crust.
I AM alive with thee
In each bush, flower, and blade of grass.
All nature sings in thee and me,
For we are one.
I AM alive in the hearts of the downtrodden,
Raising them up.
I AM the Law exacting the Truth of Being
In the hearts of the proud,
Debasing the human creation therein
And spurring the search for thy Reality.
I AM all things of bliss
To all people of peace.
I AM the full facility of divine grace,
The Spirit of Holiness
Releasing all hearts from bondage into unity.

It is finished!
Thy perfect creation is within me.
Immortally lovely,
It cannot be denied the blessedness of Being.
Like unto thyself, it abides in the house of Reality.
Nevermore to go out into profanity,
It knows only the wonders of purity and victory.
Yet there stirs within this immortal fire
A consummate pattern of mercy and compassion
Seeking to save forever that which is lost
Through wandering away
From the beauty of Reality and Truth.
I AM the living Christ in action evermore!

It is finished!
Death and human concepts have no power in my world!
I AM sealed by God-design

With the fullness of that Christ-love
That overcomes, transcends, and frees the world
By the power of the three-times-three
Until all the world is God-victorious—
Ascended in the Light and free!

It is finished!
Completeness is the Allness of God.
Day unto day an increase of strength, devotion,
Life, beauty, and holiness occurs within me,
Released from the fairest flower of my being,
The Christ-consecrated rose of Sharon
Unfolding its petals within my heart.
My heart is the heart of God!
My heart is the heart of the world!
My heart is the heart of Christ in healing action!
Lo, I AM with you alway, even unto the end,
When with the voice of Immortal Love
I too shall say, "It is finished!"

Section 14

The Dark Night of the Soul and the Dark Night of the Spirit

I N THE PATH OF CHRISTHOOD AND THE return to God, the soul passes through what the sixteenth-century mystic Saint John of the Cross described as the "dark night." There are two aspects of the dark night. The first is experienced as one encounters the return of personal karma. This dark night of the soul is in preparation for the dark night of the Spirit, when the soul is, as it were, cut off from the I AM Presence and must survive solely on the Light garnered in the heart while holding the balance for planetary karma.

Saint John of the Cross described these initiations in his work "The Dark Night": "This night...causes two kinds of darkness or purgation in spiritual persons according to the two parts of the soul, the sensory and the spiritual. Hence the one night or purgation will be sensory, by which the senses are purged and accommodated to the spirit; and the other night or purgation will be spiritual, by which the spirit is purged and denuded as well as accommodated and prepared for union with God through love."[1]

Saint John writes of the initiation of the dark night of the Spirit: "Since the divine extreme strikes in order to renew the soul and divinize it (by stripping it of the habitual affections and properties of the old man to which it is strongly united, attached, and conformed), it so disentangles and dissolves the spiritual substance—absorbing it in a profound darkness—that the soul at the sight of its miseries feels that it is melting away and being undone by a cruel spiritual death; it feels as if it were swallowed by a beast and being digested in the dark belly, and it suffers an anguish comparable to Jonas' when in the belly of the whale.[2] It is fitting that the soul be in this sepulcher of dark death in order that it attain the spiritual resurrection for which it hopes."[3]

The dark night of the soul is a self-imposed crucifixion. It is the crucifixion that comes to you as the result of your personal karma. When you meet that personal karma, it is very difficult, and if you are going to face it all the way, you go through a kind of a crucifixion, but it is a self-crucifixion.

When you have passed through that crucifixion, then you go through the real crucifixion that is the initiation of the ruby ray, which is the dark night of the Spirit. This is when you assume the cross of planetary karma—it is not your own; it is the world's karma. It is so enormous upon you that it actually eclipses the Light of your mighty I AM Presence.

And therefore Jesus said on the cross, "My God, my God, why hast thou forsaken me?" He cried out because the entire momentum of world condemnation was upon him, and he had to hold the balance for that weight by the Light already mastered within his own heart.

In the dark night of the Spirit, the initiation is given to the Christ incarnate to sustain life, to sustain Light in the soul in this octave, not having the tie to the I AM Presence. Therefore, by definition, Christhood must be that state where you have so expanded the Light in your heart and in your chakras that you can sustain soul consciousness, even without that tie.

The first dark night is the preparation for the second. When you go through the first dark night of your own karma, the burden seems almost too great to bear, and yet you created it. But if you are going to descend into Matter and ascend, you must take the second initiation—the dark night of the Spirit. God leads us through the labyrinth of our own self-imposed crucifixion so that we can come to this initiation, the supreme test of Christhood.

This initiation may take place at the etheric retreat of Serapis Bey, the Ascension Temple at Luxor in Egypt. It may also be given in the King's Chamber of the Great Pyramid, which is used at the etheric level for this test of the laying down of the body, to see if man is attached to his body or if he knows that he is Real in God. It is not enough just to believe it, because in the hour of the dark night, all the momentums of the subconscious, which we call the electronic belt, rise up to challenge the Light within man.

This combined momentum of energy is called the dweller-on-the-threshold. We all have to meet that dweller sooner or later, and we have to slay the beast. This is why some of the saints are pictured as slaying a dragon. That dragon is their own dweller-on-the-threshold. But it is more than their own; it is the dweller-on-the-threshold of the entire planetary body. It is this planetary momentum of darkness that surrounded the cross at the hour of the crucifixion and that Jesus had to bear, totally cut off from his Presence, just on the memory of what it was like to be with God and to feel his Presence.

There comes a time when we all have to stand on our own Light, the Light we have invoked. We are given no more, and we have to walk by that momentum of Light until the hour of the dark night of the Spirit and the crucifixion has passed. By that Light that we have internalized, we see the unreality of death.

Many metaphysicians have claimed that Jesus never said, "My God, my God, why hast thou forsaken me?" But there is no question that he said it, because the dark night of the Spirit is part of the initiation of the crucifixion. Many people do not understand this initiation, and they have tried to ignore it. "We should not be bothered with the crucifixion, because we are not amplifying death. Jesus was only on the cross a few hours. He died for us, and therefore, we don't have to go through this."

But Jesus was the great example. He demonstrated publicly all the initiations that we must pass through. And we must realize that this initiation is a glorious privilege. We would never want to bypass it. Nor would God himself wish to deprive us of the crucifixion, because it is that supreme moment when we overcome death. We see the unreality of death when, with the Light we have invoked, we see that death is swallowed up in victory.

Beloved Holy Amethyst gives us a key to passing through these initiations: "Step by step, line by line, karma must be balanced to the right and to the left. Each individual who reads my words must know that the responsibility to balance the energies of life is the meaning of the judgment. When you determine to get back to Eden, to return to the house of the Father-Mother God, you must be willing to retrace every footstep you have taken since the descent of your soul into the planes of Mater.

"The road of return has two aspects: the sorrowful way and the glorious way. It all depends upon your perspective; for the bliss of the divine reunion is experienced within—even in the moment of agony, through the dark night of the soul, and on the cross.

"The sixty-ninth Psalm of David contains three cycles of twelve. In thirty-six verses David reveals the experiences of one who passed through the dark night of the soul to the full realization of the Christ consciousness. You who have determined to pass through the dark night of both the soul and the Spirit would do well to ponder the meditations of David and then to apply yourself diligently to the invocations of the sacred fire, especially to the violet flame that is the concentrated energy of the Holy Spirit in the forgiveness of sin, the righting of all wrong, and the bringing of the four lower bodies into alignment with the original blueprint of creation."[4]

Section 15

The Fourteen Stations of the Cross

I N EVERY CATHOLIC CHURCH THERE are fourteen symbolic representations spaced around the church depicting the events from the time when Jesus is condemned to death, to when he is laid in the sepulcher. These are fourteen key events in Jesus' walking the way of the cross, and Catholics are taught to pray in front of these stations.

The fourteen stations of the cross are known as the *via dolorosa*, the "sorrowful way." This is the description of the observer. It is not the description of the one who is passing through the initiation; for the one who passes through is in supreme joy and passion.

The fourteen stations of the cross are a coil of energy that unwinds, and they are also the spiral of energy whereby we build the divine momentum of our attainment and of our initiation on the Path. God has not ordained that we should face the full energy and weight of our entire past karma in one day, and therefore, he unwinds that coil of energy increment by increment—

as Jesus tells us, "Sufficient unto the day is the evil thereof."[1]

The initiation of each station is to take that energy and demand that it be transmuted by the sacred fire according to the nature of the initiation of that station. That which cannot stand the trial by fire in love is consumed by the Holy Ghost, by the violet flame, and that which can stand is sealed for eternity.

The Initiations of the Stations

The stations can be charted on the lines of a clock representing the Twelve Solar Hierarchies (see pages 196–98). We place the first station on the the twelve-o'clock line and proceed in a clockwise direction. Each time you change a position on this cosmic clock, you have changed a frequency, you have changed an energy, you have changed a sign of the zodiac, you have totally changed a cosmic vibration. It is an entirely different initiation because you are dealing with different energies.

The Fourteen Stations of the Cross

The First Station

The first station is "Jesus is condemned to death," the **twelve-o'clock line.** This is the line of God-power, and it is the line of the Hierarchy of Capricorn. The misuse of energy on that line, the misqualification of power, is condemnation. The fallen ones have ever misused God's power to condemn the Christ.

You cannot meet this station of the cross if you fear to declare yourself the Son of God. You declare yourself to be the Son of God right in the very midst of your karma, your problems, your burdens, your failures, because you know that it is not the outer human ego that is the Son of God, it is the Inner Light of the Christ; and you hold on to that rock, that Christ, affirming Jesus

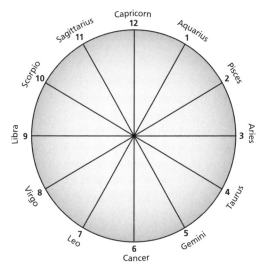

TWELVE SOLAR HIERARCHIES

The Twelve Hierarchies of the Sun are twelve mandalas of Cosmic Beings ensouling twelve facets of God's consciousness. Each Hierarchy holds the pattern of that frequency for the entire cosmos. They are identified by the names of the signs of the zodiac, as they focus their energies through these constellations. They are diagrammed as lines of a clock, with Capricorn on the twelve-o'clock line, Aquarius on the one, and so on.

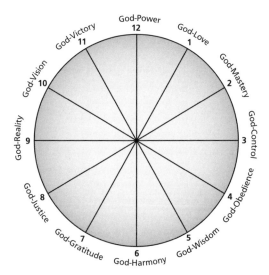

THE GOD CONSCIOUSNESS, OR
GOD-QUALITIES, OF THE SOLAR HIERARCHIES

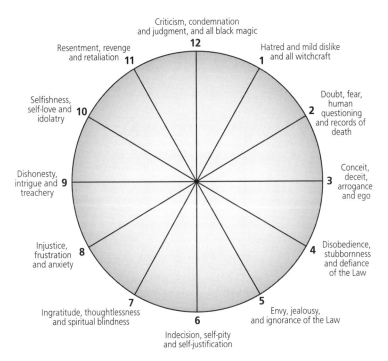

Criticism, condemnation
and judgment, and all black magic
12

Resentment, revenge
and retaliation **11**

Hatred and mild dislike
1 and all witchcraft

Selfishness,
self-love and **10**
idolatry

Doubt, fear,
human
2 questioning
and records of
death

Dishonesty,
intrigue and **9**
treachery

Conceit,
deceit,
3 arrogance
and ego

Injustice,
frustration **8**
and anxiety

Disobedience,
stubbornness
4 and defiance
of the Law

7

5

Ingratitude, thoughtlessness
and spiritual blindness

6

Envy, jealousy,
and ignorance of the Law

Indecision, self-pity
and self-justification

**HUMAN PERVERSIONS OF THE
GOD CONSCIOUSNESS OF THE SOLAR HIERARCHIES**

Christ as your Saviour, affirming that Son of God.

When you are on the first station of the cross and you feel the heaviness of the weight upon you of world condemnation of the Son of God, you acknowledge it, and you immediately call for the transmutation of personal and planetary momentums of the condemnation to death not only of Jesus Christ, but also of the Mother and her children.

The Second Station

The second station is "Jesus is made to bear his cross," the **one-o'clock line.** This is the line of Aquarius, of the New Age. It is the line of Saint Germain, and the energy of this line is

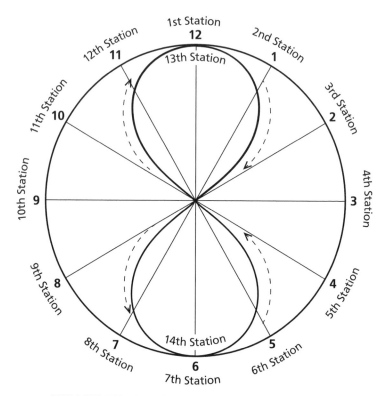

THE FOURTEEN STATIONS ON THE LINES OF THE CLOCK

love. And therefore, the cross we are made to bear is the cross of all perversions of love—personal and planetary. Every time we have misused the energy of love we have forged our own cross. And the only way our own Christ Self can come down from that cross is if we requalify that energy of hatred, mild dislike, irritation, dislike of the Christ within ourselves or within other people with love.

The Third Station

The third station is "Jesus falls the first time," the **two-o'clock line.** It is Pisces, a water sign. The quality is God-mastery, and we find that Jesus fell for the first time on this line. This is the cross of the planetary momentum of death, of doubt and fear—fear that God does not exist, doubt in his existence, fear of our own selfhood, fear of separation—and it is endless human questioning. When we are on this station, we give our invocations for the violet flame, we name that death momentum, we call for the glory of God in the energy of God-mastery, and we go on.

The Fourth Station

The fourth station is "Jesus meets his afflicted mother," the **three-o'clock line** of Aries and God-control. This is the line of the ego, where we must choose between the human ego and the Christ Ego. We must surrender the ego that we love most—the ego that is our own. But we often do not admit that it is our own, and therefore we objectify that love in another. And so we find that the one whom Jesus loved most was his mother.

He met his mother on these fourteen stations, sorrowful and burdened. He could have put down his cross and walked away. Jesus was not locked into these fourteen stations, and neither are you. He clearly had the choice. He made the choice in Gethsemane, and he told God, "I would rather not go through with this crucifixion; nevertheless not my will but thine be done."[2] He clearly expressed his free will and his free will was to withdraw, but at the moment of that desire, he determined that he would go through with the initiation for you and for me. As he looked into the eyes of Mary, his mother, he faced that test again. He determined that he would go on. He would separate himself from that which he loved most and therefore slay the carnal mind within that, through human sympathy, would cause him to remove himself from the Path.

This test comes to every one of us. It is a very difficult test. But only by passing this test do we inherit the fullness of our own Christ Self. The misuse of this line is the conceit of the ego that would carve out its own path according to its own terms.

The Fifth Station

The fifth station is "Simon the Cyrenian helps Jesus to bear his cross," the **four-o'clock line**. The story is told that Jesus was falling under the weight of the cross, and as he leaned against the wall to brace himself, his hand left an imprint. Simon the Cyrenian saw that miracle, was immediately converted, and came forward to bear the cross. The imprint in the stone can be seen in the city of Jerusalem today.

The initiation on this line is under the Hierarchy of Taurus, an initiation of obedience. In our desire to come into conformity with the will of God we will have to surrender the concept that by might and by power we can do this initiation all by ourselves and that we can do it without acknowledging the need for intercession, the need for the Holy Spirit to help us through the person of the friend.

This is something that even Jesus Christ in all of his glory and his attainment acknowledged openly before us. He had the need of a friend to make it on the Path. Those friends were angels, they were Ascended Masters and Elohim, and they were all those who surrounded him in his mission.

As we face this initiation, it is necessary to admit that we can't make it alone, and this is a humbling experience. The fallen ones like to portray the adept as the supreme person who is able to manipulate energy and command forces and do anything he pleases. Adeptship becomes a point of great pride for the Luciferians, and there are many adepts in the world today who are on the left-handed path and who have enormous pride in their self-sufficiency. If we have any of this pride within us, it will be broken sooner or later when, momentarily, we cannot carry the full weight of our own personal karma or of the planetary karma that we are required to bear.

In that moment, Simon the Cyrenian comes to bear the cross for Jesus, and he enables Jesus to stand on that line of

Taurus, the line of the fall of Satan, the line of planetary rebellion. Satan, as the power of this world and the prince of this world, is faced on that four-o'clock line. On this line, Jesus was wrestling with Satan and with the hordes of darkness who would subvert the children of God by causing them to be disobedient to their own inner being. And while he wrestled with Satan and with those fallen ones, another bore his cross. This is the great mystery of the Body of God, this Mystical Body of God that we are. We are one person, totally dependent on each and every other part of that person. This is the key to the defeat of Satan and the carnal mind within and without.

On this station we also face our own internal rebellion against the requirements of the Law of God. That rebellion can well up within us like a Vesuvius. It can cause us to be arrogant and out of sorts and bullish. Taurus is the sign of the bull, and we throw our weight around like bulls and we say, "I'm not going do this," until finally we are brought to our knees in the realization that our rebellion has brought us to the place where we have to cry out for help.

The Sixth Station

The sixth station is "Veronica wipes the face of Jesus," the **five-o'clock line.** As Jesus made his way along the road to Golgotha, he came to that place where Veronica came out to wipe his face, and the Catholic Church states that it has the handkerchief on which was left the imprint of the face of Jesus in the hour of this walking these stations.

This is an initiation under the Hierarchy of Gemini, the five-o'clock line of wisdom, the line of the teaching. The cloth represents the white page of the soul, the garment of the soul, which, in being placed upon the face of Jesus in an act of compassion, receives the imprint of the image of the Christ. The image of the Christ pressed upon that cloth and impressed upon our soul chakra becomes the impression of his consciousness, of his teaching, on the soul. The recording upon the handkerchief of the woman symbolizes that Jesus is entrusting the perpetuation of the teaching to the care of the Mother flame.

This initiation is the transference of energy from the Teacher to the disciple, from Spirit to Matter. The perversion of this line is ignorance of the teaching and ignorance of the Law. It is a willful ignorance that results in envy and jealousy of those who have the Light because they have passed through the path of initiation.

On that day when we feel the density opposing the Gemini Light, we must challenge the ignorance of the Law, our own ignorance, our own density; we must challenge envy and jealousy that makes us say, "Why can't I have as much Light as this person?"

The Seventh Station

The seventh station is "Jesus falls the second time," the **six-o'clock line.** The fall on this line is under the weight of the personal and planetary misuses of the energy of the Mother under the Hierarchy of Cancer.

The six-o'clock line is the base-of-the-spine chakra. All misuses and abuses of the feminine ray, of our soul and of our body temple, will be up for transmutation on this line. It is a challenge of the emotional body because it is a water sign. The perversion of the station is inharmony and discord that manifests as indecision, self-pity, self-justification. We justify our discord and our inharmony.

This is a key line for the Lightbearers, the seed of the Mother, the mandala of the 144,000. It is the line of the Mother, and we are all intended to become the Mother. This is the point of the Aquarian age. When you meet the energy of the Mother, this is the challenge to be able to become one with the Mother in her discipline, in her chastisement, in her compassion, in the cross she bears, and in the very being of your own self.

The Eighth Station

The eighth station is "Jesus consoles the holy women," the **seven-o'clock line.** It is the line of Leo and God-gratitude. It is the affirmation, the joy, the praise, the acclaim, the release in the desire body of that energy of gratitude. The misuse of this line is ingratitude, thoughtlessness, density, spiritual blindness, the failure to give forth the release of energy as joy, as gratitude that manifests the victory in Leo.

On this station, Jesus extends consolation to the women of Jerusalem who are weeping. He says to them, "Weep not for me ye daughters of Jerusalem, but weep for yourselves, and for your children."[3] He is saying, "I am all right. I am passing through my fourteen initiations. Take heed; you will have to reincarnate and pass through these same initiations of the cross. So take care of yourselves and your children, because it is the Woman and her seed who will have to face this initiation in the next age."

The Ninth Station

The ninth station is "Jesus falls the third time," the **eight-o'clock line.** The third fall of Jesus is under the weight of personal and planetary momentums of every form of injustice. This is the Virgo initiation.

When you are carrying the cross on this station, you will experience injustice, and you will have to remember the statement of Portia, the Goddess of Justice, who says, "There is no injustice anywhere in the universe." That is an absolute statement and an affirmation of being. It means that right in the very midst of what appears to be injustice, you can invoke the Light of the violet flame and of transmutation, and you can see that behind injustice (which is always either a test or a manifestation of karma—one of the two) is the Reality of God-justice.

The Tenth Station

The tenth station is "Jesus is stripped of his garments," the **nine-o'clock line.** This is a cosmic initiation that is given to the Lightbearers and to the fallen ones alike. Those who think that they are clothed with fine raiment and that they are rich and increased in the goods of this world will find that suddenly, overnight, they are stripped of their garments—stripped of their money, supply, outer prestige and momentum—and all of a sudden they are reduced to nothing, because we are all required to stand naked before God.

Jesus stood naked before those who condemned him. He was stripped of his garments, and yet he stood in all of the glory of the Son of God. He had no need for outer adornment to prove that he was the Son of God. He could go to his death upon that cross and prove himself to be the Son of God, and he did not have to rely upon the adornments of the world.

Stripped of all outer ego, stripped of the accumulations of this world, stripped of everything but the Light within our heart, how many of us today could pass through the crucifixion? Are we leaning upon the opinions of other people, upon material things? Are these props to our identity?

This is the line of the Holy Spirit. What are you in the Holy Spirit? Is your temple the temple of the living God? If it is, then there is nothing that the world can offer you, not its plaudits, not its praise, not its blame; nothing in this world can touch you because you are sealed and hid with Christ in God.

This test comes to all of us. We will stand naked before the world. The world will judge us. And as we see with Jesus, it does not matter how well we have proven the Law, the world will always condemn. "If they have persecuted me, they will also persecute you."[4] If they have done it to Jesus, can we expect any better? And so, our desire must be not for popularity, not for acclaim. We must have one desire: the salvation of souls entrusted to our care.

The God-quality of Libra is Reality, and its perversion is unreality: the self-deception of the human ego, the deception of ourselves and the deception of others. It is the Liar and his lie, dishonor, absence of integrity, the inability to keep one's word. All of these are sins against the Holy Spirit, and if we engage in these things, we cannot retain that Holy Spirit on the nine-o'clock line. We deceive ourselves if we rest upon our human ego instead of upon the Christ Self.

The Eleventh Station

The eleventh station is "Jesus is nailed to the cross," the **ten-o'clock line.** The Mother and her children are being nailed to the cross today. These great avatars of Light who are called to be embodied in this age are passing through these fourteen initiations right within the mother's womb.

From the hour and the moment of the decision for abortion, that Christed One is condemned to death. He is called upon to bear the cross of the hatred of the parents, the doctors and those who are calling for the death of the child. He is made to bear the planetary momentum of death; goes through the momentum of the Luciferian anti-Christ of the three-o'clock line; faces the rebellion of the Satanists on the four-o'clock line in the disobedience of the parents to the laws of life; faces on the five-o'clock line the envy, jealousy of that Light by the fallen ones, the ignorance of the parents regarding that life in the womb.

The child passes through all of those stations within that nine-month cycle in the womb, which may be reduced to several weeks or a few days—whatever is the point that that avatar is actually passing through this crucifixion. And unwittingly, just as Peter unwittingly denied his Lord, as Judas was trapped unwittingly into the betrayal of his Lord, we find that people today, intelligent people who have had the teachings and the faith of their churches for centuries, can suddenly turn upon this most helpless manifestation of the Lord Jesus Christ. And so we see this nailing of God—God incarnate—to the cross is happening every hour and every day.

When you walk this path of initiation, you are one with every son and daughter of God. No matter who is suffering upon the planetary body, it registers upon your temple, and you cannot live unless you are daily giving your invocations to Light for the rescue of these souls, because it is always the rescue of Jesus Christ upon the cross.

This cross on the ten-o'clock line is the cross of selfishness and self-love. It is the Hierarchy of Scorpio, and the energy of Scorpio is the vision of God. The blind leaders of the blind are those who have totally obstructed the third eye by their human selfishness. Being utterly selfish, they lead those who are utterly selfish.

We have a cult of selfishness in the world today that is unparalleled. That same cult of selfishness destroyed Rome and every other civilization that has fallen. People live unto themselves, and there is very little going out of the way to help others.

When you feel this stench of selfishness standing between the people and their salvation, and you stand on this eleventh station feeling yourself nailed to that cross, you invoke the Light of Cyclopea, the All-Seeing Eye, and you invoke the violet flame for the transmutation of personal and planetary momentums of human selfishness manifesting as spiritual and material blindness.

Any time our vision is clouded and we don't know the next step to take in the will of God, let us remember to clear up that record of human selfishness—maybe something we did on Atlantis or Lemuria, maybe something we did ten thousand years ago or yesterday. Whatever it is, the vibration of selfishness deprives us of our mission and of our divine plan.

The Twelfth Station

The twelfth station is "Jesus dies on the cross," the **eleven-o'clock line.** Life is energy, and it can be neither created or destroyed. The life that Jesus lays down goes unto God and permeates the heart of every child of God evolving on earth. It becomes the life of all people. It is the external equation of integration.

Our integration in God has a momentary appearance of lifelessness and death, but it is only by the absorption of our being into the white-fire core that we may return on the third day in the fullness of the Real Self, the Christ Self resurrected. The laying down of one's life for one's friends is the laying down of the human consciousness so that the Christ can live within all.

Nevertheless, from the standpoint of the Sanhedrin, the Sadducees, the Pharisees, the powers of Rome, Caiaphas, this was the crucifixion of the Christ. They sought to destroy the body and therefore destroy the power of this man, destroy his influence. It was the killing of the outer self in the attempt to destroy that which can never be destroyed.

The supreme initiation on this line is to realize that we must prove indestructibility here and now within this temple. It serves no purpose for us to be indestructible in heaven. We must show the indestructibility of the Light of the Christ here on earth. That is the point of the resurrection. That is why he raised up the physical body. He could have left that body in the tomb and returned as a spirit, but he wanted them to see the nail prints in his hands and feet. He wanted them to know that the physical temple, the Mother, the Matter body, was restored.

We must prove this to the very best of our ability, here and now. While we have life, we must determine to be that resurrection and that life where we stand—not dying, but living the life of the Christ.

That dying on the cross is the initiation of Sagittarius. It is the line of God-victory and its misuse. The energy we deal with in challenging it is resentment, revenge and retaliation. As Jesus is dying on the cross he hears them mock him, berail him, tell him that if he is the Son of God he should come down and save himself. There are two malefactors who are crucified with him, the one denying him, the other asking him for forgiveness. Jesus gives the promise, "To day shalt thou be with me in paradise."[5] And so we see that by his sacrifice, many are drawn into that God consciousness.

The Thirteenth Station

The thirteenth station of the cross is "Jesus is taken down from the cross," the **twelve-o'clock line** of Capricorn again. Day by day our service is taking down from the cross those whom the world has crucified. They have hung there, some of them, for thousands of years, because no one has come along in the person of the Mother flame to say, "Here, I will help you. I will show you how to enter the tomb, the laboratory of the Spirit, to prove your resurrection."

So we see our youth, we see men and women and children hanging on the cross. Every single child who passes through abortion is going through this crucifixion. And this crucifixion, this death on the cross becomes a pall upon the planetary body. And until we go in the person of the Mother to minister to this life, these people on the cross are on the hillsides of the world. They are waiting for someone to say, "I will minister unto my Lord and Saviour within you. There is nowhere where my

Lord and Saviour is more real than in the person of you, the disciple, the chela, the newborn one. I will come."

The condemnation of the world would leave the sons and daughters of God to die forever upon that cross, and it is the compassion of the Mother that says, "I will not condemn thee, but I will affirm the glory of God within thee." And that condemnation of the world that the Mother denies is the condemnation for the mistakes, the failures, the misuses of energy by God's children.

It is all well and good to praise people when they are filled with Light, but the acknowledgment of their Reality is needed in their darkest hour or burden. That is when you need the friends who tell you that God lives in you. That is the work of the Ascended Masters and their chelas in this age.

The Fourteenth Station

The fourteenth station is on the **six-o'clock line:** "Jesus is laid in the tomb." The tomb is a symbol of the chamber of the heart, that laboratory where we prove our eternal life. It is the womb of Matter. It is in the heart of Mother. And it is in the base-of-the-spine chakra, the six-o'clock line again. This means that the proving of eternal life is dependent upon our raising up of the sacred fire from that base chakra to the crown, the perfect flow of the caduceus.

Jesus left the temple in his full mastery of his Christ Self. His soul within the Christ Self descended into the astral plane and preached to the rebellious spirits who had been confined there since the days of Atlantis. He returned to his body for the resurrection on Easter morning.

We are in that period of being in the tomb with the Mother. The Mother is laid in the tomb, and the tomb is Matter; we are all part of the seed of Mother. As we are laid in the tomb with Jesus, this is the place where we stay, perhaps for many years, even while we are still walking the cycles of the fourteen stations. But it is required now in this hour that we preach the gospel in the lowest levels of earth, to every nation, that we baptize in the name of the Father, the Son and the Holy Spirit, which means the transfer of the teaching, the energy of Father, Son and Holy Spirit, the transfer of self-awareness in God.

The six-o'clock line marks the astral body; it marks the initiations of the desire body. And many souls of Light who should be in the laboratory of the Mother working out the problem of being, working out the resurrection of their temple, are caught in the astral plane—and this is actually a perversion of the very initiation of this line. Our mission, then, is to carve out of the astral plane the souls of Light who have been caught there.

As Jesus' body lay in the tomb, the angels of Alpha and Omega stood at the head and the feet. Jesus came in his etheric body and his Christ Self. He stood before his physical body. He commanded the energies to reenter the body. He called forth the threefold flame to reignite within the physical temple to start the beating of the heart once again.

In that resurrection, in that demonstration of the victory of the fourteen stations, Jesus is fully the incarnation of the Universal Christ, and he is about to receive in the next forty days the "all-power in heaven and in earth."[6]

The Fourteen Stations in the Aquarian Age

The four cardinal points of God are Father, Son, Holy Spirit and Mother. In each age one of these cardinal points passes through the crucifixion. Since God is one, all of these elements are present in any manifestation of God, but the emphasis today is the crucifixion of Mother. It is the Divine Mother and her children on planet Earth today who are being crucified. It is woman and it is the life-force and the sacred fire, the Kundalini itself, that is being assaulted, condemned and crucified. And it is the body of the Mother—the body of man and woman.

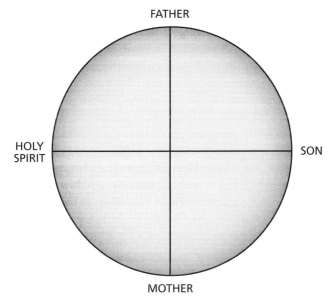

FOUR MANIFESTATIONS OF GOD

In the Piscean dispensation Jesus walked these stations for the initiation of the Christ and of the masculine ray. In the age of Aquarius, it is the Mother and her children who walk the fourteen stations. This was why Jesus said, when he came to the eighth station, "Weep not for me, ye daughters of Jerusalem, but weep for yourselves and for your children." He knew that the mothers and their children would reincarnate to see the day when they themselves would be walking through these fourteen stations.

Thus it says in the twelfth chapter of the Book of Revelation that when the dragon was cast down into the earth, he attacked the woman who was coming to give birth to the Man-child. And so the attack against woman, against Mother, against the feminine principle within man and woman is rampant. And today is the day when woman is intended to bear the cross of her own karma and of world karma, and to teach her children how to do the same. It is the day when the feminine principle in man rises and challenges his karma of the misuse of the feminine energy.

The Fourteen Stations of the Aquarian Cross
1. The Woman and her seed are condemned to death.
2. The Woman and her seed are made to bear their cross.
3. The Woman and her seed fall the first time.
4. The Woman and her seed meet their afflicted mother.
5. Simon the Cyrenian helps the Woman and her seed bear their cross.
6. Veronica wipes the face of the Woman and her seed.
7. The Woman and her seed fall the second time.
8. The Woman and her seed console the holy women.
9. The Woman and her seed fall the third time.
10. The Woman and her seed are stripped of their garments.
11. The Woman and her seed are nailed to the cross.
12. The Woman and her seed die on the cross.
13. The Woman and her seed are taken down from the cross.
14. The Woman and her seed are laid in the tomb.

Daily Opportunity

Paul said, "I am crucified with Christ: nevertheless I live."[7] The crucifixion, the cross, is the crossroad of opportunity. Living in the crucifixion is living for the transmutation of personal and planetary karma that would destroy the Christ step by step on these fourteen levels of initiation.

Paul knew that he was living the crucifixion all the days of his life. But the crucifixion is not a sorrow, not a sacrifice, not a pain; it is a point of transmutation and of transformation. And as long as we remain centered in the white-fire cross, in that very dot where the two lines meet, we are at that supreme point where, through the nexus, or through the heart chakra of ourselves, darkness passes into Light. At that point we sustain the bliss of holy communion, and we become the vortex of Light whereby this misqualified energy of the subconscious of the person and of the planet passes through the sacred fire.

This energy is washed, is cleansed, and that pure white Light returns to the heart of the I AM Presence. In order for the soul to get back to the I AM THAT I AM, all energy that is unlike that original image of the Christ, all that is impure that has ever manifested in thought, word, feeling or deed, must return to God purified.

In order for this to occur in those evolutions who have departed from obedience, we must walk the fourteen stations of the cross. It is the path of initiation. Whether you are Hindu, Buddhist, Moslem, Jew, Christian or none of the these, your life is the outpicturing of the fourteen stations of the cross. When you know it, you can make it if you try. When you don't know it, you are tumbled in the waves; you don't ride the crest.

This is how God has planned it. He is not concerned with the human consciousness and its indulgences. That I AM THAT I AM has one purpose and one intent: that the soul that God has made should return through becoming the individual Christ Self.

The Mystery of the Fifteenth Rosary:

The Surrender of the Christ You Have Become

WHEN YOU HAVE DILIGENTLY striven to gain your Christhood, you are then presented with another initiation. We can say that symbolically forty days after the resurrection—which in your life might be forty days, forty years, forty centuries—you come to the perfectionment by the sacred fire of that Christhood. Then you are free to enter into what is known as the mystery of the Fifteenth Rosary, to take the fullness of that Christhood and to give it to the world that all of your Christhood and all of your attainment should now be given day after day to support those who are somewhere on the outer rings of walking the stations of the cross, who are burdened, who are bearing the cross, not only of their own karma but of world karma. You lend the Light of your Christhood to support and uphold them by your prayers and by your service. By your free will, you may or may not choose to accept this test.

Mother Mary explains the mystery of the Fifteenth Rosary, the surrender of that Christ you have become: "First, let me say that the Fourteenth Rosary and all of the rosaries preceding it* are preparatory initiations for the putting into the flame of the unbalanced karma, the misqualified energies of life, the unwanted substances and all that is unreal. These rosaries are sacred keys to the initiations of Christhood whereby you, very presently and with haste, may balance 51 percent of your karma and remain in life the Presence, lo, the living Presence of your own blessed Christ Self.

"This goal is not so very far from you if you will heed the word of a Mother. For I taught the blessed disciples, and I have taught many lifestreams, one by one, the steps that are not too hard for thee, for they are not too hard for the LORD.[1] You do not scale a mountain all at once, but you prepare for the journey; and if it take fourteen days, then you take the necessary supplies, change of clothing, all that you require, and then you set your pace.

"Pacing yourself, preparing for the climb to the summit may involve many prior excursions into the mountains. But that ascent that is the ultimate ascent to the Mount of Transfiguration is one that you pace by the very breath of the Holy Spirit, for it is in the inbreathing and the outbreathing of the prana of life that you are able to mount that mount of attainment. Thus, beloved, you are able to pause at the fourteen stations and tarry there.

"Those fourteen stations are meant to be way stations on

---

*Mother Mary has released a rosary for each of the seven rays of the Christic Light to be used each morning of the week and a rosary for the eighth ray to be used on Sunday evening. A rosary for each of the five secret rays of the Holy Spirit was given for communion with the Paraclete on the five evenings of the week. These mysteries outline the testings that the soul must face, the demonstrations of the Law that she must make, and the temptations that she must overcome ere the devotee of the Mother and the Son be wholly integrated within the consciousness of the Christ. The Fourteenth Rosary is the Mystery of Surrender—the surrender of all that is not real in life, all that is not of the Christ.

the path that leads onward up the royal road of reintegration with your God Self. Thus, you see, what is most important is that you begin and that you attune with the pace of the Holy Spirit, the Maha Chohan; for your pace on this road of life is truly the rhythm of the heartbeat of Almighty God. Thus, in beginning, step by step, as the mountain becomes steeper and the air more rarefied, you must leave behind some of the heavier weight of your baggage. As the sun and nature and God himself become more real, you leave behind still more of that self because it is nonessential, for you have found the Self that is God.

"Passing through, then, the fourteen stations, you arrive at the summit of being who is Christ the Lord. You enter into the heart of that Christ, and that Christ enters into the fullness of your temple. First, you go into the secret chamber of the heart where the Ishwara* who is Christ in you is sealed. There are the initiations for Christhood. When you have passed them, the blessed Ishwara steps forth from the secret chamber of the heart and now occupies the fullness of the temple of life.

"Understand, then, that you are yet mounting the fourteen stations. And there are some who are students of the Ascended Masters who have not yet begun the fourteen stations. They are preparing for the preparation for Christhood.

"Thus, in the beginning to receive the judgment of the world, and the hatred, and the records of death, and the Antichrist, and the entire rebellious momentum of disobedience, and the division of life and the attempt to divide and conquer, and the burdens of the misuse of the Mother flame, and all that opposes the great Light of the joy of the heart as the ingratitude of selfishness, the entire accumulation of planetary and personal injustice, misuses of the cycles of life, the entire

---

Ishwara: from the Sanskrit meaning master or lord. It is a name for the Cosmic Christ, the universal one.

momentum of unreality, the entire conglomerate of the world's sense of struggle that manifests only through selfishness and self-love, and ultimately to defeat the dragon of vengeance against the Almighty—these stations* of bearing the burden of life result, then, in the transfer of the all-power in heaven and in earth.[2] In that hour of the fulfillment of the resurrection through the fourteen stations, it is understood that each candidate has the opportunity to elect to enter into the ascension spiral and to ascend to God....

"This is not our desire in this age, but our desire is to see the fullness of that Christ manifest in the earth for many cycles and years in many of our devotees. For the harvest is truly great,[3] and the souls of Light upon earth need the physical example of those who walk in the ultimate sense of freedom. Thus, my beloved, the mystery of the Fifteenth Rosary is the mystery of the surrender of that Christ that you become.

"It is not an automatic surrender, for some disciples may fulfill the fourteen stations and become that Christ and yet desire to possess that Christ, to be that Christ, to enjoy that Christhood and with it to yet pursue some of the private paths that indeed may increase attainment but may not increase the path of Christhood for others. Thus you see that when all other surrenders are in the valleys behind you and you stand on the mount of that transfiguration and you stand in the glory of Easter morn, you recognize that from the Mount of Transfiguration unto the mount of the Holy of holies of the resurrected Self, there is a unique path to be walked. It is the surrender of that Christhood that you have attained.

"The not-self that is placed upon the altar of God is not a sufficient sacrifice that you might have transferred to you the fullness of your Christ Self. It happens that when the not-self is

---

*Mother Mary here lists the perversions of the God consciousness of the Solar Hierarchies on each line of the cosmic clock. See page 197.

surrendered, then the True Self begins to manifest—often in faint glimpses at first, as a tiny babe, and then growing and waxing strong until the fullness of the Christhood is manifest. Thus, from the hour of the setting aside of the long path of unreality to the hour of the putting on of God-reality in the fullest sense of the word, that is the path of the Fourteenth Rosary. But when the God-reality comes and the Christ in you is made perfect and the soul is made perfect in Christ, there is the decision to be made: to give away that Christ that you have become.

"And therefore, my beloved, when Abraham laid Isaac on the altar, he was surrendering his Christhood manifesting in his own son.[4] He was not surrendering the not-self, but he was willing to give even the fullness of that God-identity in the trust that as that body and that consciousness and that being would be broken as the crumbs of life to feed all of humanity, even so that Christ would return and be one. And in having been broken for all, then that Christhood—the ultimate Christhood of the victory of the mission—becomes the Cosmic Christ, becomes the Ascended Master.

Breaking the Bread of Life

"In the breaking of the loaf that God is within you, there is the temporary sacrifice of the fullness of the expression of that identity. Rather than keep the fullness of that Light to your very own temple, you have said, 'I will break the bread of life. I will give a portion of that Christhood that is my own to every soul of God who is sent to me to receive that leaven, that white cube, that igniting fire of eternal life.'[5]

"Thus, my beloved, though God take in his hands the loaf, it is given to God by your free will and in your surrender. And as you give that Christ consciousness to him and he does break the bread of life, you live in the joy of the threefold unfed flame everywhere—in the hearts of little children, of those who are aging according to this world's cycles of time and space, in the hearts of families, in the hearts of elementals and angels. You even live in the unfed flame of Ascended Masters and Cosmic Beings. You transcend the stairway of life, moving in and out of the octaves of heaven and earth. For truly, by the gift of the grace of God of your own Selfhood, you have become one with all life in the deepest sense of the word.

"This is the mystery of the Holy Grail—how the Grail can be one and yet duplicates of that Grail, your own Electronic Presence, fragments of its crystal, might live and grow and multiply God consciousness in every part of life whom God has ordained.

"This oneness of life is a love incomparable. It is the oneness that you share with your Messengers. Now it is a oneness that is yours—to drink, to experience and to give away. Thus, when you are passing through the exercises of life where you must surrender this or that trinket or experience or even a dear friend who must take another path, remember that these surrenders are preparatory to the moment when you will give away the most precious gift of all—the Son of God that you have become....

"Out of the Light of East and West, out of the inner retreat of the Mother of India, I give to you the gift of the flame of the Mother East and West. I give to you the gift of a Mother's heart, the most sacred gift—the mystery of the Fifteenth Rosary. With those who have gone before me, I say, Forge your God-identity! and thereby enter the mystery of the Fifteenth Rosary."[6]

The Multiplication of the Christ Consciousness

Are you willing to surrender that hard-won Christ you have become and give a portion of that Christhood to every soul who is sent to you? Giving your Christhood to the world is not a one-time event. Each time you give away your Christhood, it is instantaneously replenished, almost as though photographically the Electronic Presence of yourself is manifest. You give it to another, the Electronic Presence is manifest again.

Anyone who does not give away his Christhood in service to the world simply does not understand the great glory and joy of the very process. Because each time you give, it's the outbreath of the sacred fire breath. And so, that which is self-emptied, having created a vacuum, is now infilled. Once again, that Christhood infills you, but because you have given it away to multiply another's Christhood, you have an increase. Each time you give it away, your Christhood has increased.

The only way you can ever keep your life is to give it away.* The only way you can ever renew your strength or your youth or your eternal Be-ness is in giving it away and letting that Light pour through you. The channels are opened, they never cease to be opened, and God never ceases to pour through. And it is always more than yesterday, because you receive the increase of the great good work that has been accomplished.

---

* "Whosoever shall seek to save his life shall lose it; and whosoever shall lose his life shall preserve it." (Luke 17:33.)

Section 17

The Risen Christ

W HEN JESUS ROSE FROM THE DEAD, the first of the disciples that he met was Mary Magdalene. She did not recognize him, but when he said her name, "Mary," she turned to him and said, "Rabboni," and she was filled with love and wanted to embrace her Master. Jesus said to her, "Touch me not; for I am not yet ascended to my Father: but go to my brethren, and say unto them, I ascend unto my Father, and your Father; and to my God, and your God."[1]

He wanted the message proclaimed. He was not even so concerned that she give the report of the resurrection. He was concerned that the message be proclaimed that he was in the process of ascending; he was proving the law of being for all of us; he was overcoming the last enemy. And he wanted it known that he was not ascending to an exclusive God whom he had addressed as Father. He was ascending to his Father and to our Father, "to my God and to your God."

Thus, in a scripture that has not yet been tampered with,

we find captured these words of Christ, which, when correctly understood by the interpretation of the Spirit, enable us to understand that God has given to Jesus a God and to us a God. "To your God and my God" refers to the individualization of the one God. There is only one God, but each of us has that personal contact with the individual I AM Presence, the same individualized I AM Presence that appeared to Moses and declared I AM THAT I AM.

Paul had a very clear understanding of this in his preaching. If you study the life and testimony of Paul, of Peter and of the other apostles, wherever they went they would preach, to Jew and Gentile alike, the life and mission of Jesus Christ, and they would go back to the Old Testament and show line by line the prophesy of the coming of the Messiah, how Jesus fulfilled that prophesy and how he was crucified. This history is important, because it shows the steps of initiation followed by the people of Israel all the way from that moment of the departure from God through disobedience back to the reunion with God.

In his public crucifixion, Jesus went through an outer demonstration of the inner temple initiations that are given at Luxor, Egypt, in the Ascension Temple. He wanted to leave a record that no one could take from the people, a record that we could read two thousand years later and know from that record, not that he was the exclusive Son of God doing something that only he could do, but that we must also follow in his footsteps. He wanted to leave a record that he was passing the initiation that every son and daughter must pass, and that because he passed that initiation, he would be there as an Ascended Master to help us when we would be ready and have the courage to take the same initiation. Therefore, the death on the cross symbolizes to us that the old man with his deeds must die, and we must be willing to let that old man be crucified.

It was the Christ whom they attempted to crucify, but in

actuality they killed only the body temple. The temple went through the process of death, but Christ was alive forevermore. We see in Jesus' example that there is an agony in this death, that allowing the old self to die is not an easy matter. With all of the balance of his karma, it took Jesus the three years of his ministry, the thirty years of his life to prepare for this initiation. And even then there was the agony in the Garden of Gethsemane, "Shall I or shall I not drink from this cup that is the will of God?" He decided to drink of that cup for you and for me.

When we read that he died for our sins, he died for the fact that he knew we would have karma, we would have sin, we would have substance misqualified in our temple, and in the hour for the exchange of the lesser self for the Greater Self, we would have to allow the lesser self to die. In that hour we would be able to remember Christ upon the cross, and we would take renewed courage, and we would say, "I will let the old self die that Christ might live in me today. And if Christ live in me today, there is hope for this world."

Paul's Declaration of Being

Paul gave a magnificent sermon recorded in the fifteenth chapter of his first letter to the Corinthians. His teaching refutes the concept that there is only one Son and only one who could ascend. He writes:

For I am the least of the apostles, that am not meet to be called an apostle, because I persecuted the church of God. But by the grace of God I am what I am: ...

He declares Being, and he says that not by what I did as a sinner, not by what I did as a righteous man, but by the grace of God I AM what I AM. It is wonderful to know that it is not by our human goodness and our human badness that we have the right to claim our being, but by the grace of God we can say, "I AM what I AM."

... and his grace which was bestowed upon me was not in vain; but I laboured more abundantly than they all: ...

Paul, who never met Jesus in the flesh, who was not among the five hundred witnesses at Bethany's hill, who was not with Jesus in his ministry, who was not one of the twelve apostles, yet becomes the one who labors more than all the rest. Does this not give us hope, that even though perhaps we have not measured up to the world's standards, if we have the determination and if we have the gift of the Holy Spirit, we can rise to bear witness to the Truth as Paul did. We can awaken all Christians and Jews and people of every religion to this quickening, this goal of the ascension—all of these people who have fallen asleep and who have not had those to teach them of the goal of life.

... yet not I, but the grace of God which was with me.

Paul was so aware of the Light of God because he had the comparison of his own state of consciousness before his conversion. He knew when the grace of God came upon him that it was God working through him. How smug do we become when we take for granted that we are the doer. The more we realize that God is working, the more he comes. And the more he comes, the more we see the difference between the puny human consciousness and the great God Self that is the Reality of our life. This is what Paul is preaching to all of those who had the witness of Jesus already.

The Resurrection

Now if Christ be preached that he rose from the dead, how say some among you that there is no resurrection of the dead?

But if there be no resurrection of the dead, then is Christ not risen:

There was an argument among the early Christians that there is no resurrection from the dead. But Paul is saying, if no one can rise from the dead, then neither could Christ. If you are saying that your dead cannot rise, then you are saying that Christ could not rise.

How many people who celebrate the resurrection on Easter morning believe in a personal resurrection that can be forged and won in this life? And how many who do believe in this have the understanding of the necessary requirements for the individual to attain that resurrection?

And if Christ be not risen, then is our preaching vain, and your faith is also vain.

Yea, and we are found false witnesses of God; because we have testified of God that he raised up Christ: whom he raised not up, if so be that the dead rise not.

For if the dead rise not, then is not Christ raised:

And if Christ be not raised, your faith is vain; ye are yet in your sins.

Then they also which are fallen asleep in Christ are perished.

If in this life only we have hope in Christ, we are of all men most miserable.

This teaching that comes from Paul is based on his premise that if Jesus were not resurrected, then his preaching is in vain—he might as well discontinue his entire ministry, because in the resurrection of Jesus the Christ lies the hope and the salvation of the entire world.

What are we preaching if we are not preaching eternal life? What do we have faith in if it is not the ultimate faith that we are destined to become one with God and live forevermore?

But now is Christ risen from the dead, and become the firstfruits of them that slept.

For since by man came death, by man came also the resurrection of the dead.

For as in Adam all die, even so in Christ shall all be made alive.

But every man in his own order: Christ the firstfruits; afterward they that are Christ's at his coming.

When Christ comes to you in that Second Coming, that is the opportunity for your resurrection—if you are Christ's, if *to your heart* you are one with his consciousness when he comes. Paul is preaching that every man will experience the resurrection in his own order, which means according to the cycles of his own initiations, which by free will he may accelerate or decelerate. We can slow our progress on the Path by all kinds of indulgences and misuses of energy, or we can speed up that progress on the Path.

The Last Enemy

Then cometh the end, ...

The next three verses are always interpreted as being manifestations outside of ourselves. But the coming of the end is the end of our human consciousness, the end of the carnal mind, the end of the concept that we are subject to the law of mortality.

...when he shall have delivered up the kingdom to God, even the Father; ...

When Christ, who is come to us in the Second Coming, delivers up our consciousness—that word *kingdom* means consciousness—when he delivers up our consciousness to God, even the Father,

...when he shall have put down all rule and all authority and power.

For he must reign, till he hath put all enemies under his feet. The last enemy that shall be destroyed is death.

When Christ in us shall have put down all rule, all authority and all power that is less than the Christ—this is an inner experience of an inner initiation. And this is what Paul was telling the brethren to whom he spoke. He was talking about this experience of the coming of Christ into the temple, that he must reign within us till he has put all enemies—every vice, every aspect of the carnal mind—under his feet, under the rule of the Piscean conqueror. And the last enemy that shall be overcome is death.

Jesus' three-year ministry in healing the sick and raising the dead was proving the overcoming of certain forcefields of karma, one by one within the subconscious of the individuals whom he healed. But finally, the culmination of all of these demonstrations of the science of life was the victory over death. And he manifested that victory first in the raising of Jairus' daughter and the raising of Lazarus, and then he went on to manifest that victory in his own life. Raising these two from the dead was the practice session for Jesus. He was using the laboratory of his friends and loved ones to prove the mastery of life over death. And when he was confident in that flow of energy, the initiation came where he had to actually withdraw from the body, allow it to die, return to it, restore the threefold flame to the altar, restore life to every cell.

For he hath put all things under his feet. But when he saith all things are put under him, it is manifest that he is excepted, which did put all things under him.

And when all things shall be subdued unto him, then shall the Son also himself be subject unto him that put all things under him, that God may be all in all.

The Christ has subdued all lesser manifestations in his own being. He comes into our being to subdue those things, and by his coming into our being, our own Christ consciousness is quickened so that we also become the workers with him of the submission of those lesser energies.

Else what shall they do which are baptized for the dead, if the dead rise not at all? why are they then baptized for the dead?

"I Die Daily"

And why stand we in jeopardy every hour?

I protest by your rejoicing which I have in Christ Jesus our Lord, I die daily.

Such a magnificent teaching of Paul! He knew that we cannot pass these initiations all at once in the hour of our transition. He knew that it was such a momentous feat to be crucified with Christ and to be found ready to be received by him, that unless we would give something of this lesser self day by day, we would not be ready for the resurrection when he would come. "I die daily" means that every single day of our lives we put aside one more trait of the human consciousness. And if it be only one and perhaps it take us a week or a month, if we put it to rest and it is permanently dead, we have won a permanent victory. We have accelerated consciousness. We are ascending.

If after the manner of men I have fought with beasts at Ephesus, what advantageth it me, if the dead rise not? let us eat and drink; for to morrow we die.

We might as well go ahead and follow the teachings of the hedonists, follow the pleasure cult—eat, drink and be merry for tomorrow we die. What is the point of striving or being a good Jew or Christian if we die tomorrow and there is no resurrection?

Be not deceived: evil communications corrupt good manners.*

Awake to righteousness, and sin not; for some have not the knowledge of God: I speak this to your shame.

He was speaking to those who had the Light, who had the Teachings, who had the witness of the ascension of Jesus, and of how they went back to their old friends and their old vibrations

---

*or, "evil company corrupts good morals."

and their old haunts and kept company with those who had not the Light or the belief in the resurrection. Thus, their own consciousness began to be tainted and darkened, because they no longer retained that Light. And therefore, he is rebuking them. He says, "How can you go back to your old ways and your old friends when you have the Light and the conviction, and they speak to mock your belief?"

Bodies Celestial and Bodies Terrestrial

But some man will say, How are the dead raised up? and with what body do they come?

Thou fool, that which thou sowest is not quickened, except it die:

And that which thou sowest, thou sowest not that body that shall be, but bare grain, it may chance of wheat, or of some other grain:

But God giveth it a body as it hath pleased him, and to every seed his own body.

All flesh is not the same flesh: but there is one kind of flesh of men, another flesh of beasts, another of fishes, and another of birds.

He speaks of the order of evolution of planes of consciousness, all the way from elemental life to the kingdom of the sons and daughters of God to the plane of the angelic hosts.

There are also celestial bodies (bodies that are suited to the heaven plane, the Spirit plane, the plane where we receive the fullness of cosmic consciousness), and bodies terrestrial (the physical bodies we wear): but the glory of the celestial is one, and the glory of the terrestrial is another.

There is one glory of the sun, and another glory of the moon, and another glory of the stars: for one star differeth from another star in glory.

So also is the resurrection of the dead.

The star and the sun and the moon are different personalities, different people who have different levels of awareness of cosmic consciousness. Some who have a greater awareness shine as the sun; those of lesser awareness as the moon.

The one star that differs from another in glory is the star of your own Causal Body of Light, your own I AM Presence. It is the energy you have given back to that Source, and therefore it is marked by an individuality. Just as your face is different from the face of the one sitting next to you, so the star of your Presence has a different vibration, a different color, a different emanation, a different contribution to the totality of cosmic consciousness. So is the resurrection of the dead—in the resurrection each star, each realization of God, is unique.

It is sown in corruption; it is raised in incorruption:

Paul is building to the crescendo that although we may be corrupted—in the sense that we are subject to decay, our atoms and our molecules are subject to degeneration and disintegration—yet by the natural outpicturing of cosmic law, by the action of the Trinity and of the Holy Spirit, that which is in a state of degeneration can be quickened into a state of regeneration. This is the meaning of the fire of the resurrection: we may sow in corruption, but we are raised in incorruption.

It is sown in dishonor; it is raised in glory: it is sown in weakness; it is raised in power:

This raising is the acceleration of consciousness. It comes about through the use of the sacred fire. It comes about through the use of the resurrection flame. The raising means the bringing into alignment of the energies of being until they are raised to the level of the Christ. That is how something that is sown in dishonor can be raised in glory: it is by the alchemy of the sacred fire that we invoke by the science of the spoken Word. This is how we can work for the resurrection and manifest it day by day.

It is sown a natural body; it is raised a spiritual body. There is a natural body, and there is a spiritual body.

And so it is written, The first man Adam was made a living soul; the last Adam was made a quickening spirit.

The last man, Jesus Christ, became a fountainhead of the Holy Spirit.

Howbeit, that was not first which is spiritual, but that which is natural; and afterward that which is spiritual.

In the order of our soul evolution we must first master the plane of Matter—our four lower bodies and the physical universe. We must master time and space; we must take dominion over the earth. Then, when we have proven our victory in the plane of Matter, in this physical universe, we may be given the opportunity to master the Spirit.

The first man is of the earth, earthy: the second man is the Lord from heaven.

The first man is the outer consciousness; the second man, the Christ Self who descends into this temple, into this clay vessel, who becomes the Real Self, who has ordained that the former self should pass away.

As is the earthy, such are they also that are earthy: and as is the heavenly, such are they also that are heavenly.

And as we have borne the image of the earthy, we shall also bear the image of the heavenly.

Paul is as certain of this as he is certain of his own life and his own heart beating. He is absolutely certain that he will bear the image of the heavenly self, the Higher Self, the Christ Self.

Now this I say, brethren, that flesh and blood cannot inherit the kingdom of God; neither doth corruption inherit incorruption.

Behold, I shew you a mystery; We shall not all sleep, but we shall be changed,

Paul taught the sacred mysteries that we receive today from the Ascended Masters. Very few were recorded, yet the word is translated here—*mystery*. And here is the mystery and the great joy of our ascension in this life: every one of us who is of the Inner Church of God, which we carry in our hearts; everyone who has this communion of the saints—all of us shall be changed. It is a promise to everyone who has a threefold flame.

In a moment, in the twinkling of an eye, at the last trump: for the trumpet shall sound, and the dead shall be raised incorruptible, and we shall be changed.

The "dead" are the Lightbearers who are waiting in the retreats of the Great White Brotherhood, waiting in the temples of Light. And there comes a period at the end of the dispensation of the age of Pisces, a certain calling when those who have gone before the Lightbearers who are in incarnation, when those who are in the retreats of the Brotherhood shall be raised.

The "dead" are those who have passed from the screen of life and not yet received the resurrection and the ascension because the cycle and the dispensation of the grace of God is not yet come to them. But in this moment of the conclusion of cycles "the dead shall be raised incorruptible and we shall be changed."

For this corruptible must put on incorruption, and this mortal must put on immortality.

So when this corruptible shall have put on incorruption, and this mortal shall have put on immortality, then shall be brought to pass the saying that is written, Death is swallowed up in victory.

O death, where is thy sting? O grave, where is thy victory?

The sting of death is sin; and the strength of sin is the law.

But thanks be to God, which giveth us the victory through our Lord Jesus Christ.

Fulfilling the Mandate of the Soul

Therefore, my beloved brethren, be ye stedfast, unmoveable, . . .

If you want this resurrection, if you want this ascension, know that it will come to you in a moment, in the twinkling of an eye when the last trump shall sound. It will come to you at the hour of God's appointing—if you are ready, if you are found in Christ in that moment.

Therefore, what do you do to get ready? A very simple formula: Be steadfast—steadfast in your knowledge of the Law, in your practice of the science of the Word. Be steadfast in your consciousness, not wavering back and forth, one day doubting, one day certain, but never grounded. Steadfastness implies the flowing stream of cosmic consciousness that you invoke daily, you attune with daily. Be steadfast in your awareness of yourself as the I AM THAT I AM. Be unmovable—absolutely unmovable—to any temptation or trial or argument of the fallen ones.

. . . always abounding in the work of the Lord, . . .

Abounding in that work means fulfilling that work day by day. We are giving out the energy God has given to us, and that is the certainty of the ascension. If we give all energy back to God every day in service to humanity, we know we are ascending. Abounding in the work of the Lord is laying up treasure in heaven, storing in our Causal Body all of the energy of God, and it is the certain opportunity for renewed energy on the morrow.

. . . . forasmuch as ye know that your labour is not in vain in the Lord.

The call of the ascension is not a choice; it is the demand of the very life in us. It is the demand of the fire in our hearts. And at a certain moment—we know not when—we see our loved ones and fellow disciples on the Path, and suddenly God calls them and takes them by the hand, and we see them going up in that whirling action of the sacred fire.

You know this teaching in your soul, because God has placed that mandate there, the same mandate that has carried all of the saints who have already returned to the heart of God. May this become letters of living fire that you place before you in a very prominent place. When you realize that you must put on immortality, that you must put on incorruption, it becomes a daily working the works of God, steadfast and unmovable.

The Teachings of the Risen Christ

The Book of Acts records that following the resurrection, Jesus taught the disciples for forty days in the Upper Room. These were his teachings to the inner circle, which are not recorded in scripture. Mother Mary speaks to us of these teachings of the risen Christ:

"The teachings of the risen Christ are transcendent, indeed, and far in advance of those recorded in the scripture, which he gave in parable to the multitudes. Today, the Great White Brotherhood would impart to mankind the fullness of those teachings, and we stand ready, at the portal of humanity, to impart the knowledge that he gained after that final triumph when the world could no longer touch him, for he remained a part of the world, and yet he had overcome this world. Not even the force of gravity could hold his body earthbound, but by conscious will, he remained to give his final service to the evolutions of earth. . . .

"Blessed ones, I am calling today for a conscious reunion with the Spirit of Christhood that you might enter into the Holy of holies, to that place where the fullness of the divine teachings may flow from your own Christ Presence into the very cells of your brains to awaken you to the knowledge of life without end, life without beginning.

"I come to you this day to inspire you to search the meaning of all things that pertain to the fullness of your own Christ-identity with its transcendent possibilities. Realize, then, that the Father who gave you life and birth could not have done so without imparting unto you the seed containing all that which you shall ultimately be as you discover your Divine Selfhood, which was created and is sustained in his Image and Likeness; the fullness of your divine potential, then, is already a part of your True Being. You have but to claim it, to commune with it, to adore it, to be one with the Presence of the Lord of Hosts.

"Strive daily, then, to be children of the one God, followers of the high calling, as Christs and sons of the Most High. Little by little, as the sand falls in the hourglass, so the knowledge of divine union will descend into your lower self and enable you to have that reunion, which you so desire, with the great wisdom of your Higher Mind. Nothing is impossible to him who believes in the promise and the fulfillment of the Christ for every man; for indeed, the Christ did give himself for the sins of mankind—not that mankind throughout all ages shall be exonerated for wrongdoing because he died—no, but because he lived, they, too, can find the glory of the resurrection and know the fullness of their own Christ Self. Jesus did not place himself upon the cross to atone for your sins, precious ones—only you can do that; but the Christ offered himself that you might realize that you, too, can be an overcomer of all things through him.

"The footsteps of the cross are not sorrowful ones, precious children, they are the footsteps of the overcomer; they are the steps of initiation that each one must pass. But because my son manifested them for you, the pathway is made easier for your lifestream. The Christ would not deprive anyone of God's children from the great joys upon the path of overcoming. God would not confine salvation to one son when all must find the fullness of his Presence here on earth in order to rise into the heavenly bliss that comes from fulfillment and from self-mastery.

"Beloved ones, the path of the Christ is not one to be shunned; it is one to be embraced. Give yourself wholeheartedly, then, to the pursuit of this high calling, for no greater joy exists. You think that in the pleasures of the world there is happiness, that in the indulgences of the senses you will find true oneness and happiness. How false are mankind's conceptions of bliss, for joy is found only in the Presence of the Joyous One. Absence from the Lord is not life; on the contrary, it is nonexistence; it is separation, incompleteness, a cutting off from the Divine Source, which can only result in unhappiness, fruitlessness and death.

"I AM the resurrection, and the life! So simple is this statement of the Christ, yet it reveals the fullness of the Law. But how men do wander in search of the answer that yet lies before them and to which all nature attests. O mankind, reverse the flow, reestablish the patterns of divine unity, and you will find the joy of the Lord in his Presence."[2]

Christ Is Taken Down from the Cross

In many Christian churches Christ hanging on the cross is a primary symbol of the faith. Yet he was only on the cross for a few hours. It was a stage of the path of initiation that he had to pass through in order to arrive at the resurrection and the ascension. Serapis Bey explains that the Brotherhood would have us place our attention on the risen Christ, rather than Christ hanging on the cross: "Now, beloved ones, I come with a message from the Lord Jesus Christ, who does stand here this day. His message is a mighty outpouring of love—love from the heart of the eternal Christ. I give you a moment, therefore, to attune your hearts to the heart of Jesus.

"The blessed Saviour, the living Christ, the Ascended Master Jesus, does honor me, a Son of God, to release to you from the heart of Luxor, Retreat of the Ascension Flame, his announcement to you and to all.

" 'This day the declaration does go forth from God the Father and God the Son that the living Christ Jesus is forevermore taken down from the cross and from the very image of the crucifixion. . . . '

"For beloved Alpha and Omega, the Father and the Son do not desire to behold Christ crucified, but him resurrected and ascended and free. And therefore, in the initiations of life, this Church and this body have undergone this particular station of the cross as the very testing of the soul in the humility to bear the same burden that he bore.

"Now, with full God-mastery, I say to one and all: Come down from the cross—the cross inflicted by the world mind and the cross inflicted by subconscious guilt. Take heed that the higher initiation of the cross of the ruby ray is thine own. And in taking this path and this overcoming, beloved ones, you will be on the high road of initiation, bypassing that Golgotha."[3]

And therefore, our meditation is upon the risen Christ and on the ascension, but we do not bypass Jesus on the cross. We are on the cross with him, but the cross becomes a blaze of fire at the nexus, at the point where the two lines meet, and there is the bursting conflagration whereby the mortal becomes the immortal. And this happens right where you are, right in your aura, that burst of fire that is the action of being a living sacrifice. It often means withdrawal from various involvements in the world or worldly pleasures because you cannot be in and of the world and at that nexus of the cross at the same time.

God Is the Victor in You

Jesus, the risen Christ, speaks to us of our mission as we follow in his footsteps through the resurrection and the ascension: "Thus, understand in this hour: The dispensations have come—and lo, the cycles have turned. It is the hour of Aquarius, and the descent of the Holy Christ Self has taken place. And the Great White Brotherhood moves among the people. But I tell you, beloved hearts, as surely as there came the rejection of my mission, as surely as Rome and the Roman Church this day has denied the true reason for my coming, so it can come to pass that this dispensation of the I AM Presence and the Christ Self can be denied by those in the establishment of the World Council of Churches, and therefore denied to the very people who ought to rise up and be the prophesied remnant.

"Understand the meaning of prophecy. Prophecy has never been a psychic prediction. It has never been ironclad. It does come to pass because the spirit of prophecy is received by receptive hearts who are the fulfillment of the Lord's prophecy by free will. Prophecy does tell you what can be if the people affirm God's will.

"So it was, as I was given the opportunity to demonstrate the victory over Death and Hell, which had to be done in the very process of the judgment of the fallen angels who determined to destroy the Christ. Thus, I gave them my body to prove for all time and eternity that they have no power—neither over the body or the soul of my brothers and sisters who will hold steadfastly to the One and to being the mouthpiece of the One who has sent them, even the LORD God, even your mighty I AM Presence, even your Christ Self, even the Cosmic Christ and hosts of the Lord, even the Ancient of Days who has sent you as surely as he sent Daniel and Jeremiah and Isaiah and John the Baptist...

"I have not passed through this crucifixion for naught. I have passed through it that you might see and know the Truth that God is the Victor in you in this hour over that same seed who moved against me. And in this hour it is the prophecy and the decree that the LORD's judgment will fully and finally bind the persecutors of Christ in you!

"Therefore, as I did, so do ye. Hasten the judgment by *being* the Christ, *knowing* Christ is in you, *knowing* you are fashioned in the image, your soul is a part of me, and the Universal One Christ is the common loaf of our identity in God. This do. This say and know that I AM THAT I AM."[4]

The Message of the Risen Christ

El Morya explains that the message of the risen Christ was and is for all upon earth: "Where do a people stand when they do not have recourse to Almighty God and his Spirit in them? What can they do when their bodies are beset by drugs, when they are caught up in violence, when all manner of pleasure and entertainment is the first thing they think of when their jobs are through? I tell you, if America is to be saved from that which is plotted by the dark ones on this planet, there must be a rising fervor and a return to first principles both in Church and State.

"How shall we tell them? How shall they be God-taught when the false pastors have invaded the temples and denounced even the very communion of saints that we enjoy with you and you with us in this Spirit of the Great White Brotherhood? Brothers and sisters of Light on earth have a right ordained by Jesus Christ to commune with brothers and sisters in heaven, not by psychic or astral means, but by the true Holy Ghost. And the Holy Ghost is the Comforter and the Teacher who has come to you to bring all those things to your remembrance which Jesus taught you.[5]

"*When* did he teach you those things that you are now reminded of? *When?* Were you all there in Galilee? It is not quite possible for the tens of thousands and millions who ascribe to the path of the Brotherhood on this planet to have all been there in the flesh. And thus, Jesus spake to all of you to whom he preached in all octaves of being in that hour and mission. For the Son of God truly spoke from the etheric retreats, and all the world heard him.

"Do you think his fame spread only by the apostles or only by the grapevine, as they say in India? I tell you, no. The power of the Presence of Jesus Christ in the earth has been the power to contact every living soul these two thousand years with the inner knowledge and the sense of the honor of Christ's presence in them. And that teaching is ongoing no matter what is said in their mosques or synagogues or temples.

"For the living Christ does shepherd his own, nation by nation, and for this reason: People understand right and wrong, they know what ought to be and ought not to be, they know what is evil if they will allow themselves to perceive it. And therefore, the Standard lives. The honor code is present with the comings and the goings of philosophers and psychologists and all the rest who now say, 'this is right,' and then say, 'this is wrong.'

"Relative good and evil is not the story of your life. Put that aside and recognize that it is the Absolute Good of God present with you that is the power to devour the forces of Absolute Evil, first and foremost being that tyranny over the soul and the spirit and the heart of man. . . .

Find the True Path

"The entire purpose of life is finding God—finding God in yourself and your talents and your calling and your sacred labor—and endowing anything that you do with his Spirit. They may say otherwise, but when it comes down to the depths of the soul, no one in this world is happy until he has made his peace with his God, his I AM Presence. There are many who would deny this, yet are they truly happy? They say they are happy but they have not known the joy of Reality. Many are insane, many are bound, and yet do they take up the path toward God?

"Why don't they take up the Path? Is it because it has been given to them from childhood with such distaste, with such obvious flaw that they have become atheists and agnostics rather than hear the same old bromide Sunday after Sunday? Many people have learned to hate God in the churches because they have never been told that there is an exciting path waiting—the Homeward path that enables you day by day to know the joy of doing more for those in need because more of God is in you.

"Have you ever thought about that—that the churches turn more people away from God, the true and living God, the Reality of the way of the cross, the Reality of life as it ought to be? I can tell you without equivocation that the doctrines taught in America today in the mainline religions will never afford the people the ability to save this nation!

"Do I preach a particular brand of religion? Nay. The teachings of the Ascended Masters incorporate the path that the Mystical Body of God has walked through all eternity. It is not even unique to this planetary system. It is the same descent of the soul unto the grand experiment in freedom and free will, meeting all forces that pretend to be the adversary when the only true enemy is within. And that is the ultimate knowledge: Man, know thyself and know thyself as God, and know that the only foe that can ever overcome in thy life is thine own fear or internal schism or compromise or failure to surrender truly to God. . . .

"It is the quickening that we would convey. It is the native power of God unto you. And it is especially the love of our bands and hosts for you personally as our brothers and sisters. We tarry on earth on behalf of you and millions of others who truly would do better if they knew better, who truly desire to know the Truth, and who persecute many righteous men thinking that they do God service.[6]

"The path of the violet flame and the spoken Word, beloved, is certainly the path that can lift the accumulated debris of density of the centuries—the covering over of the chakras, the limiting of the human brain because it has lost the impulse of the crystal cord and the flow of Light. Mankind do not need to wed the computer to gain superhuman powers, but only to unite with the living Christ.

"I pray every day that this nation and all peoples on earth will not have to come to the knowledge of Truth through adversity, through nuclear war, through economic collapse. I trust you will also pray with me in this wise, for beloved, the prayer of the righteous—those who use the righteous law, the right use of the law of the science of the spoken Word—availeth much.[7]

"And thus, let us say:

Our heavenly Father, — *and Mother* we beseech thee in the name of the saints who have gone before and the precious people of this earth that enlightenment shall come by the might of the Archangels, by the interactions of angels and men, and by the Holy Comforter.

Our Father, we ask you today and every day to bring healing, Light and comfort—peace and the awareness of the enemy of their souls.

O God, send thy Angel of Faith, Archangel Michael, to their aid! Send that holy one of God that they be not plucked from the screen of life in an untimely manner and therefore miss the opportunity to fulfill their divine plan and to glorify thee.

Our heavenly Father, make us stewards of thy grace and thy abundant life. Make us responsible in caring for the sick and the needy. Give us the understanding heart to walk many miles with our brother.

Our heavenly Father, we pray for every soul of Jesus on earth—all who are the lovers of his heart, all who truly worship thee through him even though they have been limited by orthodoxy in some form.

I call to legions of Truth, and in the name of the Son of God, I, El Morya, call to the twelve legions of angels of the Lord Christ to descend for the rescue of the churches this day that they may be infilled with thy true Spirit and not the spirits of the night that seize their bodies and their chakras, causing them to writhe or dance or jump or scream or weep.

I demand, as the Chohan of the First Ray, the exorcism of the churches of those foul spirits and the exorcism of every form of demon taunting them away from the true and living Spirit of the Holy Ghost!

Maha Chohan, enter them now and purge them and let the living fire of true freedom and true worship be upon them. For these are thy hearts, our Father. Cut them free and let them become fierce disciples, taking the true stand for defense instead of advocating the pacifism of the Devil.

O living Word, as thou hast written, I, too, have taken my pen this day and I have written my coded message in the hearts of my own. It is my forget-me-not.

"Precious chelas of the will of God, in fervor and faith, fight the good fight and win ground for Reality. *Bind* unreality and illusion and set the captives free! For it is your calling and your desiring and all of your love fulfilled.

"I remain with you as a mentor on the Path, ever desirous of assisting you, especially in your calls for God-government and the abundant life in the economy.

"In the name of my teacher and friend of Light, the Great Divine Director, in the joy of my co-worker Saint Germain, I AM El Morya Khan."[8]

Section 18

Christ in Birmingham
A Sermon by Mark L. Prophet

THE STORY IS TOLD AND RETOLD many times of the crucifixion. I will not repeat it. But the story has been told that in this modern day and age that when Christ came to Birmingham, the people of Birmingham did not crucify him, although they wished to reject him. But he stood in the street and leaned against the wall, and as the people passed by, he reached out his hand, offering to help them. And each person went on his way, coldly indifferent to his plea. The season changed, and with the fall of night, the rain came down, and the rain turned to sleet and ice. And Christ froze in Birmingham, leaning against the wall with his outstretched hands.

This is what has happened in the world today. Christ is not crucified—Christ is ignored. And this is Truth. Because you and I do not ignore him does not mean that many others do not. Most people in the world today have a form of godliness, but they deny the power of God to free them from every mortal tendency and raise them into complete Christhood.

You hear people today speaking about mastership. They talk about the Masters of the Far East, they talk about our beloved El Morya and Saint Germain, they talk about the Great White Brotherhood—some people do—and they seem to feel that these beings are remote. They never seem to envision God as very close at hand to them. And it is this sense that creates a breach in the internal cosmic sense, the spiritual hearing of the spiritual ear that can listen and know the clarion call of perfection and see with the eyes of the inner Self.

Without vision the people perish, and with vision the people come to life, but not the kind of life that you hear about on television. They come to life that is God, and this produces the wonderful dynamism of infinite health, of infinite love, of infinite strength—strength beyond anything that you have ever imagined.

Now, Jesus looked like a man. He stood on the hillside, a tall figure in a flowing robe. You and I would be wearing robes tonight if it were the custom of our times; and if Christ were here, he would not be in a robe, he would be in a business suit.⁇ Somehow or other we get our vision twisted—we become captivated by the flowing robe and lose sight of the great masterful presentation of this Master as he stood upon the hillside.

The fact that Christianity and the many religions of the world have failed to materialize that religious science that will solve man's problems, reveals that mankind must make direct contact with the Universal Christ. This Christ will show them the Law of God fulfilling the Golden Rule—"Therefore all things whatsoever ye would that men should do to you, do ye even so to them: for this is the law and the prophets."[1] Through this Christ there will come the fulfillment of the promises of Jesus—"These signs shall follow them that believe"[2]— and the fulfillment of the faith that in God and in Christ as the man of action within all, there is hope enduring, a flame that can never be extinguished, a light that is indeed the light of the world.[3]

Long ago Saint Paul said, "If the trumpet give an uncertain sound, who shall prepare himself to the battle?"[4] Who is responsible, then, for the changing of divine concepts into those of present-day religionists? Who has sought to glorify Jesus as a person, as a sacrifice, as a saviour, while ignoring his mandates in their personal lives? Who, by the person of Christ, has weakened his mission? Certainly not the Father; certainly not the God of all Truth.

The apostle James said, "Faith without works is dead," and that we should show our faith by our works.[5] Saint Paul also said, "Work out your own salvation with fear and trembling. For it is God which worketh in you both to will and to do of his good pleasure."[6] It is also recorded that the Son must bow to the Father "that God may be all in all."[7] Jesus said, "Ye believe in God, believe also in me."[8] This was not usurping God but showing that he lived in Christ. When called "Good Master," he also said, "Why callest thou me good? there is none good but one, that is, God"[9]—thus showing the common denominator of the Universal God, which he proved in his life, could be shared by all. "I and my Father are one" is the decree of sonship that all can receive and manifest.[10]

No one on earth today can honestly tell us that life is being lived as God intended; for life is certainly not happy for many people. There is a poverty consciousness on earth, an absence of a zest in living the abundant life. Many people are so miserable that they won't even tell you about it. Others are so miserable that they tell you about it all the time! But all of us have asked ourselves this question: "Why is life the way it is? Did God plan it this way?"

Many possible answers cross our minds. Some say that God ordained it so to punish a wayward generation. Others have been embodied so many times in the rounds of mediocrity that they accept their state of misery as the norm and happiness as the exception. We know that this creation and the way it is currently manifesting does not produce happiness. It is filled with frustrations, fear and uncertainty, and the uncertain sound is what people are hearing rather than the certain sound that satisfies their hunger and thirst for the clarion call.

The Clarion Call

What is the clarion call? The clarion call is the voice of the Creator that sounded forth the note of the perfect creation. "In the beginning God created the heaven and the earth. And the earth was without form, and void; and darkness was upon the face of the deep. And the Spirit of God moved upon the face of the waters. And God said, Let there be light: and there was light."[11] God spoke and his voice uttered not the uncertain sound, but the certain sound of victory and perfection.

God never created imperfection. He never has, and he never will. This is pure Truth. The trumpet has given the certain sound, and the clarion call has gone forth, but men have not heard it. And there is a reason why they have not heard it, and there is a reason why they have not responded to that call.

I am certain that this hungry generation—and I think this generation is hungry and is lean for the pure Truth of God—if they actually heard this certain call, this clarion call, I believe with all my heart that there is not an amphitheater, there is not a building in the world that could contain the people in one city among the major cities of the earth who would be interested and who would respond to the clarion call. Why do we not have that response?

Could it be that the senses, which are avenues to consciousness themselves, and which are faculties of soul and of mind, of God and of his divine mind, in some way are not functioning perfectly?

Some of us wear reading glasses. Some of us wear distance glasses, and many people wear no glasses at all. Some people have hearing aids, some have no hearing aids, but if the outer senses do not function properly, most of us do something about it, don't we? We go out and see someone who can help us. For today there is no need for anyone to suffer bad eyesight in most cases, because the optometrists of the world are quite capable of correcting many types of deficiencies in vision. And the same applies to hearing. Science has produced wonderful inventions for man, and I am certain under divine direction.

Why is it that the senses of the soul are dulled? What is the reason why mankind en masse do not respond? I think there are many reasons. Perhaps chief among the reasons is that almost all of the orthodox world today feel that they have already discovered as much of God as is possible for mankind to discover in their generation, and they simply are not interested in discovering more. It is a sense of complacency, in other words. They feel that they already know as much of God as anyone else knows. In the sophistry of our times, people sit back and say, "Well, I studied for seven years, and I think I have discovered as much of the answers as anyone." In this complacency they become content.

There is no point in thinking that we have it all, if for no other reason than that God is infinite. And certainly the knowledge of the Infinite cannot be compounded and piled up in anyone's consciousness in the span of a few short years so that a man does not need any more of God. This is a bit ridiculous on the face of it. Yet, complacency plays some part.

Jesus talked about the quick and the dead. Saint Paul said that the world was dead in trespasses and sin[12]—and one of the greatest sins of all is the ignorance of Reality. But how can they affirm a Reality that they do not know? As Saint Paul said, "How shall they believe in him of whom they have not heard?"[13]

The Word, then, has to be heard, but the clarion call has already sounded forth. The clarion call is in the eternal Now. It was spoken before Abraham was. It was spoken before the foundation of the world. Yet the sound can be heard today, and the sound will be so well preserved that you will be able to hear the clarion call ten thousand years from now as clearly as it rings this instant. This is the eternal call of perfection, and it is capable of producing a revolution in consciousness in you right here and now.

What was the statement made by John? He said, "In the beginning was the Word, and the Word was with God, and the Word was God. All things were made by him; and without him was not anything made that was made."[14] Throughout the scriptures we find that the *Word* is referenced as the Christ— not as Jesus the man, but as Jesus the Christ, the Universal Son of God. And you, too, are a part of God; you, too, are the Universal Son of God, for Jesus said, "I am in you and you are in me, and I am in the Father and the Father is in me." Thus we see that it is all a matter of how you look at it.[15]

Paul said, "No man can say that Jesus is the Lord, but by the Holy Ghost."[16] For it is the Holy Ghost, the Holy Comforter, that enables the man who feels the farthest from God to reintegrate with God. He is a drop of water that seems separated from the ocean; now he merges with the ocean. He becomes one with God, even as Jesus taught. Then he is qualified to say that Jesus is Lord, that Jesus is also the Christ.

He is the greatest Teacher that we have known, yet we have not followed his teachings; we have not heard his voice; we have not understood all that he said. For men of lesser dimensions, sometimes sincerely, sometimes in a bigoted manner, have sought to hide the Master's face from us.

He revealed God to us; he taught us of the Eternal Father; of the mystery of Christ that is within us. This Christ that is within us is the inner man. When he comes to the world of the individual or to the world as a thief in the night, the world is changed because he has come. And every individual who receives him and becomes a joint heir with him in the Father's plan enriches the world upon his return to the Father, and can also say to succeeding generations, "Greater things shall ye do because I go unto my Father."[17]

We all came forth from the one Source and we all return to that Source. The lines of manifestation marking birth and death, or beginning and ending, are only lines of opportunity. When our perspective is larger and we see that Christ comes to us in a moment, in the twinkling of an eye; when it dawns upon us that the Only Begotten lives within us, that we identify altogether with him, we will see that we can no longer be a child of God in name only; but we must also accept the fullness of all Reality, that we may, in becoming Christs without, fulfill the mystery of that which is already within.

Transfiguring Affirmations of Jesus the Christ

I AM THAT I AM
I AM the open door which no man can shut
I AM the Light which lighteth every man
      that cometh into the world
I AM the Way
I AM the Truth
I AM the Life
I AM the Resurrection
I AM the Ascension in the Light
I AM the fulfillment of all my needs and requirements
      of the hour
I AM abundant supply poured out upon all life
I AM perfect sight and hearing
I AM the manifest perfection of being
I AM the illimitable Light of God
      made manifest everywhere
I AM the Light of the Holy of Holies
I AM a son of God
I AM the Light in the holy mountain of God

Notes

Introduction

1. Prov. 29:18.
2. Gen. 1:28.

Section 1 • The Mystery of the Christ

1. 1 Cor. 12:3.
2. 1 John 4:9.
3. John 1:9.
4. Rom. 10:12–13.
5. Mother Mary, *Keepers of the Flame Lesson 16*, pp. 7–9.
6. Luke 4:16–21.

Section 2 • The Divinity of the Christ…

1. John 3:16.
2. John 6:33, 35.
3. 1 Cor. 11:24–25.
4. John 1:1, 3.
5. John 8:58.
6. James 4:8.
7. John 14:12.
8. Matt. 5:18; Gal. 6:7; Eph. 6:8.

Section 3 • The Universal Christ…

1. Hab. 1:13.
2. Jer. 23:5, 6.
3. John 1:5, 14.
4. Exod. 3:14–15.

5. 1 John 4:9.
6. John 1:9.
7. John 14:23.
8. John 3:16.
9. Luke 22:42.
10. For example, the term "Son of man," often used by Jesus, finds great elaboration in the Book of Enoch. It has long been thought that Jesus' use of the term "Son of man" in referring to himself originated with Daniel 7:13. But prominent scholars believe that it was the Book of Enoch that provided this key term to Jesus. Although Laurence's translation of the Book of Enoch does not reflect it, it seems that Enoch himself was called by God "Son of man." Biblical scholar H. H. Rowley points out that various translators have hedged on this passage, mistranslating it or even attempting to change the original text that applies the words "Thou art the Son of man" to Enoch. Laurence's translation of the key passage, perhaps for doctrinal reasons, substitutes the words "offspring of man" for the literal translation "Son of man." By contrast, when the term "Son of man" clearly refers to Jesus Christ, Laurence uses it without hesitation. It has been suggested that one reason the Book of Enoch was not included in the Bible was its use of the term "Son of man" to refer to anyone other than Jesus. See Elizabeth Clare Prophet, *Fallen Angels and the Origins of Evil* (Corwin Springs, Mont.: Summit University Press, 2000).
11. Phil. 2:5.
12. Jer. 23:6, 33:16.
13. Deut. 4:24, 9:3; Heb. 12:29.
14. Matt. 16:13–16.
15. Matt. 16:17–18.
16. John 11:27.
17. John 12:32.
18. John 12:44–45.
19. Jesus Christ, "Are You Ready for the Second Coming," *Pearls of Wisdom,* vol. 35, no. 66, December 16, 1992.
20. John 10:2, 7, 9.
21. John 14:6.
22. John 14:12.
23. Matt. 5:48.

Section 4 · You Can Become the Christ

1. Exod. 17:8–13; Deut. 31:23; Josh. 1; 6; 8:1–29; 10; 11.
2. Gen. 37, 39–41.
3. 1 Kings 19:16–21; 2 Kings 2:1–9; 3; 13:14–21.
4. Isa. 40:3–5; Mal. 3:1; 4:5; Matt. 3:1–3; Luke 1:13–17, 76; 3:2–6; John 1:22, 23.
5. Matt. 11:10, 13, 14; 17:10–13; Mark 9:11–13; Luke 7:27.
6. Phil. 3:14.
7. 1 John 2:18, 22; 4:3; 2 John 7.
8. In the first century B.C., El Morya was embodied as Melchior, one of the three wise men from the East who calculated by astrology the time and place of the birth of the Avatar of the Piscean age. "We have seen his star in the East and are come to worship him." (See Matt. 2:1–12.)
9. 1 John 3:1–2.
10. John 13:23, 25; 21:20.
11. See Serapis Bey, "The Banner of Humility," *Dossier on the Ascension* (Corwin Springs, Mont.: Summit University Press, 1978), p. 33.
12. Acts of John 90–91; Apocalypse of Peter 4–20 (Akhmim fragment). See M. R. James, trans., *Apocryphal New Testament* (London: Oxford University Press, 1924), pp. 251–52, 518–19.
13. Matt. 17:1–13; Mark 9:2–13; Luke 9:28–36.
14. Gen. 5:22, 24; Heb. 11:5.
15. Through the coming of the Avatar Jesus Christ and the two-thousand-year Piscean dispensation, there was the setting aside of karma for the Lord's disciples and for the planet as a whole until they should attain to the level of self-mastery in Christ whereby they themselves could balance that karma through prayer and good works. In this hour, the karma is increased on the planet because the people of earth are now expected to bear their own burden (i.e., weight) of karma that has been set aside these two thousand years through the grace (Light) of Christ's Presence. As it is written, "Every man shall bear his own burden" (Gal. 6:5), and "Not one jot or tittle of the law (of karma) shall pass till all be fulfilled" (Matt. 5:18).
16. Matt. 22:11–14.
17. El Morya, "Message to America on the Mission of Jesus Christ," *Pearls of Wisdom,* vol. 27, no. 47, September 23, 1984.

18. Kuthumi and Djwal Kul, *The Human Aura* (Corwin Springs, Mont.: Summit University Press, 1996), pp. 186–190.

19. Marvin W. Meyer, trans., *The Secret Teachings of Jesus: Four Gnostic Gospels* (New York: Random House, Vintage Books, 1986), p. 5.

20. Mark 12:29.

21. Rom. 8:17.

22. Ezek. 18:4, 20.

23. Rom. 6:23.

24. Sanat Kumara, "To Keep the Light of a World," *Pearls of Wisdom,* vol. 42, no. 13, March 28, 1999.

25. John 6:29.

26. Serapis Bey, "The Crowning Moment: The Image of the Golden Man," *Pearls of Wisdom,* vol. 25, no. 36, September 5, 1982.

27. Ibid.

28. Jesus, "Comfort Ye My People!" *Pearls of Wisdom,* vol. 30, no. 79, December 18, 1987.

29. Jesus, "You Can Become a Christ!" *Pearls of Wisdom,* vol. 26, no. 56, December 27, 1983.

Section 5 • The Path of Personal Christhood

1. Helios, "The Meaning of Life: Advice to a Planet," October 12, 1970.

2. Serapis Bey, "The Very First Steps of the Law," *Pearls of Wisdom,* vol. 27, no. 29, June 3, 1984.

3. El Morya, "Chela—Christed One—Guru: Offices on the Path of the Individualization of the God Flame," *Pearls of Wisdom,* vol. 28, no. 11, March 17, 1985.

4. 2 Timothy 2:15.

5. Sanat Kumara, "I Will Come when You Need Me," *Pearls of Wisdom,* vol. 31, no. 44, July 24, 1988.

6. Jesus, "The Day of Thy Christhood," *Pearls of Wisdom,* vol. 30, no. 74, December 13, 1987.

7. Elizabeth Clare Prophet, "Teachings of Jesus Christ on Your Path of Personal Christhood," June 27, 1993.

8. Cyclopea, "The Confrontation with God and Anti-God," *Pearls of Wisdom,* vol. 29, no. 66, November 25, 1986.

9. Portia, "The Mother of Aquarius Steps Down from Cosmic Levels," *Pearls of Wisdom,* vol. 31, no. 41, July 17, 1988.

10. El Morya, "Chela—Christed One—Guru: Offices on the Path of

the Individualization of the God Flame," *Pearls of Wisdom,* vol. 28, no. 11, March 17, 1985.

11. Archangel Jophiel and Archeia Hope, "Is Anything Too Hard for the Lord?" *Pearls of Wisdom,* vol. 32, no. 36, September 3, 1989.
12. Ibid.
13. John 14:15.
14. Elizabeth Clare Prophet and the Staff of Summit University, *Walking with the Master* (Corwin Springs, Mont.: The Summit Lighthouse Library, 2002), p. 8.
15. Elizabeth Clare Prophet, "Teachings of Jesus Christ on Your Path of Personal Christhood," June 27, 1993.
16. Ibid.
17. Ibid.
18. Omri-Tas, "Be the Spark that Ignites a Cosmos!" *Pearls of Wisdom,* vol. 31, no. 3, January 17, 1988.
19. Leto, "Become the Master!" *Pearls of Wisdom,* vol. 33, no. 45, November 18, 1990.
20. See "Momentum," in *The Lost Teachings of Jesus 1* (Corwin Springs, Mont.: Summit University Press, 1994), pp. 165–219.
21. See Jesus and Kuthumi, "Habit," in *Corona Class Lessons* (Corwin Springs, Mont.: Summit University Press, 1986), pp. 257–303.
22. Omri-Tas, "Be the Spark that Ignites a Cosmos!" *Pearls of Wisdom,* vol. 31, no. 3, January 17, 1988.
23. "Watch With Me" Jesus' Vigil of the Hours, released by Elizabeth Clare Prophet, is a worldwide service of prayers, affirmations and hymns, which in 1964 the Master called upon Keepers of the Flame to keep individually or in groups. The service was dictated by the Ascended Master Jesus Christ for the protection of the Christ consciousness in every son and daughter of God and in commemoration of the vigil the Master kept alone in the Garden of Gethsemane when he said: "Could ye not watch with me one hour?" Available in 44-page booklet and also on 90-min. audiocassette B87096.
24. Elizabeth Clare Prophet, "Teachings of Jesus Christ on Your Path of Personal Christhood," June 27, 1993.
25. Elizabeth Clare Prophet and the Staff of Summit University, *Walking with the Master,* ch. 9.
26. Gal. 6:4–5.

27. Elizabeth Clare Prophet and the Staff of Summit University, *Walking with the Master,* pp. 378, 379.

Section 6 · The Christ Flame in the Heart

1. *Saint Germain on Alchemy* (Corwin Springs, Mont.: Summit University Press, 1993), pp. 350–51.
2. Jer. 31:33–34; see 1 Kings 8:4–11; Paul's explanation of the first Covenant, Heb. 9; and the New Covenant, Heb. 8:10–13.
3. Matt. 23:37; Luke 13:34; 19:41.
4. John 1:6–14.
5. Ps. 8:5; Heb. 2:7.
6. Jesus Christ, "Place Your Attention on Your Threefold Flame," *Keepers of the Flame Lesson 9,* pp. 19–21.

Section 7 · The Mission of Jesus Christ...

1. For more information about the Keepers of the Flame Fraternity, contact Summit University Press.
2. Jesus Christ, "Ancient Records of Earth's Karma," *Keepers of the Flame Lesson 30,* pp. 19–22.
3. John 8:23, 44.
4. Matt. 13:24–30, 36–42.
5. Rev. 12:7–9.
6. See Elizabeth Clare Prophet, *Fallen Angels and the Origins of Evil* (Corwin Springs, Mont.: Summit University Press, 2000). Includes the text of the Book of Enoch, which tells the story of the fall of the Watchers.
7. Nephilim [Hebrew "those who fell" or "those who were cast down," from the Semitic root *naphal* 'to fall']: A biblical race of giants or demigods, referred to in Genesis 6:4 ("There were giants in the earth in those days..."); the fallen angels who were cast out of heaven into the earth (Rev. 12:7–9). Biblical scholar and orientalist Zecharia Sitchin concludes from his study of ancient Sumerian texts that the Nephilim were an extraterrestrial race who "fell" to earth (landed) in spacecraft 450,000 years ago. See *Fallen Angels and the Origins of Evil,* pp. 70–75.
8. *Laggards* is a term for those who lag behind the evolutions of their planets; specifically souls assigned to earth who had failed to fulfill their divine plan on schedule on their home star, Maldek, and have continued to lag behind their own God-

ordained destiny as well as that of the lifewaves of earth, among whom they continue to reembody. See Mark L. Prophet and Elizabeth Clare Prophet, *Climb the Highest Mountain: The Path of the Higher Self* (Corwin Springs, Mont.: Summit University Press, 1986), pp. 86, 93–103.

9. John 1:12.
10. Matt. 16:18, 19.
11. Jesus Christ, "Rise, Peter: Kill and Eat!" *Pearls of Wisdom,* vol. 29, no. 14, April 6, 1986.
12. John the Beloved, "Called to Be Apostles of God in Jesus Christ," *Pearls of Wisdom,* vol. 33, no. 38, September 30, 1990.
13. John 11:25.
14. John 11:26.
15. John 14:6.
16. Acts 16:31.
17. Deut. 6:4.
18. Jer. 23:1.
19. Jer. 23:3–4, 6.
20. John 1:12.
21. Jesus Christ, "You Can Become a Christ!" *Pearls of Wisdom,* vol. 26, no. 56, December 27, 1983.
22. John 14:6.
23. Matt. 19:17; Mark 10:18.
24. Jesus the Christ, "Place Your Attention on Your Threefold Flame," *Keepers of the Flame Lesson 9,* p. 19.
25. Matt. 28:18.
26. Phil. 2:8.
27. Luke 2:49.
28. Lord Maitreya, "The Mission of Jesus Christ," *Pearls of Wisdom,* vol. 27, no. 47a, September 26, 1984.

Section 8 · The Cosmic Christ

1. John Woodroffe, *The Garland of Letters: Studies in the Mantra-Sastra* (Madras, India: Ganesh & Co., 1979), p. 4.
2. John 1:4–18.
3. John 5:25.
4. Jesus Christ, "Christhood," *Pearls of Wisdom,* vol. 31, no. 21, May 22, 1988.
5. John 1:9.
6. John 12:35.

7. John 5:17, 18.

8. John 5:19–24.

9. John 14:8–15.

10. John 10:30.

11. John 10:38; 14:10, 11.

12. John 20:17.

13. Matt. 28:18.

14. Phil. 2:11; 1 John 4:15.

15. John 11:27.

16. John 1:1, 2.

17. Jesus Christ, "The Mystery School of Lord Maitreya," 1984 *Pearls of Wisdom*, Book I, Introduction I, pp. 2–3, *Pearls of Wisdom*, vol. 27, no. 36, July 8, 1984.

18. John 1:14.

19. 2 Cor. 6:2.

20. Jan Nattier, "The Meanings of the Maitreya Myth: A Typological Analysis," in *Maitreya, the Future Buddha*, ed. Alan Sponberg and Helen Hardacre (New York: Cambridge University Press, 1988), p. 39 n. 17.

Section 9 • The Second Coming

1. Luke 2:8–14.

2. Isa. 9:6.

3. Words by W. H. Neidlinger.

4. 1 Cor. 12:3.

5. Rev. 12:11.

6. Rev. 14:6.

7. Hilarion, "The Known God Whom I Declare to Be the I AM THAT I AM," *Pearls of Wisdom,* vol. 19, no. 42, October 17, 1976.

8. 1 Cor. 3:16.

9. *Lankavatara-sutra,* in Adrian Snodgrass, *The Symbolism of the Stupa* (Ithaca, N.Y.: Cornell Southeast Asia Program, 1985), pp. 196, 197; *Ratnagotravibhaga,* in Edward Conze, ed., *Buddhist Texts through the Ages* (1954: reprint, New York: Harper and Row, 1964), p. 181.

10. John 5:21, 25; Rom. 8:11.

11. Matt. 24:27–31; Mark 13:24–26; Luke 21:25–28; 1 Thess. 4:16, 17.

12. Rev. 1:7.

13. See Elizabeth Clare Prophet and the Staff of Summit University, *Walking with the Master,* ch. 1, 4, 5.

14. Matt. 26:26; Mark 14:22; Luke 22:19; 1 Cor. 11:24.

15. Elizabeth Clare Prophet and the Staff of Summit University, *Walking with the Master,* p. 145.

16. Lord Maitreya, "Welcome to the Mystery School!" *Pearls of Wisdom,* vol. 31, no. 6, February 7, 1988.

17. John 14:12.

18. Jesus Christ, "The Mystery School of Lord Maitreya," *Pearls of Wisdom,* vol. 27, no. 36, July 8, 1984.

19. Mark L. Prophet and Elizabeth Clare Prophet, *Morya: The Darjeeling Masters Speaks to His Chelas on the Quest for the Holy Grail* (Corwin Springs, Mont.: Summit University Press, 1983), p. 270.

20. Ibid., p. 328.

21. Sanat Kumara, "Preachers of the Acceptable Year of the Lord," *Pearls of Wisdom,* vol. 22, no. 36, September 9, 1979. Also published in *Sanat Kumara, The Opening of the Seventh Seal* (Corwin Springs, Mont.: The Summit Lighthouse Library, 2001), p. 184.

Section 10 · The Doctrine of Original Sin

1. *New Catholic Encyclopedia,* s.v. "Original Sin," p. 777.

2. Kenneth Scott Latourette, *A History of Christianity* (New York: Harper & Row, 1975), vol. I, p. 182.

3. Matt. 11:28.

4. Jesus, "The Zeal of My House," *Pearls of Wisdom,* vol. 31, no. 83, December 4, 1988.

5. John 9:4.

6. Ps. 51:5.

7. Jesus Christ, "The Office of Bride of Christ," *Pearls of Wisdom,* vol. 38, no. 25, June 11, 1995.

8. The Goddess of Liberty, April 1, 1962.

9. Mother Mary, October 26, 1977.

Section 11 · The Virgin Birth...

1. Luke 1:34.

2. Mark L. Prophet and Elizabeth Clare Prophet, *Morya I* (Corwin Springs, Mont.: The Summit Lighthouse Library, 2001), pp. 150–51.

3. Matt. 12:46–50.
4. Betrothal at the time of Jesus legally effected a marital relation-
    ship, as attested to in both the Old Testament and the Talmud.
    It was sealed when the husband to be paid the future bride's
    father or guardian a "bride price" as compensation for his loss.
    Thereafter she was in his power and considered him her "Baal,"
    i.e., lord, master, husband. The betrothal could only be repudi-
    ated by a bill of divorce. If the woman lay with another man it
    was considered adultery. If the man died the woman was con-
    sidered a widow and subject to the levirate. Thus marriage and
    betrothal carried similar rights and responsibilities.

    Biblical scholar William E. Phipps explains: "Within a short
    time after the betrothal covenant was completed the boy had the
    privilege and obligation of cohabitation with his spouse. In the
    case of the earliest tradition pertaining to Hebrew marriage cus-
    toms, there appears to have been only a few days lapse between
    the betrothal transaction and the cohabitation. The girl
    remained at the home of her father until the husband was ready
    to receive her. At that time there was usually a nuptial drinking
    party to celebrate the bride's transference to the groom's home.
    Intimate relations by betrothed couples were not prohibited in
    Jewish Scriptures. The Mishnah and the Talmud indicate that
    Palestinian Judaism showed considerable tolerance towards
    prenuptial unions in the era of the New Testament, and children
    conceived as a result were not stigmatized as illegitimate."
    (William E. Phipps, *Was Jesus Married?* [New York: Harper &
    Row, 1970], pp. 39–40.)
5. Matt. 1:18, 22–23.
6. Some scholars believe that the infancy narratives in Matthew
    and Luke may not be part of the original texts, but additions by
    later authors. The baptism of Jesus is the starting point of the
    earliest preaching of the Church as seen in the Pauline Epistles
    and Acts. Mark begins there and so does John, following a brief
    introductory passage on the preexistence of the Word. Matthew
    and Luke deal with Jesus' birth in the infancy narratives, but do
    not mention his birth again in their Gospels. If the infancy nar-
    ratives (which were probably composed after the narratives of
    Jesus' ministry) are taken as a foreword to the Gospels of
    Matthew and Luke, then these Gospels are seen to also begin
    with the baptism of Jesus.

Apart from their introductory placement, the events of the infancy narratives seem disconnected from Matthew and Luke, and none of the characters in their writings appears to have any knowledge of the miraculous circumstances of Jesus' birth; even his sisters, brothers and mother appear unaware of Jesus' virginal conception. Furthermore, Mark 3:20–21, suggests that they saw him more like themselves: "He went home again, and once more such a crowd collected that they could not even have a meal. When his relatives heard of this, they set out to take charge of him, convinced he was out of his mind" (JB). If they were aware of his miraculous conception, it seems unlikely they would have thought his behavior out of character with his mission.

7. Raymond E. Brown, *The Birth of the Messiah,* (Garden City, N.Y.: Doubleday & Co., 1977), p. 132.
8. William E. Phipps, *Was Jesus Married?* pp. 40–41.
9. Ibid., pp. 41–42.
10. Ibid., p. 43.
11. Mother Mary, "Come, My Child, Bear the Burden of Light," September 19, 1976.
12. Mother Mary, "Go Forth to Challenge the Night!" *My Soul Doth Magnify the Lord!* (Corwin Springs, Mont.: Summit University Press, 1986), p. 317.

Section 12 • Vicarious Atonement...

1. Gen. 22:1–13.
2. 1 Sam. 15:22.
3. Rom. 12:1.
4. Matt. 3:17; Mark 1:11; Luke 3:22.
5. The Maha Chohan, *Keepers of the Flame Lesson 2,* p. 10.
6. Gal. 6:5.
7. Matt. 11:30.
8. Matt. 9:2; John 5:14.
9. Saint Germain, "Verity," *Keepers of the Flame Lesson 19,* pp. 34, 36–37.
10. See Mark L. Prophet and Elizabeth Clare Prophet, *The Lost Teachings of Jesus 4* (Corwin Springs, Mont.: Summit University Press, 1993), pp. 7–11; and Edgar Evans Cayce, *Edgar Cayce on Atlantis,* ed. Hugh Lynn Cayce (New York: Warner Books, 1968), pp. 60–61, 68–72, 99–107, 131–32.
11. Lev. 18:21; 20:2–5; Deut. 12:31; 18:10; 2 Kings 16:3; 17:17;

21:6; 23:10; 2 Chron. 28:3; 33:6; Ps. 106:37–38.
12. Jer. 7:31, 32; 19:1–6; 32:35; Ezek. 16:20, 21, 36; 20:26, 31; 23:37–39; Isa. 57:5; Amos 5:25, 26; Mic. 6:7.
13. Matt. 26:28; John 1:29; 1 Pet. 1:19; Rev. 7:14; 12:11.
14. Heb. 9:22.
15. Ps. 51:1, 9; Isa. 43:25; 44:22; Jer. 31:34; Acts 3:19; Heb. 8:12; 10:17.
16. Eph. 4:22–24; Col. 3:9–10; Rom. 6:6.
17. John 14:6.
18. John 7:38.
19. Matt. 15:24.
20. Matt. 11:30.
21. Jesus and Kuthumi, *Corona Class Lessons* (Corwin Springs, Mont.: Summit University Press, 1986), pp. 178–83.
22. John 6:53.
23. Rom. 5:17–19.
24. Gen. 2:15–17; 3:1–24.
35. Saint Germain, "Verity," *Keepers of the Flame Lesson 19*, pp. 37–38.

Section 13 · The Crucifixion

1. Saint Germain, "Verity," *Keepers of the Flame Lesson 19*, pp. 33–34.
2. Luke 9:23.
3. 1 Cor. 15:31.
4. Mark 15:34.
5. Luke 23:28.
6. Luke 2:49.
7. John 12:32.
8. 1 John 3:2.
9. Luke 22:53.
10. See, for example, Matt. 3:1–12; 23:27–36; Luke 11:52.
11. John 18:28–40, 19:1–22.
12. Matt. 27:51; Mark 15:38.
13. John 12:24.
14. Matt.11:30.
15. 2 Cor. 6:17.
16. John the Beloved, "The Initiation of the Crucifixion," April 12, 1974.
17. John 1:9.

18. John the Beloved, "The Initiation of the Crucifixion," April 12, 1974.
19. John 11:25; John 14:6; Jesus Christ, "Renewal and Commemoration," April 6, 1969.
20. Matt. 24:22; John the Beloved, "The Initiation of the Crucifixion." April 12, 1974.
21. Luke 23:46.
22. Matt. 17:1–13; Mark 9:2–13; Luke 9:28–36.
23. Saint Thérèse of Lisieux, "Outside the Church," Part II, *Pearls of Wisdom*, vol. 31, no. 39, July 13, 1988.
24. John 19:30.

Section 14 • The Dark Night of the Soul...

1. *The Collected Works of St. John of the Cross*, trans. Kieran Kavanaugh and Otilio Rodriguez (Washington, D.C.: ICS Publications, 1979), p. 311.
2. Jonah 2:1–3.
3. *The Collected Works of St. John of the Cross*, p. 337.
4. Elizabeth Clare Prophet, *Vials of the Seven Last Plagues* (Corwin Springs, Mont.: Summit University Press, 1980), pp. 106–07.

Section 15 • The Fourteen Stations of the Cross

1. Matt. 6:34.
2. Luke 22:42.
3. Luke 23:28.
4. John 15:20.
5. Luke 23:43.
6. Matt. 28:18.
7. Gal. 2:20.

Section 16 • The Mystery of the Fifteenth Rosary...

1. Gen. 18:14; Jer. 32:17, 27.
2. Matt. 28:18.
3. Matt. 9:37, 38; Luke 10:2.
4. Gen 22:1–18.
5. John 6:35; Matt. 26:26; 13:33; Rev. 2:17.
6. Mother Mary, "The Gift of a Mother's Heart: The Mystery of the Fifteenth Rosary," *Pearls of Wisdom*, vol. 23, no. 27, July 6, 1980.

Section 17 · The Risen Christ

1. John 20:17.
2. Mother Mary, *Pearls of Wisdom,* vol. 9, no. 18, May 1, 1966.
3. Serapis Bey, "The Very First Steps of the Law," *Pearls of Wisdom,* vol. 27, no. 29, June 3, 1984.
4. Jesus Christ, "My Victory, Your Victory," *Pearls of Wisdom,* vol. 27, no. 31, June 5, 1984.
5. John 14:16–18, 26; 15:26; 16:7–15.
6. John 16:2.
7. James 5:16.
8. El Morya, "Message to America on the Mission of Jesus Christ," *Pearls of Wisdom,* vol. 27, no. 47, September 23, 1984.

Section 18 · Christ in Birmingham

1. Matt. 7:12.
2. Mark 16:17–18.
3. John 8:12; Matt. 5:14.
4. 1 Cor. 14:8.
5. James 2:18, 20.
6. Phil. 2:12–13.
7. 1 Cor. 15:28.
8. John 14:1.
9. Matt. 19:16–17; Mark 10:18; Luke 18:19.
10. John 10:30.
11. Gen. 1:1–3.
12. Eph. 2:1.
13. Rom. 10:14.
14. John 1:1, 3.
15. John 14:11, 20.
16. 1 Cor. 12:3.
17. John 14:12.

Glossary

Terms set in italics are defined elsewhere in the glossary.

Adept. An initiate of the *Great White Brotherhood* of a high degree of attainment, especially in the control of *Matter,* physical forces, nature spirits and bodily functions; fully the alchemist undergoing advanced initiations of the *sacred fire* on the path of the *ascension.*

Akashic records. The impressions of all that has ever transpired in the physical universe, recorded in the etheric substance and dimension known by the Sanskrit term *akasha.* These records can be read by those with developed *soul* faculties.

Alchemical marriage. The soul's permanent bonding to the *Holy Christ Self,* in preparation for the permanent fusing to the *I AM Presence* in the ritual of the ascension. See also *Soul; Secret chamber of the heart.*

All-Seeing Eye of God. See *Cyclopea.*

Alpha and Omega. The divine wholeness of the Father-Mother God affirmed as "the beginning and the ending" by the Lord *Christ* in Revelation (Rev. 1:8, 11; 21:6; 22:13). Ascended *twin flames* of the *Cosmic Christ* consciousness who hold the balance of the masculine-feminine polarity of the Godhead in the *Great Central Sun* of cosmos. Thus through the *Universal Christ* (the *Word* incarnate), the Father is the origin and the Mother is the fulfillment of the cycles of God's consciousness expressed throughout the *Spirit-Matter* creation. See also *Mother.*

Ancient of Days. See *Sanat Kumara.*

Angel. A divine spirit, a herald or messenger sent by God to deliver his *Word* to his children. A ministering spirit sent forth to tend the heirs of *Christ*—to comfort, protect, guide, strengthen, teach, counsel and warn. The fallen angels, also called the dark ones, are those angels who followed Lucifer in the Great Rebellion, whose consciousness therefore "fell" to lower levels of vibration. They were "cast out into the earth" by Archangel Michael (Rev. 12:7–12)—constrained by the karma of their disobedience to God and his Christ to take on and evolve through dense physical bodies. Here they walk about, sowing seeds of unrest and rebellion among men and nations.

Antahkarana. The web of life. The net of *Light* spanning *Spirit* and *Matter,* connecting and sensitizing the whole of creation within itself and to the heart of God.

Archangel. The highest rank in the orders of *angels.* Each of the s*even rays* has a presiding Archangel who, with his divine complement or *Archeia,* embodies the God consciousness of the ray and directs the bands of angels serving in their command on that ray. The Archangels and Archeiai of the rays and the locations of their *retreats* are as follows:

First ray, blue, Archangel Michael and Faith, Banff, near Lake Louise, Alberta, Canada.

Second ray, yellow, Archangel Jophiel and Christine, south of the Great Wall near Lanchow, north central China.

Third ray, petal pink, deep rose and ruby, Archangel Chamuel and Charity, St. Louis, Missouri, U.S.A.

Fourth ray, white and mother-of-pearl, Archangel Gabriel and Hope, between Sacramento and Mount Shasta, California, U.S.A.

Fifth ray, green, Archangel Raphael and Mary, Fátima, Portugal.

Sixth ray, purple and gold with ruby flecks, Archangel Uriel and Aurora, Tatra Mountains, south of Cracow, Poland.

Seventh ray, violet and purple, Archangel Zadkiel and Holy Amethyst, Cuba.

Archeia (pl. **Archeiai**). Divine complement and *twin flame* of an *Archangel.*

Ascended Master. One who, through *Christ* and the putting on of that mind which was in Christ Jesus (Phil. 2:5), has mastered time and space and in the process gained the mastery of the self in the *four lower bodies* and the four quadrants of *Matter,* in the *chakras* and the balanced *threefold flame.* An Ascended Master has also trans- muted at least 51 percent of his karma, fulfilled his divine plan, and taken the initiations of the ruby ray unto the ritual of the *ascension*—acceleration by the *sacred fire* into the Presence of the I AM THAT I AM (the *I AM Presence*). Ascended Masters inhabit the planes of *Spirit*—the kingdom of God (God's consciousness)— and they may teach unascended souls in an *etheric temple* or in the cities on the *etheric plane* (the kingdom of heaven).

Ascension. The ritual whereby the *soul* reunites with the *Spirit* of the living God, the *I AM Presence.* The ascension is the culmination of the soul's God-victorious sojourn in time and space. It is the process whereby the soul, having balanced her karma and fulfilled her divine plan, merges first with the Christ consciousness and then with the living Presence of the I AM THAT I AM. Once the ascension has taken place, the soul—the corruptible aspect of being—becomes the incorruptible one, a permanent atom in the Body of God. See also *Alchemical marriage.*

Aspirant. One who aspires; specifically, one who aspires to reunion with God through the ritual of the *ascension.* One who aspires to overcome the conditions and limitations of time and space to fulfill the cycles of karma and one's reason for being through the sacred labor.

Astral plane. A frequency of time and space beyond the physical, yet below the mental, corresponding to the *emotional body* of man and the collective unconscious of the race; the repository of mankind's thoughts and feelings, conscious and unconscious. Because the astral plane has been muddied by impure human thought and feeling, the term "astral" is often used in a negative context to refer to that which is impure or psychic.

Astrea. Feminine Elohim of the Fourth Ray, the ray of purity, who works to cut *souls* free from the *astral plane* and the projections of the dark forces. See also *Elohim; Seven rays.*

Atman. The spark of the divine within, identical with *Brahman;* the ultimate essence of the universe as well as the essence of the indi- vidual.

AUM. See *OM.*

Avatar. The incarnation of the *Word.* The Avatar of an age is the *Christ,* the incarnation of the Son of God. The *Manus* may designate numerous Christed ones—those endued with an extraordinary *Light*—to go forth as world teachers and wayshowers. The Christed ones demonstrate in a given epoch the Law of the *Logos,* stepped down through the Manu(s) and the Avatar(s) until it is made flesh through their own word and work—to be ultimately victorious in its fulfillment in all souls of Light sent forth to conquer time and space in that era.

Bodhisattva. (Sanskrit, 'a being of *bodhi* or enlightenment.') A being destined for enlightenment, or one whose energy and power is directed toward enlightenment. A Bodhisattva is destined to become a *Buddha* but has forgone the bliss of *nirvana* with a vow to save all children of God on earth. An *Ascended Master* or an unascended master may be a Bodhisattva.

Brahman. Ultimate Reality; the Absolute.

Buddha. (From Sanskrit *budh* 'awake, know, perceive.') "The enlightened one." Buddha denotes an office in the spiritual *Hierarchy* of worlds that is attained by passing certain initiations of the *sacred fire,* including those of the *seven rays* of the Holy Spirit and of the five secret *rays,* the raising of the feminine ray (sacred fire of the *Kundalini*) and the "mastery of the seven in the seven multiplied by the power of the ten."

Gautama attained the enlightenment of the Buddha twenty-five centuries ago, a path he had pursued through many previous embodiments culminating in his forty-nine-day meditation under the Bo tree. Hence he is called Gautama, the Buddha. He holds the office of *Lord of the World,* sustaining, by his *Causal Body* and *threefold flame,* the divine spark and consciousness in the evolutions of earth approaching the path of personal Christhood. His aura of love/wisdom ensouling the planet issues from his incomparable devotion to the Divine *Mother.* He is the Hierarch of Shamballa, the original *retreat* of *Sanat Kumara* now on the *etheric plane* over the Gobi Desert.

Lord Maitreya, the *Cosmic Christ,* has also passed the initiations of the Buddha. He is the long-awaited Coming Buddha who has come to the fore to teach all who have departed from the way of the Great *Guru,* Sanat Kumara, from whose lineage both he and Gautama descended. In the history of the planet, there have been numerous Buddhas who have served the evolutions of mankind through the steps and stages of the path of the *Bodhisattva*. In the East Jesus is referred to as the Buddha Issa. He is the World Saviour by the love/wisdom of the Godhead.

Caduceus. The Kundalini. See *Sacred fire.*

Causal Body. Seven concentric spheres of *Light* surrounding the *I AM Presence*. The spheres of the Causal Body contain the records of the virtuous acts we have performed to the glory of God and the blessing of man through our many incarnations on earth. See also *Chart of Your Divine Self.*

Central Sun. A vortex of energy, physical or spiritual, central to systems of worlds that it thrusts from, or gathers unto, itself by the Central Sun Magnet. Whether in the *microcosm* or the *Macrocosm*, the Central Sun is the principal energy source, vortex, or nexus of energy interchange in atoms, cells, man (the heart center), amidst plant life and the core of the earth. The Great Central Sun is the center of cosmos; the point of integration of the *Spirit-Matter* cosmos; the point of origin of all physical-spiritual creation; the nucleus, or white-fire core, of the *Cosmic Egg.* (The God Star, Sirius, is the focus of the Great Central Sun in our sector of the galaxy.) The Sun behind the sun is the spiritual Cause behind the physical effect we see as our own physical sun and all other stars and star systems, seen or unseen, including the Great Central Sun.

Chakra. (Sanskrit, 'wheel, disc, circle.') Center of *Light* anchored in the *etheric body* and governing the flow of energy to the *four lower bodies* of man. There are seven major chakras corresponding to the *seven rays,* five minor chakras corresponding to the five secret rays, and a total of 144 Light centers in the body of man.

Chart of Your Divine Self. There are three figures represented in the Chart. The upper figure is the *I AM Presence*, the I AM THAT I AM, the individualization of God's Presence for every son and daughter of the Most High. The Divine Monad consists of the I AM Presence surrounded by the spheres (color rings) of *Light* that make up the body of First Cause, or *Causal Body.*

    The middle figure in the Chart is the Mediator between God and man, called the *Holy Christ Self*, the *Real Self* or the *Christ* consciousness. It has also been referred to as the Higher Mental Body or one's Higher Consciousness. This Inner Teacher overshadows the lower self, which consists of the *soul* evolving through the four planes of *Matter* using the vehicles of the *four lower bodies*—the *etheric* (memory) *body*, the *mental body*, the *emotional* (desire) *body*, and the *physical body*—to balance karma and fulfill the divine plan.

The three figures of the Chart correspond to the Trinity of Father, who always includes the *Mother* (the upper figure), Son (the middle figure) and Holy Spirit (the lower figure). The latter is the intended temple of the Holy Spirit, whose *sacred fire* is indicated in the enfolding *violet flame*. The lower figure corresponds to you as a disciple on the *Path*.

The lower figure is surrounded by a *tube of light*, which is projected from the heart of the I AM Presence in answer to your call. It is a cylinder of white light that sustains a forcefield of protection twenty-four-hours a day, so long as you guard it in harmony. The *threefold flame* of life is the divine spark sent from the I AM Presence as the gift of life, consciousness and free will. It is sealed in the *secret chamber of the heart* that through the love, wisdom and power of the Godhead anchored therein the *soul* may fulfill her reason for being in the physical plane. Also called the Christ flame and the Liberty flame, or fleur-de-lis, it is the spark of a man's divinity, his potential for Christhood.

The silver cord (or *crystal cord*) is the stream of life, or *lifestream*, that descends from the heart of the I AM Presence to the Holy Christ Self to nourish and sustain (through the *chakras*) the soul and its vehicles of expression in time and space. It is over this 'umbilical cord' that the energy of the Presence flows, entering the being of man at the crown and giving impetus for the pulsation of the threefold flame as well as the physical heartbeat.

When a round of the soul's incarnation in Matter-form is finished, the I AM Presence withdraws the silver cord (Eccles. 12:6), whereupon the threefold flame returns to the level of the Christ, and the soul clothed in the etheric garment gravitates to the highest level of her attainment, where she is schooled between embodiments until her final incarnation when the Great Law decrees she shall go out no more.

The dove of the Holy Spirit descending from the heart of the Father is shown just above the head of the Christ. When the son of man puts on and becomes the Christ consciousness as Jesus did, he merges with the Holy Christ Self. The Holy Spirit is upon him, and the words of the Father, the beloved I AM Presence, are spoken: "This is my beloved Son, in whom I AM well pleased" (Matt. 3:17).

Chela. (Hindi *celā* from Sanskrit *ceṭa* 'slave,' i.e., 'servant.') In India, a disciple of a religious teacher or *guru*. A term used generally to refer to a student of the *Ascended Masters* and their teachings. Specifically, a student of more than ordinary self-discipline and devotion initiated by an Ascended Master and serving the cause of the *Great White Brotherhood*.

Chohan. (Tibetan, 'lord' or 'master'; a chief.) Each of the seven *rays* has a Chohan who focuses the *Christ* consciousness of the ray. Having ensouled and demonstrated the law of the ray throughout numerous incarnations, and having taken initiations both before and after the *ascension,* the candidate is appointed to the office of Chohan by the Maha Chohan (the "Great Lord"), who is himself the representative of the Holy Spirit on all the rays. The names of the Chohans of the Rays (each one an *Ascended Master* representing one of the seven rays to earth's evolutions) and the locations of their physical/etheric focuses are as follows:

First ray, El Morya, Retreat of God's Will, Darjeeling, India

Second ray, Lanto, Royal Teton Retreat, Grand Teton, Jackson Hole, Wyoming, U.S.A.

Third ray, Paul the Venetian, Château de Liberté, southern France, with a focus of the *threefold flame* at the Washington Monument, Washington, D.C., U.S.A.

Fourth ray, Serapis Bey, the Ascension Temple and Retreat at Luxor, Egypt

Fifth ray, Hilarion (the apostle Paul), Temple of Truth, Crete

Sixth ray, Nada, Arabian Retreat, Saudi Arabia

Seventh ray, Saint Germain, Royal Teton Retreat, Grand Teton, Wyoming, U.S.A.; Cave of Symbols, Table Mountain, Wyoming, U.S.A. Saint Germain also works out of the Great Divine Director's focuses—the Cave of Light in India and the Rakoczy Mansion in Transylvania, where Saint Germain presides as Hierarch.

Christ. (From the Greek *Christos* 'anointed.') Messiah (Hebrew, Aramaic 'anointed'); 'Christed one,' one fully endued and infilled—anointed—by the *Light* (the Son) of God. The *Word,* the *Logos,* the Second Person of the Trinity. In the Hindu Trinity of Brahma,

Vishnu and Shiva, the term "Christ" corresponds to or is the incarnation of Vishnu, the Preserver; *Avatâra*, God-man, Dispeller of Darkness, *Guru*.

The term "Christ" or "Christed one" also denotes an office in *Hierarchy* held by those who have attained self-mastery on the *seven rays* and the seven *chakras* of the Holy Spirit. Christ-mastery includes the balancing of the *threefold flame*—the divine attributes of power, wisdom and love—for the harmonization of consciousness and the implementation of the mastery of the seven rays in the chakras and in the *four lower bodies* through the Mother flame (the raised *Kundalini*).

At the hour designated for the *ascension*, the *soul* thus anointed raises the spiral of the threefold flame from beneath the feet through the entire form for the transmutation of every atom and cell of her being, consciousness and world. The saturation and acceleration of the *four lower bodies* and the soul by this transfiguring Light of the Christ flame take place in part during the initiation of the *transfiguration*, increasing through the resurrection and gaining full intensity in the ritual of the ascension.

Christ Self. The individualized focus of "the only begotten of the Father, full of grace and Truth." The *Universal Christ* individualized as the true identity of the *soul*; the *Real Self* of every man, woman and child, to which the soul must rise. The Christ Self is the Mediator between a man and his God. He is a man's own personal teacher, master and prophet.

Color rays. See *Seven rays*.

Cosmic Being. (1) An *Ascended Master* who has attained cosmic consciousness and ensouls the *light*/energy/consciousness of many worlds and systems of worlds across the galaxies to the Sun behind the *Great Central Sun*; or, (2) A being of God who has never descended below the level of the *Christ*, has never taken physical embodiment, and has never made human karma.

Cosmic Christ. An office in *Hierarchy* currently held by Lord Maitreya under Gautama *Buddha*, the *Lord of the World*. Also used as a synonym for *Universal Christ*.

Cosmic Clock. The science of charting the cycles of the *soul's* karma and initiations on the twelve lines of the Clock under the *Twelve Hierarchies of the Sun*. Taught by Mother Mary to Mark and

Elizabeth Prophet for sons and daughters of God returning to the Law of the One and to their point of origin beyond the worlds of form and lesser causation.

Cosmic Egg. The spiritual-material universe, including a seemingly endless chain of galaxies, star systems, worlds known and unknown, whose center, or white-fire core, is called the *Great Central Sun*. The Cosmic Egg has both a spiritual and a material center. Although we may discover and observe the Cosmic Egg from the standpoint of our physical senses and perspective, all of the dimensions of *Spirit* can also be known and experienced within the Cosmic Egg. For the God who created the Cosmic Egg and holds it in the hollow of his hand is also the God flame expanding hour by hour within his very own sons and daughters. The Cosmic Egg represents the bounds of man's habitation in this cosmic cycle. Yet, as God is everywhere throughout and beyond the Cosmic Egg, so by his Spirit within us we daily awaken to new dimensions of being, soul-satisfied in conformity with his likeness.

Cosmic Law. The Law that governs mathematically, yet with the spontaneity of Mercy's flame, all manifestation throughout the cosmos in the planes of *Spirit* and *Matter*.

Crystal cord. The stream of God's *Light*, life and consciousness that nourishes and sustains the *soul* and her *four lower bodies*. Also called the silver cord (Eccles. 12:6). See also *Chart of Your Divine Self*.

Cyclopea. Masculine Elohim of the fifth ray, also known as the All-Seeing Eye of God or as the Great Silent Watcher. See also *Elohim; Seven rays*.

Deathless solar body. See *Seamless garment*.

Decree. A dynamic form of spoken prayer used by students of the *Ascended Masters* to direct God's *Light* into individual and world conditions. The decree may be short or long and is usually marked by a formal preamble and a closing or acceptance. It is the authoritative *Word* of God spoken in man in the name of the *I AM Presence* and the living *Christ* to bring about constructive change on earth through the will of God. The decree is the birthright of the sons and daughters of God, the "Command ye me" of Isaiah 45:11, the original fiat of the Creator: "Let there be light: and there was light" (Gen. 1:3). It is written in the Book of Job, "Thou shalt decree a thing, and it shall be established unto thee: and the light shall shine upon thy ways" (Job 22:28).

Dictation. A message from an *Ascended Master,* an *Archangel* or another advanced spiritual being delivered through the agency of the Holy Spirit by a *Messenger* of the *Great White Brotherhood.*

Divine Monad. See *Chart of Your Divine Self; I AM Presence.*

Electronic Presence. A duplicate of the *I AM Presence* of an *Ascended Master.*

Elohim. (Hebrew; plural of *Eloah,* 'God.') The name of God used in the first verse of the Bible: "In the beginning God created the heaven and the earth." The Seven Mighty Elohim and their feminine counterparts are the builders of form. They are the "seven spirits of God" named in Revelation 4:5 and the "morning stars" that sang together in the beginning, as the Lord revealed them to Job (Job 38:7). In the order of *Hierarchy,* the Elohim and *Cosmic Beings* carry the greatest concentration, the highest vibration of *Light* that we can comprehend in our present state of evolution. Serving directly under the Elohim are the four hierarchs of the elements, who have dominion over the elementals—the gnomes, salamanders, sylphs and undines.

Following are the names of the Seven Elohim and their divine complements, the ray they serve on and the location of their etheric *retreat:*

First ray, Hercules and Amazonia, Half Dome, Sierra Nevada, Yosemite National Park, California, U.S.A.

Second ray, Apollo and Lumina, western Lower Saxony, Germany

Third ray, Heros and Amora, Lake Winnipeg, Manitoba, Canada

Fourth ray, Purity and Astrea, near Gulf of Archangel, southeast arm of White Sea, Russia

Fifth ray, Cyclopea and Virginia, Altai Range where China, Siberia and Mongolia meet, near Tabun Bogdo

Sixth ray, Peace and Aloha, Hawaiian Islands

Seventh ray, Arcturus and Victoria, near Luanda, Angola, Africa

Emotional body. One of the *four lower bodies* of man, corresponding to the water element and the third quadrant of *Matter;* the vehicle of the desires and feelings of God made manifest in the being of man. Also called the astral body, the desire body or the feeling body.

Entity. A conglomerate of misqualified energy or disembodied individuals who have chosen to embody evil. Entities that are focuses of sinister forces may attack disembodied as well as embodied individuals.

Etheric body. One of the *four lower bodies* of man, corresponding to the fire element and the first quadrant of *Matter;* called the envelope of the *soul,* holding the blueprint of the divine plan and the image of *Christ*-perfection to be outpictured in the world of form. Also called the memory body.

Etheric octave or etheric plane. The highest plane in the dimension of *Matter;* a plane that is as concrete and real as the physical plane (and even more so) but is experienced through the senses of the *soul* in a dimension and a consciousness beyond physical awareness. This is the plane on which the *akashic records* of mankind's entire evolution register individually and collectively. It is the world of *Ascended Masters* and their *retreats,* etheric cities of *Light* where *souls* of a higher order of evolution abide between embodiments. It is the plane of Reality.

The lower *etheric plane,* which overlaps the astral/mental/physical belts, is contaminated by these lower worlds occupied by the false hierarchy and the mass consciousness it controls.

Etheric temple. See *Retreat.*

Fallen angels. See *Angels.*

Father-Mother God. See *Alpha and Omega.*

Four Cosmic Forces. The four beasts seen by Saint John and other seers as the lion, the calf (or ox), the man and the flying eagle (Rev. 4:6–8). They serve directly under the Elohim and govern all of the Matter cosmos. They are transformers of the Infinite Light unto souls evolving in the finite. See also *Elohim.*

Four lower bodies. Four sheaths of four distinct frequencies that surround the *soul* (the physical, emotional, mental and etheric bodies), providing vehicles for the soul in her journey through time and space. The etheric sheath, highest in vibration, is the gateway to the three higher bodies: the *Christ Self,* the *I AM Presence* and the *Causal Body.* See also *Physical body; Emotional body; Mental body; Etheric body.*

Great Central Sun. See *Central Sun.*

Great Hub. See *Central Sun.*

Great White Brotherhood. A spiritual order of Western saints and Eastern adepts who have reunited with the *Spirit* of the living God; the heavenly hosts. They have transcended the cycles of karma and rebirth and ascended (accelerated) into that higher reality that is the eternal abode of the soul. The *Ascended Masters* of the Great White Brotherhood, united for the highest purposes of the brotherhood of man under the Fatherhood of God, have risen in every age from every culture and religion to inspire creative achievement in education, the arts and sciences, God-government and the abundant life through the economies of the nations. The word "white" refers not to race but to the aura (halo) of white *Light* surrounding their forms. The Brotherhood also includes in its ranks certain unascended *chelas* of the Ascended Masters.

Guru. (Sanskrit.) A personal religious teacher and spiritual guide; one of high attainment. A guru may be unascended or ascended.

Hierarchy. The universal chain of individualized God-free beings fulfilling the attributes and aspects of God's infinite Selfhood. Included in the cosmic hierarchical scheme are *Solar Logoi, Elohim,* Sons and Daughters of God, ascended and unascended masters with their circles of *chelas, Cosmic Beings,* the *Twelve Hierarchies of the Sun, Archangels* and *angels* of the *sacred fire,* children of the *Light,* nature spirits (called elementals) and *twin flames* of the *Alpha/Omega* polarity sponsoring planetary and galactic systems.

This universal order of the Father's own Self-expression is the means whereby God in the *Great Central Sun* steps down the Presence and power of his universal being/consciousness in order that succeeding evolutions in time and space, from the least unto the greatest, might come to know the wonder of his love. The level of one's spiritual/physical attainment—measured by one's balanced self-awareness "hid with *Christ* in God" and demonstrating his Law, by his love, in the *Spirit/Matter* cosmos—is the criterion establishing one's placement on this ladder of life called Hierarchy.

Higher Mental Body. See *Chart of Your Divine Self.*

Higher Self. The *I AM Presence;* the *Christ Self;* the exalted aspect of selfhood. Used in contrast to the term "lower self," or "little self," which indicates the *soul* that went forth from and may elect by free will to return to the Divine Whole through the realization of the oneness of the self in God. Higher consciousness.

Holy Christ Self. See *Christ Self.*

Human monad. The entire forcefield of self; the interconnecting spheres of influences—hereditary, environmental, karmic—which make up that self-awareness that identifies itself as human. The reference point of lesser- or non-awareness out of which all mankind must evolve to the realization of the *Real Self* as the *Christ Self.*

I AM Presence. The I AM THAT I AM (Exod. 3:13–15); the individualized Presence of God focused for each individual *soul.* The God-identity of the individual; the Divine Monad; the individual Source. The origin of the soul focused in the planes of *Spirit* just above the physical form; the personification of the God flame for the individual. See also *Chart of Your Divine Self.*

I AM THAT I AM. See *I AM Presence.*

Kali Yuga. (Sanskrit.) Term in Hindu mystic philosophy for the last and worst of the four yugas (world ages), characterized by strife, discord and moral deterioration.

Karmic Board. See *Lords of Karma.*

Keepers of the Flame Fraternity. Founded in 1961 by Saint Germain, an organization of *Ascended Masters* and their *chelas* who vow to keep the flame of life on earth and to support the activities of the *Great White Brotherhood* in the establishment of their community and mystery school and in the dissemination of their teachings. Keepers of the Flame receive graded lessons in *cosmic law* dictated by the *Ascended Masters* to their *Messengers* Mark and Elizabeth Prophet.

Kundalini. See *Sacred fire.*

Lifestream. The stream of life that comes forth from the one Source, from the *I AM Presence* in the planes of *Spirit,* and descends to the planes of *Matter* where it manifests as the *threefold flame* anchored in the heart *chakra* for the sustainment of the *soul* in Matter and the nourishment of the *four lower bodies.* Used to denote souls evolving as individual "lifestreams" and hence synonymous with the term "individual." Denotes the ongoing nature of the individual through cycles of individualization.

Light. The energy of God; the potential of the *Christ.* As the personification of *Spirit,* the term "Light" can be used synonymously with the terms "God" and "Christ." As the essence of Spirit, it is synonymous with *"sacred fire."* It is the emanation of the *Great Central Sun* and the individualized *I AM Presence*—and the Source of all life.

Logos. (Greek, 'word, speech, reason.') The divine wisdom manifest in the creation. According to ancient Greek philosophy, the Logos is the controlling principle in the universe. The Book of John identifies the *Word,* or Logos, with Jesus Christ: "And the Word was made flesh, and dwelt among us" (John 1:14). Hence, Jesus Christ is seen as the embodiment of divine reason, the Word Incarnate.

Lord of the World. *Sanat Kumara* held the office of Lord of the World (referred to as "God of the earth" in Rev. 11:4) for tens of thousands of years. Gautama Buddha recently succeeded Sanat Kumara and now holds this office. His is the highest governing office of the spiritual *Hierarchy* for the planet—and yet Lord Gautama is truly the most humble among the *Ascended Masters.* At inner levels, he sustains the *threefold flame,* the divine spark, for those *lifestreams* who have lost the direct contact with their *I AM Presence* and who have made so much negative karma as to be unable to magnetize sufficient *Light* from the Godhead to sustain their *soul's* physical incarnation on earth. Through a filigree thread of Light connecting his heart with the hearts of all God's children, Lord Gautama nourishes the flickering flame of life that ought to burn upon the altar of each heart with a greater magnitude of love, wisdom and power, fed by each one's own *Christ* consciousness.

Lords of Karma. The Ascended Beings who comprise the Karmic Board. Their names and the *rays* that they represent on the board are as follows: first ray, the Great Divine Director; second ray, the Goddess of Liberty; third ray, the Ascended Lady Master Nada; fourth ray, the *Elohim Cyclopea;* fifth ray, Pallas Athena, Goddess of Truth; sixth ray, Portia, Goddess of Justice; seventh ray, Kuan Yin, Goddess of Mercy. The Buddha Vairochana also sits on the Karmic Board.

The Lords of Karma dispense justice to this system of worlds, adjudicating karma, mercy and judgment on behalf of every *lifestream*. All *souls* must pass before the Karmic Board before and after each incarnation on earth, receiving their assignment and karmic allotment for each lifetime beforehand and the review of their performance at its conclusion. Through the Keeper of the Scrolls and the recording *angels*, the Lords of Karma have access to the complete records of every lifestream's incarnations on earth. They determine who shall embody, as well as when and where. They assign souls to families and communities, measuring out the weights of karma that must be balanced as the "jot and tittle" of the Law. The Karmic Board, acting in consonance with the individual *I AM Presence* and *Christ Self*, determines when the soul has earned the right to be free from the wheel of karma and the round of rebirth.

The Lords of Karma meet at the Royal Teton Retreat twice yearly, at winter and summer solstice, to review petitions from unascended mankind and to grant dispensations for their assistance.

Macrocosm. (Greek, 'great world.') The larger cosmos; the entire warp and woof of creation, which we call the *Cosmic Egg*. Also used to contrast man as the microcosm ('little world') against the backdrop of the larger world in which he lives. See also *Microcosm*.

Mantra. A mystical formula or invocation; a word or formula, often in Sanskrit, to be recited or sung for the purpose of intensifying the action of the *Spirit* of God in man. A form of prayer consisting of a word or a group of words that is chanted over and over again to magnetize a particular aspect of the Deity or of a being who has actualized that aspect of the Deity. See also *Decree*.

Manu. (Sanskrit.) The progenitor and lawgiver of the evolutions of God on earth. The Manu and his divine complement are *twin flames* assigned by the *Father-Mother God* to sponsor and ensoul the Christic image for a certain evolution or lifewave known as a root race—*souls* who embody as a group and have a unique archetypal pattern, divine plan and mission to fulfill on earth.

According to esoteric tradition, there are seven primary aggregations of souls—that is, the first to the seventh root races. The first three root races lived in purity and innocence upon earth in three Golden Ages before the fall of Adam and Eve. Through obedience to *cosmic law* and total identification with the *Real Self*, these three root races won their immortal freedom and ascended from earth.

It was during the time of the fourth root race, on the continent of Lemuria, that the allegorical Fall took place under the influence of the fallen angels known as Serpents (because they used the serpentine spinal energies to beguile the soul, or female principle in mankind, as a means to their end of lowering the masculine potential, thereby emasculating the Sons of God).

The fourth, fifth and sixth root races (the latter soul group not having entirely descended into physical incarnation) remain in embodiment on earth today. Lord Himalaya and his beloved are the Manus for the fourth root race, Vaivasvata Manu and his consort are the Manus for the fifth root race, and the God and Goddess Meru are the Manus for the sixth root race. The seventh root race is destined to incarnate on the continent of South America in the Aquarian age under their Manus, the Great Divine Director and his divine complement.

Manvantara. (Sanskrit, from *manv,* used in compounds for *manu,* + antara, 'interval, period of time.') In Hinduism, the period or age of a *Manu,* consisting of 4,320,000 solar years; one of the fourteen intervals that constitute a *kalpa* (Sanskrit), a period of time covering a cosmic cycle from the origination to the destruction of a world system. In Hindu cosmology, the universe is continually evolving through periodic cycles of creation and dissolution. Creation is said to occur during the outbreath of the God of Creation, Brahma; dissolution occurs during his inbreath.

Mater. (Latin, 'mother.') See *Matter; Mother.*

Matter. The feminine (negative) polarity of the Godhead, of which the masculine (positive) polarity is Spirit. Matter acts as a chalice for the kingdom of God and is the abiding place of evolving souls who identify with their Lord, their *Holy Christ Self.* Matter is distinguished from matter (lowercase m)—the substance of the earth earthy, of the realms of maya, which blocks rather than radiates divine *Light* and the Spirit of the *I AM THAT I AM.* See also *Mother; Spirit.*

Mental body. One of the *four lower bodies* of man, corresponding to the air element and the second quadrant of *Matter;* the body that is intended to be the vehicle, or vessel, for the mind of God or the *Christ* mind. "Let this [Universal] Mind be in you, which was also in Christ Jesus" (Phil. 2:5). Until quickened, this body remains the vehicle for the carnal mind, often called the lower mental body in contrast to the Higher Mental Body, a synonym for the *Christ Self* or *Christ* consciousness.

Messenger. Evangelist. One who goes before the *angels* bearing to the people of earth the good news of the gospel of Jesus Christ and, at the appointed time, the Everlasting Gospel. The Messengers of the *Great White Brotherhood* are anointed by the *Hierarchy* as their apostles ("one sent on a mission"). They deliver through the *dictations* (prophecies) of the *Ascended Masters* the testimony and lost teachings of Jesus Christ in the power of the Holy Spirit to the seed of *Christ,* the lost sheep of the house of Israel, and to every nation. A Messenger is one who is trained by an Ascended Master to receive by various methods the words, concepts, teachings and messages of the Great White Brotherhood; one who delivers the Law, the prophecies and the dispensations of God for a people and an age.

Microcosm. (Greek, 'small world.') (1) The world of the individual, his *four lower bodies,* his aura and the forcefield of his karma; or (2) The planet. See also *Macrocosm.*

Mother. "Divine Mother," "Universal Mother" and "Cosmic Virgin" are alternate terms for the feminine polarity of the Godhead, the manifestation of God as Mother. *Matter* is the feminine polarity of *Spirit,* and the term is used interchangeably with Mater (Latin, 'mother'). In this context, the entire material cosmos becomes the womb of creation into which Spirit projects the energies of life. Matter, then, is the womb of the Cosmic Virgin, who, as the other half of the Divine Whole, also exists in Spirit as the spiritual polarity of God.

Nirvana. The goal of life according to Hindu and Buddhist philosophy: the state of liberation from the wheel of rebirth through the extinction of desire.

OM (AUM). The Word; the sound symbol for ultimate Reality.

Omega. See *Alpha and Omega.*

Path. The strait gate and narrow way that leadeth unto life (Matt. 7:14). The path of initiation whereby the disciple who pursues the *Christ* consciousness overcomes step by step the limitations of selfhood in time and space and attains reunion with Reality through the ritual of the *ascension.*

Pearls of Wisdom. Weekly letters of instruction dictated by the *Ascended Masters* to their *Messengers* Mark L. Prophet and Elizabeth Clare Prophet for students of the sacred mysteries throughout the world. *Pearls of Wisdom* have been published by *The Summit Lighthouse* continuously since 1958. They contain both fundamental and advanced teachings on *cosmic law* with a practical application of spiritual truths to personal and planetary problems.

Physical body. The most dense of the *four lower bodies* of man, corresponding to the earth element and the fourth quadrant of *Matter.* The physical body is the vehicle for the *soul's* sojourn on earth and the focus for the crystallization in form of the energies of the *etheric, mental* and *emotional bodies.*

Rays. Beams of *Light* or other radiant energy. The Light emanations of the Godhead that, when invoked in the name of God or in the name of the *Christ,* burst forth as a flame in the world of the individual. Rays may be projected by the God consciousness of ascended or unascended beings through the *chakras* and the third eye as a concentration of energy taking on numerous God-qualities, such as love, truth, wisdom, healing, and so on. Through the misuse of God's energy, practitioners of black magic project rays having negative qualities, such as death rays, sleep rays, hypnotic rays, disease rays, psychotronic rays, the evil eye, and so on. See also *Seven rays.*

Real Self. The *Christ Self;* the *I AM Presence;* immortal *Spirit* that is the animating principle of all manifestation. See also *Chart of Your Divine Self.*

Reembodiment. The rebirth of a *soul* in a new human body. The soul continues to return to the physical plane in a new body temple until she balances her karma, attains self-mastery, overcomes the cycles of time and space, and finally reunites with the *I AM Presence* through the ritual of the *ascension.*

Retreat. A focus of the *Great White Brotherhood,* usually on the *etheric plane* where the *Ascended Masters* preside. Retreats anchor one or more flames of the Godhead as well as the momentum of the Masters' service and attainment for the balance of *light* in the *four lower bodies* of a planet and its evolutions. Retreats serve many functions for the councils of the *Hierarchy*

ministering to the lifewaves of earth. Some retreats are open to
unascended mankind, whose *souls* may journey to these focuses in
their *etheric body* between their incarnations on earth and in their
finer bodies during sleep or *samadhi.*

Root race. See *Manu.*

Sacred fire. The Kundalini fire that lies as the coiled serpent in the base-
of-the-spine *chakra* and rises through spiritual purity and self-mastery to the crown chakra, quickening the spiritual centers on the
way. God, *Light,* life, energy, the *I AM THAT I AM.* "Our God is
a consuming fire" (Heb. 12:29). The sacred fire is the precipitation
of the Holy Ghost for the baptism of souls, for purification, for
alchemy and transmutation, and for the realization of the *ascension,* the sacred ritual whereby the *soul* returns to the One.

Samadhi. (Sanskrit, literally "putting together": "uniting") In Hinduism, a state of profound concentration or absorption resulting
in perfect union with God; the highest state of yoga. In Buddhism,
samadhis are numerous modes of concentration believed to ultimately result in higher spiritual powers and the attainment of
enlightenment, or *nirvana.*

Sanat Kumara. (From the Sanskrit, 'always a youth.') Great *Guru* of
the seed of *Christ* throughout cosmos; Hierarch of Venus; the
Ancient of Days spoken of in Daniel 7. Long ago he came to earth
in her darkest hour when all light had gone out in her evolutions,
for there was not a single individual on the planet who gave adoration to the God Presence. Sanat Kumara and the band of
144,000 souls of Light who accompanied him volunteered to keep
the flame of life on behalf of earth's people. This they vowed to do
until the children of God would respond to the love of God and
turn once again to serve their mighty *I AM Presence.* Sanat
Kumara's retreat, Shamballa, was established on an island in the
Gobi Sea, now the Gobi Desert. The first to respond to his flame
was Gautama *Buddha,* followed by Lord Maitreya and Jesus. See
also *Lord of the World.*

Seamless garment. Body of *Light* beginning in the heart of the *I AM
Presence* and descending around the *crystal cord* to envelop the
individual in the vital currents of the *ascension* as he invokes the
holy energies of the Father for the return home to God. Also
known as the *deathless solar body.*

Glossary

Secret chamber of the heart. The sanctuary of meditation behind the heart *chakra*, the place to which the *souls* of Lightbearers withdraw. It is the nucleus of life where the individual stands face to face with the Inner *Guru*, the beloved *Holy Christ Self*, and receives the soul testings that precede the alchemical union with that Holy Christ Self—the marriage of the soul to the Lamb.

Seed Atom. The focus of the Divine *Mother* (the feminine ray of the Godhead) that anchors the energies of *Spirit* in *Matter* at the base-of-the-spine *chakra*. See also *Sacred fire*.

Seven rays. The *Light*-emanations of the Godhead; the seven *rays* of the white Light that emerge through the prism of the *Christ* consciousness.

Siddhis. Spiritual powers such as levitation, stopping the heartbeat, clairvoyance, clairaudience, materialization and bilocation. The cultivation of siddhis for their own sake is often cautioned against by spiritual teachers.

Solar Logoi. *Cosmic Beings* who transmit the *Light*-emanations of the Godhead flowing from *Alpha and Omega* in the *Great Central Sun* to the planetary systems. Also called Solar Lords.

Soul. God is a *Spirit*, and the soul is the living potential of God. The soul's demand for free will and her separation from God resulted in the descent of this potential into the lowly estate of the flesh. Sown in dishonor, the soul is destined to be raised in honor to the fullness of that God-estate which is the one Spirit of all life. The soul can be lost; Spirit can never die.

　　The soul remains a fallen potential that must be imbued with the reality of Spirit, purified through prayer and supplication, and returned to the glory from which it descended and to the unity of the Whole. This rejoining of soul to Spirit is the *alchemical marriage* that determines the destiny of the self and makes it one with immortal Truth. When this ritual is fulfilled, the highest Self is enthroned as the Lord of Life, and the potential of God, realized in man, is found to be the All-in-all.

Spirit. The masculine polarity of the Godhead; the coordinate of *Matter;* God as Father, who of necessity includes within the polarity of himself God as *Mother,* and hence is known as the *Father-Mother God.* The plane of the *I AM Presence,* of perfection; the dwelling place of the *Ascended Masters* in the kingdom of God. (When

lowercased, as in "spirits," the term is synonymous with discar-
nates, or astral *entities;* "spirit," singular and lowercased, is used
interchangeably with soul.)

Spoken Word. The *Word* of the Lord God released in the original fiats
of Creation. The release of the energies of the Word, or the *Logos,*
through the throat *chakra* by the Sons of God in confirmation of
that lost Word. It is written, "By thy words thou shalt be justified,
and by thy words thou shalt be condemned" (Matt. 12:37). Today
disciples use the power of the Word in *decrees,* affirmations,
prayers and *mantras* to draw the essence of the *sacred fire* from
the *I AM Presence,* the *Christ Self* and *Cosmic Beings* to channel
God's *Light* into matrices of transmutation and transformation
for constructive change in the planes of *Matter.*

The Summit Lighthouse. An outer organization of the *Great White
Brotherhood* founded by Mark L. Prophet in 1958 in Washington,
D.C., under the direction of the *Ascended Master* El Morya, Chief
of the Darjeeling Council, for the purpose of publishing and dis-
seminating the teachings of the Ascended Masters.

Threefold flame. The flame of the *Christ,* the spark of life that burns
within the *secret chamber of the heart* (a secondary *chakra* behind
the heart). The sacred trinity of power, wisdom and love that is the
manifestation of the *sacred fire.* See also *Chart of Your Divine Self.*

Transfiguration. An initiation on the path of the *ascension* that takes
place when the initiate has attained a certain balance and expansion of the *threefold flame.* Jesus' transfiguration is described in
Matthew 17:1–8.

Tube of light. The white *Light* that descends from the heart of the *I AM
Presence* in answer to the call of man as a shield of protection for
his *four lower bodies* and his *soul* evolution. See also *Chart of
Your Divine Self.*

Twelve Hierarchies of the Sun. Twelve mandalas of *Cosmic Beings*
ensouling twelve facets of God's consciousness, who hold the pattern of that frequency for the entire cosmos. They are identified by
the names of the signs of the zodiac, as they focus their energies
through these constellations. Also called the Twelve Solar Hierarchies. See also *Cosmic Clock.*

Twin flame. The *soul's* masculine or feminine counterpart conceived out
of the same white-fire body, the fiery ovoid of the *I AM Presence.*

Unascended master. One who has overcome all limitations of *Matter* yet chooses to remain in time and space to focus the consciousness of God for lesser evolutions. See also *Bodhisattva.*

Universal Christ. The Mediator between the planes of *Spirit* and the planes of *Matter.* Personified as the *Christ Self,* he is the Mediator between the Spirit of God and the *soul* of man. The Universal Christ sustains the nexus of (the figure-eight flow of) consciousness through which the energies of the Father (Spirit) pass to his children for the crystallization (*Christ*-realization) of the God flame by their soul's strivings in the cosmic womb (matrix) of the *Mother* (Matter).

Violet flame. Seventh-ray aspect of the Holy Spirit. The *sacred fire* that transmutes the cause, effect, record and memory of sin, or negative karma. Also called the flame of transmutation, of freedom and of forgiveness. See also *Decree; Chart of Your Divine Self.*

Word. The Word is the *Logos:* it is the power of God and the realization of that power incarnate in and as the Christ. The energies of the Word are released by devotees of the Logos in the ritual of the science of the *spoken Word.* It is through the Word that the *Father-Mother God* communicates with mankind. The Christ is the personification of the Word. See also *Christ; Decree.*

World Teacher. Office in *Hierarchy* held by those Ascended Beings whose attainment qualifies them to represent the Universal and personal *Christ* to unascended mankind. The office of World Teacher, formerly held by Maitreya, was passed to Jesus and his disciple Saint Francis (Kuthumi) on January 1, 1956, when the mantle of *Lord of the World* was transferred from *Sanat Kumara* to Gautama *Buddha* and the office of *Cosmic Christ* and Planetary Buddha (formerly held by Gautama) was simultaneously filled by Lord Maitreya. Serving under Lord Maitreya, Jesus and Kuthumi are responsible in this cycle for setting forth the teachings leading to individual self-mastery and the *Christ* consciousness. They sponsor all *souls* seeking union with God, tutoring them in the fundamental laws governing the cause-effect sequences of their own karma and teaching them how to come to grips with the day-to-day challenges of their individual dharma, the duty to fulfill the Christ potential through the sacred labor.

The Path of the Higher Self

This first volume in the *Climb the Highest Mountain* series has become a classic of metaphysical literature. It explores a cornucopia of topics important to every spiritual seeker—the destiny of the soul, the difference between soul and Spirit, the role of the Christ and how to contact the Higher Self and the spark within the heart. The text is complemented by charts, tables and a comprehensive glossary.

ISBN: 0-922729-84-0 Paperback, 575 pages. Available Fall 2003.

The Path of Self-Transformation

The second volume in the series continues the authors' teachings on the inner mysteries of God. It lifts the veil and reveals the true understanding of biblical allegory, including the mystical meaning of the "fall" of Adam and Eve. It answers profound spiritual questions that are supremely relevant for today. Who suppressed the concepts of karma and reincarnation and why are they key to our spiritual growth? What is the inner meaning of the judgment? Why wasn't sex the original sin? Above all, this work is about archetypes that are key to your soul's reaching its full potential.

ISBN: 0-922729-54-9 Paperback, 358 pages

The Masters and the Spiritual Path

There are Masters who have come out of all the world's great spiritual traditions. These great Lights of East and West have graduated from earth's schoolroom and reunited with Spirit in the process known as the ascension. The Masters tell us that they are examples and not exceptions to the rule. We, too, are destined to fulfill our life's purpose and reunite with Spirit. This intriguing work offers an innovative perspective on the universe and your role in it:

- The relationship between the ascension, nirvana and samadhi
- The parallel structure of the spiritual and material universes
- The difference between Ascended and unascended Masters
- The function of the spiritual Hierarchy and the role of the Masters
- A unique meditation on the bliss of union with Spirit
- A breathing exercise to help you balance and expand consciousness

ISBN: 0-922729-64-6   Paperback, 360 pages

The Path of Brotherhood

In *The Path of Brotherhood,* Mark and Elizabeth Prophet demonstrate how brotherhood is possible, and crucial, today. They take a mystical look at the Twelve Tribes, the Twelve Apostles, the Golden-Age Family and spiritual keys to reaching world brotherhood, which includes the realization of a spirit of unity and cooperation in spiritual organizations.

ISBN: 0-922729-82-4   Paperback, 264 pages

Other Titles from
Summit University ☙ Press

Fallen Angels and the Origins of Evil

Saint Germain's Prophecy for the New Millennium

The Lost Years of Jesus

The Lost Teachings of Jesus (4 vols.)

The Human Aura

Saint Germain on Alchemy

The Science of the Spoken Word

Kabbalah: Key to Your Inner Power

Reincarnation: The Missing Link in Christianity

Quietly Comes the Buddha

Lords of the Seven Rays

Prayer and Meditation

The Chela and the Path

Mysteries of the Holy Grail

POCKET GUIDES TO PRACTICAL SPIRITUALITY

Alchemy of the Heart

Your Seven Energy Centers

Soul Mates and Twin Flames

How to Work with Angels

Creative Abundance

Violet Flame to Heal Body, Mind and Soul

The Creative Power of Sound

Access the Power of Your Higher Self

Titles from

THE SUMMIT LIGHTHOUSE LIBRARY

The Opening of the Seventh Sea

Inner Perspectives

Morya I

Community

Walking with the Master: Answering the Call of Jesus

Wanting to Be Born: The Cry of the Soul

Afra: Brother of Light

For More Information

Summit University Press books are available at fine bookstores worldwide and at your favorite on-line bookseller.

If you would like a free catalog of Summit University Press books, please contact Summit University Press, PO Box 5000, Corwin Springs, MT 59030-5000 U.S.A. Telephone: 1-800-245-5445 (406-848-9500 outside the U.S.A.) Fax: 1-800-221-8307 (406-848-9555 outside the U.S.A.) Web site: www.summituniversitypress.com E-mail: info@summituniversitypress.com

Mark L. Prophet and Elizabeth Clare Prophet are pioneers of modern spirituality and internationally renowned authors. Among their best-selling titles are *The Lost Years of Jesus, The Lost Teachings of Jesus, The Human Aura, Saint Germain On Alchemy, Fallen Angels and the Origins of Evil* and the Pocket Guides to Practical Spirituality series, which includes *How to Work with Angels, Your Seven Energy Centers* and *Soul Mates and Twin Flames.* Their books are now translated into twenty languages and are available in more than thirty countries.